GW01044072

The Scale of Interest Organization in Democratic Politics

Interest Groups, Advocacy and Democracy Series

Series Editor
Darren Halpin, Aarhus University, Denmark

The study of interest groups and their role in political life has undergone something of a renaissance in recent years. Long-standing scholarly themes such as interest groups' influence, mobilization, formation and 'bias' are being addressed using novel data sets and methods. There are also exciting emerging themes, such as the role of Information and Communication Technologies (ICTs) in enabling collective action and the growth of global advocacy networks. Contemporary debates about the role of commercial lobbyists and professionalized interest representation are also highly salient. Together, these themes draw an ever larger and broader constituency to the study of interest groups and advocacy. This series seeks to capture both new-generation studies addressing long-standing themes in original ways and innovative scholarship posing challenging questions that emerge in a rapidly changing world.

The series encourages contributions from political science (but also abutting disciplines such as economics, law, history, international relations and sociology) that speak to these themes. It welcomes work undertaken at the level of sub-national, national and supra-national political systems, and particularly encourages comparative or longitudinal studies. The series is open to diverse methodologies and theoretical approaches. The book series will sit alongside and complement the new journal *Interest Groups and Advocacy*.

The Scale of Interest Organization in Democratic Politics

Data and Research Methods

Edited by

Darren Halpin
Associate Professor, Department of Political Science,
University of Aarhus, Denmark

and

Grant Jordan
Emeritus Professor, Department of Politics and International Relations,
University of Aberdeen, UK

Editorial matter, selection, introduction and conclusion © Darren Halpin and
Grant Jordan 2012
All remaining chapters © respective authors 2012

All rights reserved. No reproduction, copy or transmission of this
publication may be made without written permission.

No portion of this publication may be reproduced, copied or transmitted
save with written permission or in accordance with the provisions of the
Copyright, Designs and Patents Act 1988, or under the terms of any licence
permitting limited copying issued by the Copyright Licensing Agency,
Saffron House, 6–10 Kirby Street, London EC1N 8TS.

Any person who does any unauthorized act in relation to this publication
may be liable to criminal prosecution and civil claims for damages.

The authors have asserted their rights to be identified as the authors of this work
in accordance with the Copyright, Designs and Patents Act 1988.

First published 2012 by
PALGRAVE MACMILLAN

Palgrave Macmillan in the UK is an imprint of Macmillan Publishers Limited,
registered in England, company number 785998, of Houndmills, Basingstoke,
Hampshire RG21 6XS.

Palgrave Macmillan in the US is a division of St Martin's Press LLC,
175 Fifth Avenue, New York, NY 10010.

Palgrave Macmillan is the global academic imprint of the above companies
and has companies and representatives throughout the world.

Palgrave® and Macmillan® are registered trademarks in the United States,
the United Kingdom, Europe and other countries.

ISBN: 978–0–230–28443–2

This book is printed on paper suitable for recycling and made from fully
managed and sustained forest sources. Logging, pulping and manufacturing
processes are expected to conform to the environmental regulations of the
country of origin.

A catalogue record for this book is available from the British Library.

A catalog record for this book is available from the Library of Congress.

10 9 8 7 6 5 4 3 2 1
21 20 19 18 17 16 15 14 13 12

Printed and bound in Great Britain by
CPI Antony Rowe, Chippenham and Eastbourne

Contents

Tables

Figures

Acknowledgments

The cooperation of our contributors made this exercise a pleasure. Some of them are part of a wider grouping that participated in meetings in Aberdeen and Newcastle and on the fringes of various European and US conferences. We thank these colleagues for their contributions to this volume, but we also thank them – and the wider informal association – for agreeing there was something of interest in counting groups and organized interests. Other contributors have been persuaded to participate, and we are grateful to them for enriching the menu and demonstrating that these issues have wider interest. We congratulate ourselves that our hunch that there were others out there with something illuminating to say on these matters was so fruitful! We thank our research collaborators, Jamie Greenan, Dr Liu Yang, Graeme Baxter, and Iain MacLeod. Grant Jordan specifically wants to record his thanks to CBD Research Ltd. for access to their data and for the proof that universities have no monopoly on research skills or interesting research questions. Darren Halpin wants to thank the various individuals in the Scottish government who provided access to (often long forgotten) data sources. Thanks also are due for the hard work of Anja Dalsgaard and Annette Andersen, from Aarhus University, who carefully prepared the draft chapters for submission to Palgrave. Both the Halpin (RES-000-22-1932) and Jordan (RES-000-22-1959) projects were based on UK Economic and Social Research Council (ESRC) research awards. Finally, we thank the editorial staff at Palgrave Macmillan.

Notes on Contributors

Frank R. Baumgartner is the Richard J. Richardson Distinguished Professor of Political Science at the University of North Carolina at Chapel Hill. His most recent books include *Lobbying and Policy Change* (2009), *Agendas and Instability in American Politics* (2nd edn., 2009), and *The Decline of the Death Penalty and the Discovery of Innocence* (2008).

Graeme Baxter is a research fellow in the Department of Information Management at the Aberdeen Business School, Robert Gordon University. His research interests include the provision of, need for, and use of government, parliamentary, and citizenship information; freedom of information legislation; the use of the Internet by political parties and candidates during election campaigns; organizational participation in government consultation exercises; barriers to equality and inclusion in the creative industries; and the social and economic impact of the creative industries.

Shaun Bevan is a research associate at the Institute for Political and Economic Governance at the University of Manchester. He is the project coordinator for the UK Policy Agendas Project. His research focuses on the lifecycle of voluntary associations in the US, and on comparative analyses of policy agendas and government responsiveness to public opinion in the US and the UK.

Jan Beyers is a professor in the Department of Political Science at the University of Antwerp. His research interests include European interest group politics and, more generally, multilevel politics, political organizations, and institutions. He has published articles in several journals, including *International Organization*, *Journal of European Public Policy*, *European Journal of Political Research*, *Comparative Political Studies*, *West European Politics*, and *European Union Politics*.

Caelesta Braun is a postdoctoral researcher in the Department of Political Science at the University of Antwerp. Her research interests include the policy impact and political strategies of interest groups in multilevel governance systems and stakeholder management by public agencies. Her recent articles have appeared in *Governance*, *West European Politics*, and *Administration & Society*.

Jamie Greenan graduated with a Master's in Sociology from Aberdeen University in 2004 and subsequently gained a Master's in Social Research in 2005, also from Aberdeen. In addition to the British associational population, his areas of interest include the Internet and political activism, and the measurement of European social exclusion.

Darren Halpin is an associate professor in the Department of Political Science at Aarhus University. He was formerly Professor of Public Policy at the Robert Gordon University, Aberdeen, where he is now a visiting professor at the Institute for Management, Governance and Society. He has published widely on the topics of interest groups and organized interests, including recent articles in *Governance, British Journal of Political Science, Journal of European Public Policy* and *Public Administration*. He has recently published *Groups, Representation and Democracy: Between Promise and Practice* (2010).

Marcel Hanegraaff is a PhD student in the Department of Political Science at the University of Antwerp. His dissertation focuses on interest group mobilization patterns at the international level. His research interests include interest group politics, international decision making, and the relationship between religion and politics.

Grant Jordan is Emeritus Professor in the Department of Politics and International Relations at the University of Aberdeen. His first book, *Governing under Pressure* (with Jeremy Richardson), was published in 1979. The belief in the centrality of British consensus and consultation is developed with empirical illustration in *Engineers and Professional Self-Regulation* (1992) and in 'Accounting for Sub Governments: Explaining the Persistence of Policy Communities', *Administration & Society* (with William Maloney, 1997).

David Lowery is the Bruce R. Miller and Dean D. LaVigne Professor of Political Science at Pennsylvania State University. He was previously Professor of Public Administration at the University of Leiden and Thomas J. Pearsall Professor in the Department of Political Science at the University of North Carolina at Chapel Hill. Lowery teaches and conducts research on the politics of interest representation, subnational politics, and bureaucratic politics. He has authored a number of papers on these and other topics and co-authored *The Politics of Dissatisfaction* (with William E. Lyons and Ruth Hoogland DeHoog, 1992), *The Population Ecology of Interest Representation* (with Virginia Gray, 1996), and *Organized Interests and American Politics* (with Holly Brasher, 2004).

John D. McCarthy is Professor of Sociology and Head of the Department of Sociology at Pennsylvania State University. His work on social movements, protest, and collective action has been widely published. He is currently at work on projects that focus on the dynamics of US protest, 1960–1995; US campus public order disturbances during the past decade; the growth of US advocacy organizations; and spiritual entrepreneurs. In 2007 he received a Lifetime Scholarly Achievement Award, named in his honor, from the Center for the Study of Social Movements and Change at Notre Dame University.

Iain MacLeod is a researcher at the Institute for Management, Governance and Society at Robert Gordon University, Aberdeen. His research interests include Scottish devolution, the theory and practice of participatory democracy and institutional design/change, and the political participation/representation of marginalized communities, particularly children and young people.

William A. Maloney is Professor of Politics at Newcastle University. His research interests include interest groups, civil society organizations, and social capital. His recent publications include *Democracy and Interest Groups* (with Grant Jordan, 2007), *Interest Group Politics in Europe: Lessons from EU Studies and Comparative Politics* (edited with Jan Beyers and Rainer Eising, 2010), *Contextualizing Civil Society: A Comparative Analysis of Active Citizens in European Communities* (edited with Jan van Deth, 2009), and *New Participatory Dimensions in Civil Society: Professionalization and Individualized Collective Action* (edited with Jan van Deth, 2011).

John Mohan is Professor of Social Policy at the University of Southampton and Deputy Director of the Third Sector Research Centre. His research interests currently involve the distribution of voluntary resources (voluntary organizations and volunteering) and the development of long-run data resources on third sector organizations. Previously he worked on various aspects of health policy, including historical studies of the growth and distribution of voluntary hospitals in the UK, and a study of the pre-NHS hospital contributory scheme movement.

Peter Munk Christiansen is Professor of Political Science in the Department of Political Science at Aarhus University. He was member of the management board of the Danish Power and Democracy Study, to which he contributed several books. His present research interests include interest group politics, political decision-making processes, and institutional reform. He has published articles in *Scandinavian Political Studies, Governance, Government & Opposition, Local Government Studies,*

Voluntas, and *Journalism and Mass Communication Quarterly,* among other journals.

Anthony J. Nownes is Professor of Political Science at the University of Tennessee, Knoxville. He has studied lobbying and interest groups extensively, and his work has appeared in *British Journal of Political Science, Journal of Politics,* and *American Politics Research.* His latest book, *Total Lobbying: What Lobbyists Want (and How They Try to Get It),* was published in 2006.

Kay Lehman Schlozman is the J. Joseph Moakley Endowed Professor of Political Science at Boston College. A specialist in American politics, she has written numerous articles in professional journals and is editor of *Elections in America* (1987), co-editor of *The Future of Political Science* (with Gary King and Norman H. Nie, 2009), and co-author of *Injury to Insult: Unemployment, Class and Political Response* (with Sidney Verba, 1979), *Organized Interests and American Democracy* (with John T. Tierney, 1986), *Voice and Equality: Civic Voluntarism in American Politics* (with Sidney Verba and Henry E. Brady, 1995; winner of the American Political Science Association's Philip Converse Prize), and *The Private Roots of Public Action: Gender, Equality, and Political Participation* (with Nancy Burns and Sidney Verba, 2001; co-winner of the APSA's Schuck Prize). She won the APSA's 2004 Rowman and Littlefield Award for Innovative Teaching in Political Science and the APSA's 2006 Frank Goddnow Award for Distinguished Service to the Profession of Political Science. She is a fellow of the American Academy of Arts and Sciences.

Jan W. van Deth is Professor of Political Science and International Comparative Social Research at the University of Mannheim. His main research areas are political culture (especially social capital, political engagement, and citizenship), social change, and comparative research methods. He was Director of the Mannheim Centre for European Social Research, convenor of the international network Citizenship, Involvement, Democracy of the European Science Foundation, and series editor of the Studies in European Political Science for the European Consortium for Political Research. He is a corresponding member of the Royal Netherlands Academy of Arts and Sciences and national coordinator of the German team for the European Social Survey. His recent publications include *Foundations of Comparative Politics* (with Ken Newton, 2009) and 'Civicness, Equality, and Democracy: A "Dark Side" of Social Capital?', a special issue of *American Behavioral Scientist* (edited with Sonja Zmerli, 2010).

1
Estimating Group and Associational Populations: Endemic Problems but Encouraging Progress

Darren Halpin and Grant Jordan

Delineating and accounting for a sense of scale

This introductory chapter raises issues that are central to population-level studies of organized interests, interest groups, and associations. In draft form the text served as a reference point for the contributors to this volume, which seeks both to report on conclusions drawn from recent studies and to reflect on problems (theoretical, definitional, and practical) in researching this area. The volume is intended to prompt comparison in the field – both by those contributing here and in wider research.

Already, however, language poses a problem. The first sentence rushed over the terms 'organized interests', 'interest groups', and 'associations' – when lengthy discussion of different uses could have then followed. As will become evident in this volume, the contributors take varied approaches, yet there is something close to a convergence on a professional language we can use to present decisions on the counting criteria for inclusion to one another. Second, the editors (and also Hanegraaff *et al.*, Chapter 9) are using 'population' as essentially a synonym for 'total'. In this conversational use a population is a figure telling us 'how many'. However, in this volume uses differ. As expanded upon by Lowery (Chapter 3) and Nownes (Chapter 5), an important sub-literature on population ecology (PE) is very precisely saying that a population is not simply 'a summation of mobilization events'.

By default, to date, much description in this area has consisted of no more than assertions there are 'more of these' or 'fewer of those'.

The goal in this volume is that the research community will have at least a *sense of scale* and will be able to say more than 'more'. In terms of this aspiration, the projects in this volume can be crudely divided into

- what might be termed 'scale' exercises, where the aim is simply to map roughly *how many* and to consider such information in the context of working democracy (trends over time are particularly important), and
- what might be termed 'comprehension' or 'explanatory' accounts that seek to understand *why* these phenomena are of the scale that is found.

Of course there are links and overlaps, and not all chapters follow the same agenda.

The PE perspective is certainly in the comprehension camp. A population in the more technical sense is the result of an interaction between the frequency of reproduction and the environment in it occurs. A population in this PE sense is determined by something other than procreation: the context determines the final total. A simple example of this interaction is the case of cane toads, which were found to be useful to agriculture in Hawaii, but which became a problem when they were introduced into Australia because their numbers expanded rapidly in the absence of any natural predators. How many cane toads there are in a specific location is determined not by the mechanics of birth, but by the ecological balance where the births take place. The PE approach applies observations from biology on the control limits of animal populations. In a well-known discussion, the key factor determining Indian rat populations was identified as the regular but very occasional fruiting of the *Melocanna* bamboo. The plants seed more or less in unison every 48 years. This leads to a (temporary) superabundance of food that allows the rat population to explode because there is no resource limit (rats normally suppress breeding when their food supply is reduced). When the bamboo food stock once again declines, the rat super-population extends its territories into human habitations, and in particular rice fields, to find food supplies to sustain the expanded numbers. The rats and humans then directly compete in a way inhibited by the 'normal' rat population control mechanisms that operate when there is no bamboo glut. The key transferable conclusion for political science is that the rat population is limited not by the frequency of births, but by the environment in which these births take place. But the lesson does not stop there. The rats' pursuit of rice leads to a second population effect when seed shortages caused by the proliferation of rats lead to starvation in the human population. PE stresses the importance of competition (for limited resources) in understanding the rate of group generation and the longevity of established groups, but the literature is still relatively unclear on the relevant 'pool' of competing groups (and by extension on what precisely is being competed over). Is it a pool of like groups with similar constituencies (see Nownes, Chapter 5), or can the ideas be used to interpret wider sets of disparate organizations (perhaps) competing over political ends rather than for support (see Hanegraaff *et al.*, Chapter 9)?

Work by Gray and Lowery (2000) over the past 15 years has illuminated group research using a PE perspective. They have clarified the importance of not simply looking at individual group-level traits and characteristics (e.g., formation issues and incentive structures), but examining group *environments*. Lowery and Gray observe that the actual population of groups at any one time is regulated by a complex range of forces, including 'the nature of interest representation, the distribution of issues on the agenda and public opinion about them, the size and composition of the population of interests in society, and economies of scale of subpopulations of interests organized for political action', to which the 'dynamic properties of the interest community itself' – so-called endogenous factors – are added (2004, pp. 18–19). This basic insight has been extended in new ways (Nownes 2004) in political science, and has also been subjected to sympathetic constructive critique (Halpin and Jordan 2009). Whether framed as a study of explaining 'bias' or around explaining group populations, data on group populations are still crucial.

The 'scale' projects in this collection are perhaps particularly interested in change over time, as exemplified by the contributions by Jordan and Greenan (Chapter 4) and Jordan *et al.* (Chapter 7). There are simple reasons why directory-based studies pursue the time aspect. If some of the research 'chore' of data collection can piggy-back on earlier work, then there is research space to explore other things. And unless a research design is set up with decades-long horizons, the only way to have contemporaneously collected past data is to use someone else's (for instance, Chapter 8, by Christiansen, *de facto* becomes a time series exercise utilizing earlier research).

The overall purpose of this volume is no less than sevenfold. The first, and broadest, goal is to collect in one place the state of the art (whether comprehension or scale). The volume aims to set out the relevant theoretical questions, the data sources that are available, the methodological debates concerning how to design studies, and, most importantly, what empirical range is in fact covered by terms such as 'organized interest', 'interest group', or 'associational population' (it will be a recurring theme that comparison requires equivalence and consistency across studies). This volume is intended to provide an up-to-date overview of the group/associational territory, a field that is widely seen to be of enhanced importance in the light of reported party decline.

The second purpose of this collection is to build a bridge between the work of US scholars and that of their counterparts in Europe and beyond. There are important recent US additions to the portfolio of quantification attempts that deserve coverage. In the past decade European political science too has begun to address quantitatively the scale and pattern of organized interests. Works have recently been completed, or are substantially underway, at the European Union, national, and subnational levels. It is timely to integrate this work with the (newly extended) US corpus. It is of course also a feature of the subdiscipline that there is growing internationalization of research (well evidenced by the Comparative Agendas Project, www.comparativeagendas.org).

Third, the volume aims to start to bring together those working, in their related ways, across the 'separate tables' of the social sciences. There are literatures assessing populations of social movement organizations, voluntary associations, and civil society groups. Such work is as likely to be produced by sociologists or historians as by political scientists. Even within this fairly restricted (mainly political science) set of chapters, the bibliographies reveal strikingly discrete sub-literatures. At the minimum there is benefit in juxtaposing these separate 'conversations', as the process of linkage suggests connections. This volume aims at bringing scholars with different concerns together in one place so that the challenges of different approaches can be more clearly appreciated – and the differences in results indicated by these varied sorts of exercises better understood. A pessimist might assume that scholars are almost always bound by the limits of the data sets to which they have access, but the aspiration here is at least to have an agreed lexicon that allows omissions, additions, and differences to be communicated. The introduction seeks to develop this vein.

Fourth, the volume seeks, somewhat paradoxically, to celebrate the growth in knowledge in this area while emphasizing a lack of information. As is evident in all chapters, progress has been remarkable in such a short period, yet there remain very real limits on what can be achieved with existing tools (especially data). Small steps, such as attention to a shared professional lexicon, offer real advantages, especially in terms of the aspiration to cross-national comparison. The broad message is that the field is in better shape than before, but that growing knowledge reveals further weaknesses to tackle.

Fifth, the volume offers health warnings and hints on the practicalities of this sort of research. All participants have found frustration in the operationalization of the appealing ambition of 'nice to generate numbers', as trivial-sounding issues can be serious impediments to progress. The aim is not to sidestep or footnote such concerns, but to highlight and capture their dimensions so that they can constitute a focal point for collective scholarly discussions going forward.

A sixth ambition for this collection is set out in more detail in the next section: it is to encourage researchers to move on from a few random snapshots to systematic histories. While the exercise of taming the number problem in this field is in initial rather than polished form, the preliminary efforts represent a major advance. Political science has given prominence to groups and associations, but in no political system is there a satisfactory quantitative handle on the phenomena. The aspiration is to broach the 'what' and 'how' of this move to more dynamic accounts of populations.

Finally, the volume seeks to controversialize terms that might be seen as simple and self-defining. The meanings of terms such as 'association' or 'interest group population' are not self-evident, and care is required. Yet, as will become evident from the contributions to this volume, when care is taken to offer clear guidance to the reader on what is included in populations – and to do so using a basic vocabularly – getting a handle on the phenomena being addressed is vastly easier. Authoritative lessons can be more easily drawn. Where the volume cannot offer authoritative definitions it can at least offer warnings that common definitions remain elusive.

These aims represent a concerted attempt to address gaps that are already remarkably well identified in the literature. Some time ago Walker noted that there were 'almost no comprehensive descriptions of the world of interest groups in America at any historical period' (1983, p. 391). Berry more recently observed, 'unfortunately for scholars studying interest groups, there is no standard data base to measure the population of lobbying organizations over time. ... *Even measuring the participation of groups in a single year is difficult*' (1999, p. 18; emphasis added). Gray and Lowery (2000, p. 5) called attention to the very real difficulties of measuring population-level properties, quoting Cigler's point that 'In large measure, data availability has been the major determinant of the interest group politics agenda, framing both the questions we explore, and the topics we avoid' (1994, p. 29). And Lowery and Gray (2004, p. 5) point to the limitations in moving beyond nontrivial conclusions 'from one-shot lists of organizations'. In other words there have been well-articulated concerns about the limited state of knowledge. The lack of existing, publicly available data is a disincentive for the would-be interest group scholar. To date, then, this field has lacked both one-off snapshots and trends over time. But these weaknesses are being addressed.

Why count populations of organized interests?

As most people can imagine, and as the authors of these chapters can attest, counts of group populations are large undertakings in respect of their demands on resources and time. Practical problems in answering 'How many?' will be expanded upon below. Most of the data sets used are not off-the-shelf products: their use involves investment of time in sorting, sifting, collating, and checking. Even the use of existing encyclopedia-type sources involves substantial, perhaps surprising, effort in tracking cases over time. Scholars of interest groups and associations can only look enviously at other areas of political science where the relevant data are delivered from official sources – such as election returns. For instance, the *EJPR Annual Special Edition Political Data Yearbook* seeks 'to provide an indispensable and ongoing source of reliable up-to-date information on political developments in contemporary democracies' (Koole and Katz 2000, p. 227), but it contains no information about interest group activity. A similar point can be made using a US source (Stanley and Niemi 2001): in explaining some of the lack of scholarly attention to group studies, Ainsworth argues that

> Within American politics, the prominence of the American National Election Studies program no doubt bolstered the careers of countless scholars who eagerly awaited every new release of data. In the midst of the behavioral revolution, one should not be surprised when scholars move towards subfields with readily available data. (2010, p. 78)

Given the inherent difficulty, the question becomes 'Why, then, count group populations?'

The primary rationale is that representation via collective organizations is an important element of working democracies. The composition of the group system – what E. E. Schattschneider (1960) famously (and critically) characterized as the 'heavenly chorus' – has been the subject of a well-established, but predominantly US, genre of research that seeks to quantify (variously) the organized interest, group, or pressure 'system' (see Schattschneider 1960; Schlozman and Tierney 1986; Browne 1990; Walker 1991; Heinz *et al.* 1993; Gray and Lowery 2000; Baumgartner and Leech 2001; Schlozman 2010). Counting allows us better to address the nature of the system.

At one level the counting reflects a 'train-spotting' tendency: it is simply interesting for students of politics to move toward the completion of the picture of social and political organizations. But there is a more direct political science reason to develop such work. As Schlozman notes:

> Organized interests are such an essential part of the process by which policymakers in a democracy learn about the preferences and needs of citizens that barriers to entry into the political fray have potential consequences for the representation – and, in particular, for the equal representation – of citizen interests. (2010)

In other words, there has been an expansion in the research focus of political science in the past century. Initially the focus was the in-house study of legislatures and their legislative texts, but over time that was augmented by the study of parties and pre-legislative decision making. There is now an appreciation that social order and political consent rely on a wider range of institutions; what interests political scientists has shifted from the study of speeches, bills, acts, amendments, and legislative and public votes. While students of politics have looked exhaustively at major political parties and election campaigns, influential and convincing depictions of the political process now assume that the political system is in part dependent on the 'cast of thousands' of wider organizations that are relevant as part of the process of agenda setting and policy influencing, but also as part of the connection between individuals and the society. Indeed the assumption here is that the associational cacophony better represents individuals' concerns than their occasional involvement in electoral choice between professionalized vote-gathering machines.

This volume reports the results of significant US work. Grant Jordan and colleagues (Chapter 7) report the outcomes of a large-scale effort to map the associational universe as captured in the US *Encyclopedia of Associations*. With a different data source, Kay Schlozman (Chapter 2) generates a picture of policy-active organizations engaged in Washington politics that updates her much-cited work from the 1980s. In both chapters there is interest in the problems of researching the field as well as in the substantive results, but this 'craft' focus is even more central to the contribution by Anthony Nownes (Chapter 5) on researching in the gay, lesbian, and transgender communities. Nownes explains the difficulties in logging entry and exit from populations (both conceptual and methodological). Also, writing about population ecology, David Lowery (Chapter 3) providing insights into *how* counting can be done and *what* can be counted. This volume is aimed as much at sharing research difficulties (and solutions) as at reporting on past research outcomes.

The relative scarcity of European contributions in the quantification area *might* simply reflect the fact that groups and organized interests are a less important subject of study in non-congressional systems. Yet there is a strong thread in the literature which says that organized interests are (and always have been) important in, for example, even 'majoritarian' British public policy (see McKenzie 1958; Finer 1967; Richardson and Jordan 1979; Rose 1984; Wilson 1990). The absence of attempts to map the organized interest system is attributable not to a lack of salience for British (or European) scholarship but probably to intimidation by the complexity. So part of the reason for the absence of such studies could be simply that data collection is difficult (see May *et al.* 1998, fn. 9). This, of course, is a problem shared by US colleagues; however, in the US the push toward quantification has been given momentum by the availability of lobbying lists. Reinforcing practical impediments to UK research may be a lack of a UK disciplinary consensus over what data sources are legitimate (see Halpin *et al.*, Chapter 6). Colleagues in the US have a well-worn path directing them to congressional lobby registers, but work on these tempting sources has been subject to criticism precisely because their convenience might have led to studies of the available rather than the desirable.

This volume includes studies at the country (US, Germany, Denmark, UK) and global levels, and also at different geographical levels within countries. Variation with regard to focus is also introduced, self-consciously, in relation to different interpretations of the target population. This variation is intended to put the consequences of different definitions in the foreground of our attention. The Danish, UK, and US material also starts to explore differences over time.

In connection with the definitional variation, an important issue running through these different research approaches is the *formality* that is needed before a case is included. John Mohan (Chapter 10) was invited to contribute precisely because his approach, in mapping the activities of unregulated third sector organizations in England (those that do not appear in institutional registers), means constructing a relevant population where there is no 'hard' list of participants. William Maloney and Jan van Deth (Chapter 11) face similar problems in looking comparatively at all organizations active in selected localities without any kind of regulated or official listing. Should researchers exclude informal organizations because there are problems in systematically counting them, rather than make such decisions on the basis of the intrinsic importance of the cases? In summary the contributions all share an ambition to provide a sense of scale – at the national, global, local, or sectoral level – but the individual exercises reflect very different definitions of what to count. Is this still an academic Tower of Babel, or are we beginning to devise appropriate methods for particular circumstances?

Assuming interest diversity?

The effort expended in producing this volume is justified by the belief that assessing the size and diversity of the organized interest system is crucial to addressing a range of fundamental questions about the plurality of interests voiced in policymaking arenas that potentially shape policy outputs. The research hunch is that the proliferation of bodies involved in policymaking is an essential part of the character of policymaking and not policy 'noise'. This research seam appears to demand that we finally abandon the simple and rigid corporatist picture that was inserted in our heads by Schmitter:

> Corporatism can be defined as a system of interest representation in which the constituent units are organized into a limited number of singular, compulsory, non-completive, hierarchically ordered and functionally differentiated categories, recognized or licensed (if not created) by the state and granted a deliberate representational monopoly within their respective categories in exchange for observing certain controls on their selection of leaders and articulation of demands and supports. (1979, p. 13)

As recent uprisings in Tunisia and Egypt show, functioning democracy may be as rooted in everyday, and apparently minor, qualities of the policy process, procedures of a culture of respect for minorities, rule of law, consultation with affected interests, and so on as in crude electoral choice. So the argument in this chapter is that far from routine consultation among organized interests (which the contributors to this volume seek to map) being so unimportant it should be disregarded, it is the sort of micro-process that reflects the consensual values and inter-group respect that democracy requires. It follows that the broad range of varied and individually peripheral associations may be, in sum, part of the democratic essence. Our assumption is that our cast of thousands of groups and associations are the partners of the cast of thousands of middle-range civil servants identified in UK government by Page and Jenkins (2005). According to Page and Jenkins:

> Much policy work is usually conducted with few direct and specific instructions from ministers and senior officials. Since ministers do not give a detailed steer of all the things in the policy process, bureaucrats should produce precise legal clauses, specific regulations, and various forms of protocols about how policies should work in practice. (p. 79)

Given the generalist nature and lack of substantive expertise of many of those civil servants at the policy development level, in our view the system assumes an input of detail from the external organizations.

One regular target of attention among those seeking to quantify in this area is the assessment of 'bias' in the 'system' – with the unsurprising finding that (more often than not) business interests numerically dominate populations of organized interests (and therefore the implication is that business dominates outcomes). Since Schattschneider's (1960) observation regarding bias, measurements of group populations have generally reconfirmed his conclusion (or at least the preponderance of business interests; see also Schlozman and Tierney 1986; Browne 1990; Walker 1991; Baumgartner and Leech 2001; Schlozman 2010). However, as Lowery and Gray (2004) persuasively observe, authors convinced that the group system is biased surely imply the existence of a natural and unbiased relationship between interests in society and organized interests. With what unbiased reference point could empirical findings be contrasted?

Other important research agenda items include the size of populations (and subpopulations) over time, their diversity, the mix of specialist organizations versus generalist ones, and the degree to which organized interests enhance political participation (the social capital aspect). System-wide accounts of bias differ significantly depending on what is counted. Reflecting upon Tierney and Schlozman's US study, Mundo notes that they counted lobbyists as 'representing an interest';

he suggests that if one includes 'only formal interest groups [this] produces a more balanced distribution of interest groups in national politics' (1992, p. 9). Thus the conclusion, and sense of bias, reflects the definitional focus of the research: what is counted. This turns out to be a bigger problem in this field than might be anticipated. What to count proves to be less obvious than common sense might lead us to expect.

Another point is the assumption that a preponderance of groups of a certain type in an area is an indicator of the power of that set of groups. Just as plausibly, such group proliferation could show that interests are subject to state pressures that demand defensive mobilization. The stimulus to organization is often reactive. And indeed the most effective form of mobilization might be fewer rather than more units. Having the numbers to hand adds to the pressure to come to conclusions about what the numbers mean. Yet it is probably the case that the appropriate metric of power and influence remains one of the key – and also most longstanding (see Dahl 1957) – debates among group scholars.

What is counted? Which organizations are included? How are they labeled?

In this volume the object of study shifts regularly from association to group (and to organized interests). Is this a superficial labeling matter or a fundamental inconsistency across the chapters? One of the core problems bedeviling group scholarship (and comparison) has been the absence of any consistency with respect to what is, and is not, counted as part of the population. As discussed above, much of this is bound up with the type of data that are available. Sometimes, where data sets are opportunistically utilized by researchers as population proxies, the decisions have already been made. These proxy data sets come in-built with a set of ready-made decisions about what is included. Results are reported as 'group', 'association', or 'organized interest' populations, but often only the (very) small print reveals what is actually captured. In reality this makes meaningful comparison between most idiosyncratic data sets effectively impossible. Until comparison is built into research at the planning stage, the temptation will be to make do with comparison of apples and oranges.

The enterprise of mapping a 'group system', or even the 'system' of 'organized interests', implies that one should be able to catalog a more or less stable set of participants. Precisely what constitutes an *interest group* is heavily contested (or at least constantly reinterpreted), yet the label gestures toward a collection of organizations

- that are not part of the state,
- that are not seeking election or to form a government (i.e., not a political party),
- that are collective in their aggregation of interests,
- that have members or affiliates, and
- for whom influencing public policy or policy advocacy is a significant part of their reason for mobilizing or identity (see review in Jordan *et al.* 2004).

Some rightly suggest that the emphasis on 'collective organizations' leaves out bodies (e.g., corporations) that are possibly more influential, and likely more numerous, in political life. Salisbury (1984) noted that on the 'input side' of the equation, most scholarly emphasis was on interest groups and political parties. He suggested that this emphasis had led to an ignoring of the breadth of the system of organized interests: many policy-influential bodies are neither parties nor collective interest groups as conventionally understood. Salisbury argued that 'The American political universe, in fact, contains a considerably more diverse array of actors than these conventional headings suggest' (1984, p. 64). The omissions he had in mind were 'individual corporations, state and local governments, universities, think tanks, and most other *institutions* of the private sector' (p. 64; emphasis in original). The challenge, according to Salisbury, is to reconcile the scholarly orthodoxy with the observables of the Washington political system. To reserve the 'interest group' term, to preserve it from being stretched to include such institutions, Jordan *et al.* (2004) term the full array of policy-influencing bodies 'pressure participants'. They tie the 'interest group' term (primarily) to collective-action, multi-member, *policy-dedicated* organizations set up expressly to articulate a political message or defend an interest. However, many quite important examples of collective organizations may be set up for no political purposes, but nonetheless become relevant when policy is made in their areas. These may be seen as *policy-interested* if not policy-dedicated. They are still worth including under the interest group umbrella.

At core, quantification requires a choice as to what criterion of inclusion to use to construct data sets. Researchers quantifying populations have to consider whether the count subsumes both non-collective institutions and collective interest groups of the sort described above. What threshold test should apply in logging a specific case as part of a given population or community? The criterion can be an active public-policy-intervening dimension or simply presence or existence with collective structures. The consequences for coverage – what types of actors are included – depend on the precise option chosen. And ready-made sources may end up utilizing a mix of both.

A second distinction that can be made is between exploiting existing lists and generating data sets *de novo*. The literature has often used databases, handbooks, and encyclopedias to identify the boundaries of, and thus the organizations within, the organized interest system. For example, the *Encyclopedia of Associations* (Martin *et al.* 2006) limits itself to voluntary associations (by structure), and the *Washington Representatives* directory covers all organizations that have a Washington office or hire Washington lobbyists to represent them (includes by activity) (Schlozman and Tierney 1986; Schlozman 2010). For the UK, Jordan and Greenan (Chapter 4) map associations by coding time series data from the UK *Directory of British Associations* (by structure).

These categories overlap and are not entirely discrete. The *Encyclopedia of Associations* and the *Directory of British Associations* cover those organizations deemed to be associations: they need not be engaged in policy advocacy but must be collective. In contrast, the *Washington Representatives* directory covers only policy-active organizations; some may not be associations, but 'institutions' in Salisbury's terminology (e.g., government agencies, corporations). The two exercises sound somewhat similar, but they cover very different populations with different qualities. Halpin and colleagues' approach (Chapter 6) counts the organizations involved in Scottish public policy consultations over a 25-year period. A policy-active rule is applied. Hanegraaff and colleagues (Chapter 9) take a broadly similar approach to Halpin *et al.*'s Scottish work on the policy-active, but at the international level. Their analysis of changes in nongovernmental organization attendance at World Trade Organization ministerial conferences paints an innovative picture of fluid, policy-engaged associational populations. Christiansen, writing on Denmark (Chapter 8), focuses on politically relevant groups – that is, interest groups who want to affect political and administrative processes and output. He assesses political relevance in the following terms:

> the group must have as part of its purpose/strategy to affect political decisions regardless of how this endeavor is pursued. If it is not obvious whether the group is politically relevant, its statutes are examined and must state that it is part of the group's purpose to somehow affect political decisions.

Schlozman's chapter (Chapter 2) also adopts an action-based definition: counting 'organizations that get involved politically'. She says:

> we focus exclusively on organizations that in some way take part in politics – by lobbying public officials, making campaign contributions, participating in hearings at regulatory agencies, mobilizing the public on behalf of a preferred position, and so on.

By using a particular published directory (*Washington Representatives*), Schlozman includes 'all organizations that *are active* in Washington politics by virtue either of having an office in the DC area or hiring DC-area consultants or counsel to represent them' (italics added).

Thus, some exercises focus on the policy-active only, but the measure of activity may be directory inclusion or may require more manipulation by the researcher to construct an *ad hoc* listing. The studies based on US lobbying lists are looking at action as the criterion, but such lists often include institutions (firms, local governments, individuals) that do not meet the collective action expectation. Baumgartner and Leech (2001) used Congressional lobbying registration records for 1996 to look at the mix of interests that actually *engaged* in the act of lobbying. Gray and Lowery (2000) adopted a similar technique for US states. Such sources map populations on the basis of whether an organization is active at a given point of time in a given policy arena. They vary in terms of the types of organizations covered, and inevitably not all end up being collective associations. Skocpol, in an important, historically aware contribution, tracks large voluntary *membership* associations in the US (in Skocpol and Fiorina 1999, p. 34). The focus is on participation by individuals, but a size threshold limiting inclusion to organizations enrolling 1 percent or more of the US adult population means this too is a useful part of the patchwork rather than the finished quilt. A recent data set relating to the EU is outlined in Wonka *et al.* (2010). This combines the Commission's CONECCS list, which records the voluntary registration of groups participating in Commission hearings or committees (749 cases); the European Parliament accreditation system for entry passes for accessing the EP buildings and interaction with members (1,534 cases); and the Landmarks commercial *European Public Affairs Directory* (2,522 cases). (After removing duplication, the total was 3,700.) This is an activity-based list in the sense that all three primary sources are recorded because of an EU focus, yet the first two components capture the cases in action while the directory is more reputational.

What constitutes 'active' differs, and is another crucial point in assessing comparability. A mixed approach is pursued by Nownes (2004), who counts US gay and lesbian organizations by triangulating between directories and public policy sources. Such an approach seems most viable when quantifying the population of a specific 'species'. Other alternatives – used principally in the study of nongovernmental organizations or the voluntary sector – include using the legal form of a set of organizations as a basis to select populations (see Kendall and Knapp 1996; Lyons and Hocking 2001). However, this has obvious problems, including the fact that legal forms vary markedly across jurisdictions (see Martens 2002).

It goes without saying that choice of source, and choice of inclusion criterion, matter. A recent comparison of guides, handbooks, and databases in the EU context reveals different coverage (Berkhout and Lowery 2008). The study points to different populations when directories are compared with actual group interactions with the Commission (and parts thereof) and the Parliament (and members thereof). There is no sense in which the debate here is about proving what is the 'best' source; it is simply that 'different' has consequences that need to be appreciated and discussed.

Different research strategies are defensible, but even valid differences still make aggregation and comparison difficult. Practice of the type employed by Scholzman and Halpin *et al.* is concerned with populations of policy-engaged organizations, while the Jordan and Greenan type of studies are interested in the reservoir of collective associations (irrespective of policy engagement) which may speak to social capital questions. Neither may be 'wrong', but what is decidedly in error is simply assuming they are equivalent.

Even if one thinks one has a viable set of distinctions, putting them into research practice may be difficult. One dimension commonly assumed to be necessary for inclusion is that the organizations are mobilized or engaged in policy activity, but this would, for instance, cover organizations, such as recreational clubs, who become temporarily drawn into policy activity, or businesses pursuing their private ends. Are these interest groups? At the other extreme, the researcher could insist on a 'policy-dedicated' test, where policy advocacy is more or less the sole reason for the collective organization to exist. But very few of the collective organizations that researchers would unequivocally call interest groups engage solely in advocacy: a hard policy-dedicated test just doesn't work. It appears too exclusive. These considerations force us to pursue something more ambiguous (and more realistic), such as 'policy-interested' or 'policy-relevant' (rather than policy-dedicated), to indicate that policy advocacy (or even 'softer', policy responsiveness) is to some degree a recognized organizational role.

The second basic characteristic frequently attributed to the interest group is that it is a collective organization. That is, it has members, and in the 'extreme' these members are fully enfranchised in terms of internal policy influence (Jordan and Maloney 1997; Halpin 2010). Again, this distinction appears conceptually crisp; however, there are several common gray areas that make its application problematic. For instance, many voluntary sector organizations would be accepted as interest groups, and have 'members' in their articles of association, but operate through a small set of trustees and fund themselves via large numbers of small donations (and often from government service delivery contracts). Should they be treated as collective organizations or as not-for-profit businesses (i.e., types of institutions)? Other organizations are set up principally to lobby but may seek funding from patronage rather than members.

In other words, the focus of counting exercises is not self-generated. Researchers have adopted different ways to operationalize this interest. A general orientation such as the number of collective organizations leaves unresolved the precise scope of the exercise. In particular is it sufficient that the organization exists – with the *potential* to intervene politically[1] – or is the aim to capture groups directly intervening politically? Is the goal to record *presence* (with an implication of potential for action), or is there a need to record *action in pursuit of public policy* (some type of actual policy behavior)? Different sources adopt different strategies – but with what implications?

The argument for a 'presence' test for inclusion rests on two legs. The first is that almost any formal organization will be involved to some extent in a public policy field that impacts it. Policy initiatives stimulate or provoke interests, and policy amateurs may become mobilized to defend their corner as conflict expansion processes kick in. The dog breeding association is largely disinterested in politics until laws to protect the public from 'dangerous dogs' are proposed. A supporting argument has been given new impetus by a well-developed social capital literature: that associations or groups enable face-to-face engagement among individual citizens. The 'virtues of association' proposition is that associations provide schools of democracy, sensitizing individuals to the value of working together, and in this way developing citizen skills that potentially spill over into overt political advocacy (see Pateman 1970). The argument for the social capital approach was famously proposed by Tocqueville in *Democracy in America*:

> In democratic countries knowledge of how to combine is the mother of all other forms of knowledge; on its progress depends that of all the others. ... So one may think of political associations as great free schools to which all citizens come to be taught the general theory of association.

This is a perspective that sees associational activities as indirectly important to politics simply in inculcating values and skills that are functionally useful when transferred to more immediately political settings. In seeing the political implications of the nonpolitical, the social capital/comprehensive reading broadens coverage beyond the explicitly policy-active or policy-oriented. From such a starting point *all* associations may be relevant, with an educative virtue – even if the organization is 'politics-lite'.

The point at issue may appear technical, and even pedantic, but the decision on whether to count as groups those identified as actively influencing public policy, or to include as relevant all organizations because of their presence and social capital potential (or a combination of both), generates very different populations. Resolving the *prior* question of scope is vital.

At the outset of this section, the term 'system' was used. It conjures up the notion that there is an ever-present set of organizations – essentially collective interest groups – that are more or less exclusively and permanently engaged in policy work of some kind. What we count has very real implications for whether the term 'system' fosters the right image. Data which directly track the policy actions of the organizations demonstrate a great deal of volatility in populations over time, which arises mostly from the inclusion of what Salisbury called 'institutions' (see Halpin *et al.*, Chapter 6). Such data render the basic notion of a more or less permanent 'system' hard to sustain.

Geographical level

One major distinction in the scope of inclusion in a counting exercise – breadth – has been considered above: is inclusion based on direct (policy-active) political orientation or open to all organizations (comprehensive)? An equally important (but very different) dimension is whether the focus is on national bodies or includes local organizations (level).

Level of research is further examined in this volume in Chapter 11, by Maloney and van Deth. Maloney *et al.* (2008) compare local associations in Mannheim and Aberdeen. Their comparison demonstrates that mapping particular locales is difficult: indeed, covering 'everywhere' might in practical terms be impossible. Richardson (2008) suggested there were 600,000 organizations in the UK not-for-profit sector in 2002 (including registered charities and others). Of these, up to 360,000 were community-level organizations not even registered as charities. A National Council for Voluntary Organisations report on *The State and the Voluntary Sector* (Clark *et al.* 2009) estimated there were over 170,900 voluntary sector organizations, up 6,180 from the previous year. Of these, 40,000 were described as having 'a very close financial relationship with the state': over 27,000 received more than 75 percent of their funding from statutory sources. Most of these were rated medium or large in size.

Knapp and Saxon-Harrold (1989; cited by Hall 2002) found a 27 percent growth in the number of voluntary organizations in the 1980s – reflecting the creation of 3,000–4,000 each year. Hall (2002) also cites Knight's survey of voluntary social service organizations in 14 localities, which found 3,691 organizations servicing just under 1 million people. Back-of-the-envelope arithmetic suggests that scaled up this equates to 200,000 voluntary organizations in the social service area (in the UK) alone. Information from the voluntary sector in Scotland suggests that Scotland has about 45,000 voluntary organizations, of which about 20,000 are regulated as charities. In total, 64 percent of the 45,000 have an annual income of less than £25,000. Perhaps these different sources with different definitions and assumptions reach disparate totals, but the ballpark number is large. Thus the number of bodies that *could* be labeled 'interest groups' is (hyper-)dependent on the definition used. Common sense is not enough; whatever sense is used has to be delineated (and well communicated).

Retro-fitting consistency: fitting definitions to data

In practice scholars have often discovered data sources or discovered practical ways to count populations and adopted definitions to fit the data. This opportunism has illuminated the area and should not be dismissed, but it does imply a health warning that research is often arguing from proxy information rather than the 'ideal' population. The discussion above establishes what many already know: that there is immense difficulty in applying sharp distinctions between interest group organizations and 'others'. The fact that group organizations do not stay stable challenges researchers to take a more flexible approach to definitions. It is not just settling on a crisp definition that is problematic; it is impossible to insist that such a definition is applied across the field. Researchers are stuck with an empirical reality that often fails to respect carefully crafted 'laboratory' definitions.

One approach could be to delineate the *extent* or *level* to which an organization belongs to the set of organizations (1) for which policy advocacy is a highly important part of their identity and (2) that have voluntary affiliates that are fully enfranchised as members (whether the members be individual citizens or institutions). This implies distinctions between groups with different levels of membership of this set of organizations. This approach explicitly acknowledges the reality that most population studies cannot prescribe a definition against which they will collect cases; most have to settle for ready-made data sets that are inscribed with one or other definitional threshold. The approach advocated here is that researchers can set the population they have counted against some objective standards so that others know what has been included (and excluded).

To add to the difficulty, organizations may change the extent to which policy advocacy is a significant facet of their organizational identity and how collective they are. So, at what point in time is an organization judged to be an interest group? And how often do we need to reassess an organization's fit with these definitions? These questions are particularly relevant in assessments of population levels over time. The ambition to give a sense of scale is an instinct that leads to practical difficulties being easily underestimated. But, for all that, we believe that the varied methods and disparate conclusions of the following chapters lead to some advances of knowledge in these areas, and some more sophisticated appreciations of problems.

Plan of the book

While individual studies in this collection might emphasize questions of scale or of explanation, it is rare for any contribution not to touch on both these themes. Thus, the book is organized loosely by region and level. We have a set of North America and European contributions, and these vary in terms of the political level of their scope: international, national, and subnational. Chapter 7 is the only explicitly cross-national comparative study, comparing data on US and UK national interest group populations. Chapter 9 looks at the policy

participant population at WTO ministerial meetings. The last two contributions (Chapters 10 and 11) focus on local-level voluntary associations: the first in the UK and the latter comparatively across regions of
several EU member states. The concluding chapter draws lessons from
these contributions and attempts to sketch the research agenda moving forward.

Note

1. The social capital argument would accept that the experiences of members
   within groups might alter their behavior in wider, but unrelated, political
   situations.

References

Ainsworth, S. (2010) 'Methodological Perspectives on Interest Groups', in
J. Berry (ed.) *The Oxford Handbook of American Political Parties and Interest
Groups* (Oxford: Oxford University Press).
Baumgartner, F. and B. Leech (2001) 'Interest Niches and Policy Bandwagons:
Patterns of Interest Group Involvement in National Politics', *Journal of Politics*,
63, 1191–1213.
Berkhout, J. and D. Lowery (2008) 'Counting Organized Interests in the
European Union: A Comparison of Data Sources', *Journal of European Public
Policy*, 15, 489–513.
Berry, J. (1999) 'The Rise of Citizen Groups', in T. Skocpol and M. Fiorina (eds.)
Civic Engagement and American Democracy (Washington, DC: Brookings
Institution Press).
Browne, W. P. (1990) 'Organized Interests and Their Issue Niche: A Search for
Pluralism in a Policy Domain', *Journal of Politics*, 52, 477–509.
Cigler, A. (1994) 'Research Gaps in the Study of Interest Representation', in
W. Crotty, M. Schwatz, and J. Green (eds.) *Representing Interests and Interest
Group Representation* (Lanham, MD: University Press of America).
Clark, J., J. Dobbs, D. Kane, and K. Wilding (2009) *The State and the Voluntary
Sector*, Report of the National Council for Voluntary Organizations (London:
NCVO).
Dahl, R. A. (1957) 'The Concept of Power', *Behavioral Science*, 2, 201–15.
de Tocqueville, A. (1969) *Democracy in America* (New York: Doubleday).
Finer, S. (1967) 'Interest Groups and the Political Process in Great Britain',
in H. W. Ehrmann (ed.) *Interest Groups on Four Continents* (Pittsburgh, PA:
University Press of Pittsburgh).
Gray, V. and D. Lowery (2000) *The Population Ecology of Interest Representation:
Lobbying Communities in the American States*, paperback edn. (Ann Arbor:
University of Michigan Press).
Hall, P. (2002) 'Great Britain: The Role of Government and the Distribution
of Social Capital', in R. Putnam (ed.) *Democracies in Flux* (Oxford: Oxford
University Press).

Halpin, D. (2010) *Groups, Representation and Democracy: Between Promise and Practice* (Manchester: Manchester University Press).

Halpin, D. and G. Jordan (2009) 'Interpreting Environments: Interest Group Response to Population Ecology Pressures', *British Journal of Political Science*, 39, 243–65.

Heinz, J. P., E. O. Laumann, R. L. Nelson, and R. H. Salisbury (1993) *The Hollow Core* (Cambridge, MA: Harvard University Press).

Jordan, G. and W. Maloney (1997) *Protest Businesses? Mobilizing Campaigning Groups* (Manchester: Manchester University Press).

Jordan, G., D. Halpin, and W. Maloney (2004) 'Defining Interests: Disambiguation and the Need for New Distinctions?', *British Journal of Politics and International Relations*, 6(2), 195–212.

Kendall, J. and M. Knapp (1996) *The Voluntary Sector in the UK* (Manchester: Manchester University Press).

Knapp, M. and S. Saxon-Harrold (1989) 'The British Voluntary Sector', Discussion Paper 645 (Canterbury, UK: Personal Social Services Unit, University of Kent).

Koole, R. and R. Katz (2000) 'Political Data in 1999', *EJPR Annual Special Edition Political Data Yearbook*, 38, 303–12.

Lowery, D. and V. Gray (2004) 'Bias in the Heavenly Chorus: Interest in Society and Before Government', *Journal of Theoretical Politics*, 16, 5–30.

Lyons, M. and S. Hocking (2001) 'Dimensions of the Australian Third Sector', First Report of Australian Nonprofit Data Project (Sydney: University of Technology, Sydney).

Maloney, W., J. W. van Deth, and S. Rossteutscher (2008) 'Civic Orientations: Does Associational Type Matter?', *Political Studies* 56(2), 261–87.

Martens, K. (2002) 'Mission Impossible? Defining Nongovernmental Organizations', *Voluntas*, 13, 271–85.

Martin, A. W., F. R. Baumgartner, and J. McCarthy (2006) 'Measuring Association Populations Using the *Encyclopedia of Associations*: Evidence from the Field of Labor Unions', *Social Science Research*, 35, 771–78.

May, T. C., J. McHugh, and T. Taylor (1998) 'Business Representation in the UK since 1979: The Case of Trade Associations', *Political Studies*, 46, 260–75.

McKenzie, R. T. (1958) 'Parties, Pressure Groups and the British Political Process', *Political Quarterly*, 29, 5–16.

Mundo, P. A. (1992) *Interest Groups: Cases and Characteristics* (Chicago, IL: Nelson-Hall).

Nownes, A. J. (2004) 'The Population Ecology of Interest Group Formation: Mobilizing Gay and Lesbian Rights Interest Groups in the Unites States, 1950–98', *British Journal of Political Science*, 34, 49–67.

Pateman, C. (1970) *Participation and Democratic Theory* (Cambridge: Cambridge University Press).

Page, E. and B. Jenkins (2005) *Policy Bureaucracy: Government with a Cast of Thousands* (Oxford: Oxford University Press).

Richardson, J. J. and A. G. Jordan (1979) *Governing under Pressure* (Oxford: Martin Robertson).

Richardson, L. (2008) *DIY Community Action: Neighbourhood Problems and Community Self-Help* (CASE Studies on Poverty, Place and Policy; Bristol: Policy Press).

Rose, R. (1984) *Do Parties Make a Difference?* 2nd edn (London: Macmillan and Chatham).

Salisbury, R. H. (1984) 'Interest Representation: The Dominance of Interest Groups', *American Political Science Review*, 78, 64–78.

Schattschneider, E. E. (1960) *The Semi-Sovereign People* (New York: Holt, Reinhart, and Winston).

Schlozman, K. L. (2010) 'Who Sings in the Heavenly Chorus? The Shape of the Organized Interest System', in J. Berry (ed.) *The Oxford Handbook of American Political Parties and Interest Groups* (Oxford: Oxford University Press).

Schlozman, K. L. and J. T. Tierney (1986) *Organized Interests and American Democracy* (New York: Harper & Row).

Schmitter, P. (1979) 'Still the Century of Corporatism?', in P. Schmitter and G. Lehmbruch (eds.) *Trends Towards Corporatist Intermediation* (New York: Sage).

Skocpol, T. and M. Fiorina (eds.) (1999) *Civic Engagement and American Democracy* (Washington, DC: Brookings Institution Press).

Stanley, H. and R. Niemi (2001) *Vital Statistics on American Politics* (Washington, DC: CQ Press).

Walker, J. L. (1983) 'The Origins and Maintenance of Interest Groups in America,' *American Political Science Review*, 77, 390–406.

Walker, J. L. (1991) *Mobilizing Interest Groups in America* (Ann Arbor: University of Michigan Press).

Wilson, G. K. (1990) *Interest Groups* (Oxford: Basil Blackwell).

Wonka, A., F. Baumgartner, C. Mahoney, and J. Berkhout (2010) 'Measuring the Size and Scope of the EU Interest Group Population', *European Union Politics*, 11(3), 463–76.

2
Counting the Voices in the Heavenly Chorus: Pressure Participants in Washington Politics

Kay Lehman Schlozman

The research project reported on in this chapter began with a pledge: No new data. But asking me and my long-time collaborators Sidney Verba and Henry Brady not to collect new data is akin – to paraphrase Calvin Trillin – to suggesting that the customs official exhibit no curiosity about the plastic bag containing the white powder. We soon broke that initial vow and now find ourselves with an extensive database of Washington pressure participants – organizations that have sought policy influence in Washington – assembled to serve as the complement to individual-level data in a study of inequalities of political voice in American democracy.[1] In this chapter, I address the twin tasks of explaining how the findings from the data set inform the objectives of our inquiry and suggesting lessons from the massive challenge of data gathering that might assist those conducting subsequent efforts in this vein.

Political voice and democracy

So that members of the public can communicate information about their experiences, needs, and preferences and hold public officials accountable for their conduct in office, all democracies require mechanisms for the expression of political voice – which my collaborators and I construe as the sum total of a variety of activities, undertaken individually or collectively, that have 'the intent or effect of influencing government'.[2] Citizens in American democracy who want to have an impact on politics have a variety of options for exercising political voice. They can communicate their concerns and opinions to policy makers in order to have a direct effect on public policy, or they can attempt to affect policy indirectly by influencing electoral outcomes. They can act on their own or work with others in informal efforts, in formal organizations, in political parties, or in looser aggregates in social movements. They can donate their time or their money. They can use conventional techniques or protest tactics. They can work locally or nationally. They can even have political input as an unintended by-product when, for reasons entirely outside politics, they affiliate with an organization or institution that is politically active.

While it matters for American democracy that there be sufficiently high levels of participation across various political acts, the distribution of that participation across individuals and groups is also significant. It is well known not only that not all citizens are equally likely to take part politically, but also that political activists, taken together, are not representative of the citizenry at large. In particular, those who are disadvantaged by low levels of income and education are less likely to take part politically.

Verba, Brady, and I are in the final stages of a sprawling investigation that considers inequalities of political voice in American democracy from a variety of perspectives.[3] Among other topics, we consider how the democratic commitment to political equality among citizens articulates with the individualistic themes of the American Dream of equality of opportunity; how inequalities of political voice are passed down through generations and how they have changed in an era of increasing economic inequality; how the possibilities for political participation on the Internet affect the extent to which political voice underrepresents younger citizens and those who are disadvantaged in terms of socioeconomic status; how the processes of recruitment by which friends, workmates, neighbors, and fellow organization and church members ask one another to take part politically affect the socioeconomic stratification of political voice; and whether various procedural reforms hold the potential to alleviate participatory inequalities.

One significant – and unusual – aspect of our study is that it brings together information about political voice as expressed through both individual-level and organizational activity. Those concerned with the representativeness of political voice ordinarily focus either on individual citizens or on organizations. We consider the two in tandem.

Organizations that seek policy influence in Washington

Social scientists study organizations for many reasons: they might be concerned, for example, with how organizational membership influences individuals' health, tolerance of racial or religious differences, adjustment to a new community, or political participation; with how social networks that develop within voluntary associations function to assist members with other goals such as finding a new job; with how internal processes within membership groups operate to sort leaders from the rank and file; with how organizations emerge from social movements and then relate to the movement base; with how the free-rider problem inhibits the emergence of large organizations, especially large organizations that seek public goods; with how organizations undertake enterprises and provide services that, in other polities, are government responsibilities; or with how the relative density of voluntary associations within a community affects its capacity to provide public goods. Such varied intellectual questions imply different research designs and a focus on different kinds of organizations.

Our concern with investigating inequalities of political voice as expressed through the medium of organizations that get involved politically places limits on the kinds of collectivities and institutions of interest. First, we focus exclusively on organizations that in some way take part in politics – by lobbying public officials, making campaign contributions, participating in hearings at regulatory agencies, mobilizing the public on behalf of a preferred position, and so on. Organizations in the United States range along a wide continuum with respect to the importance attached to political influence among their organizational goals. At one end are organizations, such as the American Civil Liberties Union or Americans for Tax Reform, for which both organizational objectives and the means of attaining those objectives are exclusively political. At the other are organizations, such as a local softball league or garden club, that never get involved in politics. In between are the vast majority of influence-seeking organizations – among them, corporations, professional associations, and labor unions – that combine political and nonpolitical means for achieving organizational goals.

Second, we expand our purview beyond membership associations of individuals to include other organizational forms. The organizations that seek national-level political influence include subnational governments; institutions such as corporations, hospitals, and museums; and associations of such institutions – for example, trade and other business associations.[4] In fact, the overwhelming majority of organizations that represent citizen interests before governments in the United States are not voluntary associations composed of individuals.

Third, we are interested only in formal organizations. Various social groups – public housing tenants, the obese, residents of a community in which a toxic waste facility is to be constructed – might be assumed to have joint policy interests, but we include them only if they are represented by formal organizations.

The puzzle of political equality when representation is by organizations

The problems in specifying what political equality among individuals would look like are formidable. However, moving from consideration of individuals to consideration of organizations that have radically different numbers of members – and, sometimes, no members at all in the ordinary sense – and that are arrayed along a variety of dimensions of political cleavage introduces a number of additional complicating factors which make it not just difficult, but impossible to know when a condition of political equality has been achieved. Nevertheless, it is possible to identify when we have substantial departures from political equality and to make comparative assessments of relative inequality. Moreover, the domain of organized interest representation is fundamentally so far from a circumstance approximating equality of political voice that the appropriate intellectual task is not to specify what equality of political voice would look like but to explore systematically the boundaries of a very unequal system.

With respect to norms of political equality, even if we were to confine ourselves to voluntary associations of individuals, how would we compare the relative political weight of the AARP (formerly the American Association of Retired Persons), which has more than 30 million members, and the American Beekeeping Federation, which has 1,200?[5] What is more, beyond the obvious differences in numbers of members are differences in resources, especially money. Such disparities in resources are not necessarily proportional to the number of members, the number of politically relevant issues, or the intensity of political concerns.

A further dilemma in seeking to understand the implications of collective representation for political equality is that even groups of people who have important attributes in common are rarely uniform in their interests, needs, and preferences. Those who focus on what is sometimes called 'intersectionality' point out the tendency to overlook such differences within groups. We would expect, for example, veterans who served during the Korean War to have different health care needs from those who served in Iraq; Hispanics to be divided along lines of national origin; elderly people with pensions to have different concerns from those who rely solely on Social Security.[6] This issue is germane for formal organizations as well as for looser collectivities. Because the preferences and concerns of the members of an association are unlikely to coincide on all relevant issues, there may be ambiguity in knowing for whom the organization is speaking. It is easy to imagine circumstances in which younger workers and retirees in the Service Employees International Union or chemists in industry and chemists at universities in the American Chemical Society might part company with one another. Such divisions of opinion and interest are even more common when a voluntary association implicitly seeks to represent a constituency beyond its dues-paying members. Thus, when an organization takes a stand in politics, there are ambiguities as to whose voice is being heard.

Such ambiguities are multiplied when we move beyond associations of individuals. In fact, the majority of the organizations that seek influence in Washington are not associations of individuals.[7] They may be policy-relevant entities such as corporations or museums, which have no members at all, or associations of these entities such as the Snack Food Association, which has firms as members, or the National Association of Children's Hospitals. That the preponderance of organizations in the pressure system have no members in the ordinary sense raises knotty questions for equality of political voice. When representation is by institutions such as corporations or universities, whose concerns and preferences are being represented? Those of the stockholders, executives, employees, or customers of a corporation? Those of the administration, professors, staff, graduates, or students of a university? Certainly, there are many occasions when the interests of these various stakeholders coincide. Nevertheless, evidence that ranges from the number of labor–management disputes before the National Labor Relations Board to student protests over tuition hikes suggests that what is good for one part of an institutional constituency is not necessarily good for all.

An additional complexity is that the set of organizations that seek political influence is structured around multiple axes of cleavage. It is complicated enough to characterize political equality considering only the dimension around which the largest portion of pressure participant representation takes place: economic interests associated with making a living. It becomes even more complicated when the framework includes the many other dimensions around which interests are organized. In achieving equality of political voice, how much of the total organizational space should be allocated to organizations based on race? On sexual orientation? On attitudes toward capital punishment or the rights of homeowners? On hobbies?

The *Washington Representatives* database

In light of our understanding of the kinds of organizations with which we were concerned, we decided that the *Washington Representatives* directory, which constitutes the closest approximation to an annual census of organizations that provide political representation, was the appropriate starting point for data collection.[8] The *Washington Representatives* directory is the most nearly comprehensive listing of politically active organizations in Washington.[9] The 1991 General Accounting Office (GAO) report that was used as justification for the 1995 Lobbying Disclosure Act made the point that, of the 13,500 people named as lobbyists in the *Washington Representatives* directory, fewer than 4,000 were registered with Congress (Salant 1995a, p. 2239).

The fact that the GAO relied on the directory for its evidence about lobbyists suggests its significance as a source of information. Using the listings in the 1981, 1991, 2001, and 2006 *Washington Representatives* directories of organizations with a presence in national politics – either by maintaining an office in the capital or by hiring Washington-based consultants or counsel to manage their government relations activities – we have built an extensive data archive containing information about the characteristics, organizational histories, and political activity of organizations involved in national politics.[10] This database covers more than 27,000 organizations.

For each organization, we entered information about its date of founding, the other sources in which it was listed, and, where possible, information that would allow us to trace its history: previous names, mergers with and spinoffs from other organizations, and so on. For all organizations except corporations in the 2001 and 2006 directories, we recorded their status in 1981 – that is, whether they were listed in the 1981 edition and, if not, whether they were in existence in 1981. Similarly, for all organizations except corporations listed in 1981 we noted their status as of 2006 and, if they were not listed in the 2006 edition, whether they still existed as organizations. Unfortunately, because of the frequency with which corporations are bought and sold, merged with and spun off from other corporations, and subject to name changes, we were unable to trace the organizational histories of corporations.

This process was, of course, made immeasurably easier by the Web. Most organizations listed in recent directories have their own Web sites. At this point, if they do not, there is reason to be suspicious that they are trying to obscure something about their organizational goals and activities or the sources of their support. In addition, many relevant library resources that were once available only in print can now be searched on the Web.[11]

Although the *Washington Representatives* directory has many advantages for our purposes, even this extensive listing has limitations. First, for those interested in making cross-national comparisons, the directory is published in the United States only and does not have a counterpart in other democracies. Second, it is not a complete listing of organizations that are politically active in the United States. It does not include organizations that drop in on Washington politics on an occasional basis but do not maintain an ongoing presence. Third, it focuses on Congress and thus does not list organizations whose participation is confined to writing checks to campaigns, filing amicus briefs, or, in recent editions, testifying at hearings in executive agencies. Fourth, the directory does not list organizations active only in state or local politics, an omission with possible consequences for our concern with socioeconomic status inequalities of political voice. It is possible that, compared with national politics, the disadvantaged achieve greater voice – for example, through neighborhood groups – in local politics.

Finally, the *Washington Representatives* series had two sources of discontinuity that restrict its utility for making comparisons over time: one had the effect of deflating the total number of organizations listed; the other the effect of inflating the total. The first occurred in the late 1980s, with consequences for the 1991 census of organizations. At the time the 1981 directory was assembled, its editor gathered information from the dockets of such regulatory agencies as the Federal Trade Commission, the Nuclear Regulatory Commission, and the Federal Maritime Commission about organizations that used outside attorneys to represent their interests before the agency. Later, this practice was discontinued because the reward in terms of additional organizations listed was deemed too costly to justify the effort involved.[12] This change of procedure would have had the effect of systematically overlooking organizations that hired outside counsel to deal with executive branch agencies but not with Congress. We have good reason to suspect that such organizations are not distributed evenly across organizational categories and that, in particular, the number of corporations is diminished by this modification.

The second discontinuity in the data derives from the impact of the 1995 Lobbying Disclosure Act. The LDA closed loopholes in the 1946 Federal Regulation of Lobbying Act and extended coverage in a variety of ways.[13] Not unexpectedly, the result was to increase the number of registered lobbyists. From 1995 to 1996, the number of entries increased

12 percent. Obviously, some of this increase reflects the jump in the number of registrations. Nevertheless, the number of entries in the 2006 directory was 19 percent higher than it was in 2001, a time when no external factor would have affected the enumeration of organizations.

Categorizing organizations in the pressure system

Given our concern with political voice, one crucial part of this data collection was to place each organization into one or more of 96 organizational categories. The primary goal in designing these categories, which are listed in Appendix 2.2, was to capture the nature of the interest being represented – business, an occupation, a foreign government, a group of universities, a religious or ethnic group, a conservative think tank, and so on. In particular, in designing categories, we were self-consciously sensitive to E. E. Schattschneider's famous observation that 'the flaw in the pluralist heaven is that the heavenly chorus sings with a strong upper-class accent' (1960, p. 35). Schattschneider pointed to the underrepresentation in pressure politics of two kinds of interests: the resource-disadvantaged and broad public interests (or public goods) that are widely beneficial to all in society. We were concerned to make sure that our categories permitted us to make an empirical test of Schattschneider's observations.

A secondary objective was to differentiate among organizations on the basis of organizational structure. Thus, in categorizing organizations in the health field, we distinguished among membership associations of health professionals (for example, nurses or ophthalmologists), which were coded as professional associations; individual health institutions (for example, hospitals or nursing homes); and other health organizations (for example, the Hospice Association of America or the National Association of Epilepsy Centers).

In contrast to most studies of pressure participants, which rely on highly aggregated categories, we deliberately proliferated the number of categories in order to capture fine distinctions. For example, the interests of business are represented by several categories of organizations: corporations, both domestic and foreign; trade and other business associations, again both domestic and foreign, which have corporations as members; occupational associations of business executives and professionals, such as human resources specialists, employed in corporate settings; and business-related research organizations.

By multiplying the number of categories we were successful in finding a home for the overwhelming share of the organizations: of the nearly

12,000 organizations in the 2001 directory, less than a half percent had to be consigned to 'Other'.

The significance of the large number of categories is worth underlining. Observers of American politics have emphasized the emergence of large numbers of citizens' groups since the 1960s. However, the aggregate category 'citizens' groups' obscures important distinctions with theoretical importance for the understanding of American politics: for example, between organizations that seek public goods and organizations that seek benefits for more limited constituencies; between organizations that seek liberal public interests and those seeking conservative ones; between organizations that advocate on behalf of the disadvantaged on the basis of economic need as opposed to some non-economic identity such as race, religion, or gender, which may be associated with economic need. While this extensive categorization reflects the 'facts on the ground' of pressure participants in American national politics, many of these distinctions are relevant for other advanced democracies.

Despite the large number of categories, there were, inevitably, organizations that seemed to fit comfortably into more than one category. To accommodate such cases – for example, the National Medical Association, Mothers Against Drunk Driving, or the American Indian Higher Education Consortium – we permitted an organization to be coded into as many as three categories. Thus, the NMA, a membership group of African American physicians, was coded as both a professional association and an African American organization.[14]

The categories in this classification scheme accommodate many distinctions. However, as might be expected, the boundaries between categories are sometimes imprecise. For example, it is not always possible to differentiate two kinds of business-related membership associations: trade associations, which bring together companies in the same industry on an ongoing basis to cooperate on multiple issues that confront the industry, and other business associations, a category that includes 'broad church', peak business associations such as the National Association of Manufacturers as well as *ad hoc* coalitions and single-issue groups joining firms from several industries. To resolve ambiguities, we often dug deeply – considering mission statements, FAQs, organizational histories, and the composition of the board or the staff. Nevertheless, the construction of this database required many judgment calls. Moreover, despite repeated efforts to clean the database, the volume of the data coded means that, inevitably, it is not error-free.

Coding political activity by pressure participants

A final addition to the database was extensive systematic empirical information to map the terrain of political activity by organizations, and thus to understand something about the political voice emerging from organized involvement in various domains of national politics. Using 2001 as the base year, we recorded data from the 2001 *Washington Representatives* directory, organizations' Web sites, congressional sources, the Federal Election Commission, Supreme Court records, opensecrets.org, and politicalmoneyline.com about the resources and political activities of organizations active in national politics. These data permit us to measure whether organizations got involved in a particular way – and, if so, to what extent – in the following respects: using their Web sites to inform potential supporters about policy issues and to urge them to take political action, hiring Washington representatives, spending on lobbying, testifying at congressional hearings, filing amicus briefs, and making donations to political action committees.[15] The sources used to compile these data were as follows:

- for all organizations listed in the 2001 *Washington Representatives* directory, the number of lobbyists on staff and the number of outside law and consulting firms hired as listed in the directory;
- for all organizations listed in the 2001 *Washington Representatives* directory, lobbying expenses for 2000 and 2001 as presented on the publicly accessible Web site of the Center for Responsive Politics, opensecrets.org;[16]
- all testimonies by representatives of organizations at congressional hearings during the 107th Congress (2001–2002) as listed in the Congressional Information Service's Abstracts;[17]
- all amicus briefs by political organizations in cases in which petitions of certiorari were submitted to the Supreme Court between October 1, 2000 and September 30, 2002 (the 2000–2001 and 2001–2002 terms) as recorded in the *U.S. Supreme Court Records and Briefs* microfiche collection;
- political action committee contributions contained in the Itemized Committee Contributions Files of the Federal Election Commission for the 1999–2000 and 2001–2002 electoral cycles.[18]

Because there is no obvious source that gives systematic information across organizations and issues about grassroots lobbying efforts, we were unable to assemble data about grassroots lobbying analogous to the data we present about other forms of political activity by pressure participants. As a surrogate measure, we searched the Web sites of the organizations in the 2001 directory and recorded whether they used their Web sites in any of several ways to inform and activate potential political supporters: by discussing current political issues, by encouraging those who visited the Web site to take a specific political action such as getting in touch with their legislators in Congress, by offering visitors the option of uploading an e-mail address so that they could receive e-mail updates about issues of concern to the organization or information about its political activities, and by providing information – for example, an interactive map – to help visitors to register or vote.[19]

What do we learn from the *Washington Representatives* database?

What has been learned from the *Washington Representatives* data? A detailed description involving 96 categories of organizations and a half-dozen measures of organizational capacity and political involvement yields a dizzying number of micro-findings. As a teaser, let me set out a few.

The contours of the Washington pressure community

With respect to the kinds of organizations that make up the Washington pressure system, the data show an astonishing number of organizations representing an astonishing number of interests. However, representation of politically relevant interests is not inevitable, and many constituencies with an apparent stake in federal policy – parents of children in Head Start programs, women at home, office receptionists, Walmart associates, recipients of Temporary Assistance for Needy Families (TANF) benefits or food stamps, parking lot attendants – have no organization of their own. Furthermore, the contours of the pressure system confirm Schattschneider's long-standing description:

* Considering the set of organizations that act on behalf of public goods, it seems, on the one hand, that a wide variety of such causes receive organized advocacy. On the other, public-goods-seeking organizations are less common than might be expected on the basis of the number of people who would potentially benefit from the conditions being sought.

- Compared with those well endowed with resources, especially business interests, economically disadvantaged constituencies – including economically disadvantaged groups defined by another characteristic such as race or gender – have limited representation in pressure politics, if they are represented at all. Two especially notable findings in this regard bear mentioning: first, unless they are members of a union, those whose work is unskilled have no occupational associations at all to represent their interests in Washington; second, although there are a small number of organizations that advocate for the poor, there is no single organization that brings together recipients of means-tested government benefits such as Medicaid acting on their own behalf.

Such findings articulate with well-known regularities regarding inequalities of political voice among individuals.

Changing Washington representation

When it comes to how the shape of the set of pressure participants has changed over time, the overall finding is a march to Washington by organized interests entailing expansion but not metamorphosis:

- There has been a notable increase in the number of organizations active in Washington politics: more than twice as many organizations were listed in the *Washington Representatives* directory in 2006 as in 1981. At the same time, the overall distribution of kinds of organizations shows a great deal of continuity.
- Rates of growth for the kinds of organizations that have traditionally dominated in Washington politics – for example, corporations, trade associations, professional associations, and unions – have not been particularly rapid. Instead, there have been notably strong rates of increase in the ranks of politically active organizations in the education and health fields, categories dominated by institutions rather than voluntary associations, and in state and, especially, local governments taking part in Washington politics.
- The pressure system is fluid, with organizations constantly entering and leaving. Organizations not listed in one directory but listed in a subsequent one were much less likely to have been newly formed organizations than to have been existing, but politically inactive, organizations that were mobilized into politics. Thus, it seems to be much harder to get a new organization off the ground than to take an ongoing organization into politics. Organizations listed in

one directory but not subsequent ones are relatively unlikely to have died. They are more likely to have gone into political hibernation – exiting Washington politics but continuing as organizations.

In sum, as the heavenly chorus has gotten bigger, neither its accent nor the mix of voices has been transformed.

Activity by pressure participants

Organized interests get involved in politics in a number of ways, and no single pattern obtains for the distribution of organized interest activity across different kinds of organizations. In general, business organizations tend to be extremely well represented in forms of involvement – for example, lobbying spending or campaign contributions by political action committees – for which the medium of input is cash. Nevertheless, unions account for about a quarter of all political action committee contributions, a far larger share than for any other form of input from pressure participants. Overall, the following generalizations can be made about the activity of organizations seeking policy influence in Washington:

- Most of the pressure participants in Washington politics do not conform to a stereotype of the well-heeled operation with resources to burn. On the contrary, a majority involve one or two in-house lobbyists or the services of a single outside firm.
- In no domain of organized interest activity does activity by organizations that provide services to or political representation of the poor register more than a trace. Activity on their own behalf by recipients of means-tested government benefits barely exists at all. Unless they are union members, the economic interests of nonprofessional, nonmanagerial workers receive very little representation in any arena of organized interest activity. The interests of unskilled workers receive none at all.
- In the multidimensional issue space of American politics, it is impossible to specify what share of activity should represent public goods. Activity by organizations seeking public goods weighs more heavily in congressional testimonies or amicus briefs than in, for example, lobbying spending. However, in no domain does activity by public interest organizations outweigh activity by organizations representing business, and activity by conservative public interest organizations is a more substantial share of activity on behalf of diffuse public interests than is generally acknowledged.

These findings about the activity of organized interests in pursuit of policy influence dovetail with our findings about unequal political voice through the medium of individual participation. Of the many kinds of individual political activity, the vote places American citizens on the most nearly level playing field. Even then, electoral turnout in the United States is not especially high and is characterized by stratification on the basis of education and income. The skewing by socioeconomic status is even more pronounced for other forms of individual political activity – for example, contacting public officials or working in electoral campaigns – and the rules governing campaign finance give wide latitude for the conversion of market resources into political resources. When we add the results of our review of organized interest activity in Washington, we must conclude that Schattschneider was right. The heavenly chorus does sing with an upper-class accent, and the voices of advocates of broad publics and the less privileged are much more muted.

Appendix 2.1   Instructions for the coding of organizations

1. Check the entry in the *Washington Representatives* directory, which may give the information needed to code the organization. If not, it may indicate a Web site or, for later use, a phone number.
2. Using a search engine such as Google, find any information about the organization on the Web. If the organization has a Web site, the necessary information can usually be located on the home page or under 'About Us' or 'FAQs'. If there are ambiguities, see what can be learned from the information about membership categories, lists of members, or the names and institutional affiliations of board or staff members. If there is no Web site, you may be able to learn about the organization from other materials on the Web.
3. Consult *Associations Unlimited* online.
4. Check the electronic archives (for appropriate dates) of publications such as *CQ*, the *National Journal*, the *New York Times*, the *Washington Post*, and the *Wall Street Journal*. Do a search on LexisNexis. Check the Supreme Court briefs in Lexis.
5. Check any other relevant Web sites – for example, the FEC PACronyms file; guidestar.org, which lists nonprofits; or influence.biz.
6. If the directory lists a location, use infousa.com to search for the organization.
7. Check the hard copies of the *Almanacs of Federal PACs*.

8. If there is a phone number, use a search engine to search on the phone number. Use infousa.com to do a reverse lookup to see whether the organization can be located. Call the organization.
9. For organizations in the 1981 or 1991 directory, consult bound copies of the *Encyclopedia of Associations* for 1980–1982 or 1990–1992.
10. Make a list of the cases where there are two or three entities with the same name. We can call the editor at Columbia Books and ask her which one was referenced in the listing.
11. If no other information is available and the organization is listed in the 1981 directory, use the 1981 code from the archives from the Organized Interests project. If no categorization was made then ('DK'), classify as 101 ('Don't Know') and give up.
12. If no information is available and the organization is not listed in the 1981 directory, classify as 101 ('Don't Know') and give up.

Appendix 2.2 Categories for the coding of the *Washington Representatives* directory

A. DON'T KNOW

B. BUSINESS
  1. Corporations
  2. US subsidiary of a foreign corporation
  3. Cooperative
  4. Trade association
  5. Other business association
  6. Firm of professionals

C. OCCUPATIONAL ASSOCIATIONS
  1. Association of business professionals
  2. Association of public employees
  3. Professional association
  4. Other occupational association
  5. Association of administrators and managers of nonprofits
  6. Association of public employees – military

D. UNION
  1. Blue-collar union – public
  2. White-collar union – public
  3. Blue-collar union – private
  4. White-collar union – private

5. Public sector union – mixed blue- and white-collar
6. Private sector union – mixed blue- and white-collar
7. Peak union, union consortium

E. FARM
  1. Farm – commodity specific
  2. Other farm

F. EDUCATION
  1. Students
  2. Educational institution – public
  3. Educational institution – private
  4. Educational institution – for-profit
  5. Educational institution – DK public or private
  6. Other educational

G. HEALTH
  1. Health institution
  2. Other health

H. US GOVERNMENT
  1. State government
  2. Local government
  3. Government corporation
  4. Consortium of governments
  5. Airport
  6. Other government

J. FOREIGN
  1. Foreign government
  2. Foreign corporation
  3. Foreign business association
  4. Transnational partnership
  5. Other foreign
  6. International organization

K. PUBLIC INTEREST
  1. Consumer
  2. Environmental
  3. Wildlife
  4. Liberal public interest group – single issue
  5. Liberal public interest group – multi-issue
  6. Liberal public interest group – international
  7. Conservative public interest group – single issue
  8. Conservative public interest group – multi-issue

9. Conservative public interest group – international
10. Other public interest group – single issue
11. Other public interest group – international
12. Civil liberties international
13. Citizenship empowerment
14. Government reform
15. School choice organization

L. ELECTORAL AND PARTISAN
1. PAC or candidate organization
2. Party or partisan organization

M. VETERANS
1. Veterans association
2. Military reserves

N. CIVIL RIGHTS, RACIAL, RELIGIOUS, AND NATIONALITY GROUPS
1. Minorities
2. African Americans
3. Latinos
4. Asians
5. Native Americans
6. European ethnic groups
7. Jewish
8. Islamic or Arab groups
9. Other nationality groups
10. Christian
11. Protestant – mainline
12. Protestant – evangelical
13. Protestant – other or DK
14. Catholic
15. Other Christian
16. Other religion
17. Interfaith
18. Islamic group

O. AGE
1. Children or youth
2. Elderly

P. GENDER-SPECIFIC
1. Men
2. Women

Q. SEXUAL ORIENTATION – LGBT

R. DISABLED AND HEALTH ADVOCACY
   1. Disabled
   2. Particular illness
S. SOCIAL WELFARE/POOR
   1. Social welfare or poor
   2. Benefits recipients
   3. Service providers
T. RECREATIONAL
U. ARTS–CULTURAL
V. CHARITY–PHILANTHROPY
W. THINK TANKS AND OTHER NONPROFIT POLICY RESEARCH
   1. Think tank – liberal
   2. Think tank – conservative
   3. Business-affiliated research
   4. Other nonprofit research
X. OTHER

Notes

1. In referring to 'pressure participants', I am following the terminology in Jordan *et al.* (2004). Because the research project described here uses information about both individuals and organizations in analyzing inequalities of political voice in the United States, the term 'pressure participants' is not fully appropriate. When they get in touch with public officials to express their views on policy matters or make contributions to the campaigns of ideologically compatible candidates for office, individuals can reasonably be said to be 'pressure participants'. I will sometimes substitute the locution 'organized interests', which is the term that John Tierney and I originally used in Schlozman and Tierney (1986) to denote any organization that gets involved in influencing political outcomes in Washington.
2. This definition is drawn from Verba *et al.* (1995, p. 38).
3. This study – which has the working title of 'The Unheavenly Chorus: Political Voice and American Democracy' – builds upon work undertaken previously, in particular Verba *et al.* (1995) and Schlozman and Tierney (1986).
4. Many students of pressure politics in the United States follow Salisbury (1984), who first used the term 'institution' in a specialized way to refer to any of a large group of for-profit and not-for-profit economic entities that sometimes get involved in the Washington pressure community and pointed to their significance for interest representation. Even though it is perfectly reasonable to refer to Congress or the Department of Agriculture as 'political institutions', in this context the term 'institutions' refers to such entities as corporations, universities, hospitals, and museums. What Salisbury called 'institutions', Jordan *et al.* (2004) call 'policy participants'. The ambiguity of this usage is

that many politically involved voluntary associations of individuals – for example, a professional association such as the American Dental Association or a recreational organization such as the National Rifle Association – would seem to be accurately designated as 'policy participants'.

5. These figures were taken from the online version of the *Encyclopedia of Associations*, searched on November 27, 2006. Throughout this chapter, I use the names of real organizations. However, the names listed in the 2001 *Washington Representatives* directory may have changed since its publication. In addition, organizations do sometimes go out of business. Therefore, some of the organizations chosen for illustrative purposes may no longer be in existence.

6. While the concept is relevant to all groups, regardless of circumstance of advantage, the term 'intersectionality' is usually used to refer to internal divisions within groups of the disadvantaged. There is now a large literature on intersectionality. For brief discussions and bibliographical references see Burns *et al.* (2001, pp. 274–76) and Strolovitch (2007, pp. 24–28).

7. On this point, which is often overlooked in discussions of organized interest politics, see Lowery *et al.* (2004).

8. The directory, *Washington Representatives* (Washington, DC: Columbia Books), is published annually. According to Valerie Sheridan, the editor of the *Washington Representatives* directory at Columbia Books, in an interview on November 10, 2003, the directory includes all organizations that are active in Washington politics by virtue either of having an office in the DC area or of hiring DC-area consultants or counsel to represent them. The out-of-town organization – a corporation in Dayton, union local in Seattle, or hospital in Tallahassee – that sends a VP on a day trip to Washington to testify before a Senate committee is not listed.

The publisher sends a form annually to each organization listed in the book giving the current information and asking for an update. If the form is not returned, it follows up with additional inquiries. The editor relies on congressional lobby registrations as the first line of defense in listing organizations. She also reads several journals: *CQ, National Journal, Influence* (which has an online newsletter, influenceonline.com), *Legal Times*, and *Association Trends*. She uses editorial judgment in including organizations that are not registered with the House or Senate. Political action committees are included if the organization (or its PAC) has an office in the Washington area; PACs that are run out of a home office elsewhere are not included. The directory also lists registered foreign agents, but not organizations that file amicus briefs with the Supreme Court. The publisher believes that organizations generally want to be listed in the directory and often get in touch with them to let them know about changes in information.

Verba, Brady, and I are grateful to Valerie Sheridan for her assistance and for her informative answers to our questions.

9. It has been suggested that we should have used the *Encyclopedia of Associations* rather than the *Washington Representatives* directory. The *Encyclopedia*, used elsewhere in this volume, is an invaluable resource for those interested in voluntary associations. We used it, and its Web-based counterpart, *Associations Unlimited*, extensively in assembling background information about the associations in the directories. Nevertheless, it has two disadvantages for our

purposes. First, as we have mentioned, a majority of the organizations in the *Washington Representatives* directory are not associations at all, whether composed of institutional or individual members, but are instead institutions of some kind. These institutions – corporations, universities, hospitals and the like – are not listed in the *Encyclopedia of Associations*. Second, except when an organizational category – for example, environmental organizations – is inherently political, it is impossible to discern from the *Encyclopedia* whether an organization is politically active. Since many organizations move in and out of politics, the failure to designate organizations as politically active is a serious shortcoming for our purposes. It would, however, be interesting to combine information from the *Encyclopedia* about the universe of membership associations with information from our databases to predict which membership associations eventually make their way into national politics.

10. Collection of these data was supported by Boston College and Harvard University. This enterprise has benefited from the industry, enthusiasm, and talents of an extraordinary group of research assistants: Will Bacic, Jeremy Bailey, John Barry, Patrick Behrer, Traci Burch, Ageliki Christopher, Lauren Daniel, Joshua Darr, Sarah Debbink, Lee Drutman, Lauren Escher, Glen Feder, John Gattman, Daniel Geary, Heitor Gouvea, Gail Harmon, Caitlyn Jones, Philip Jones, Lora Krsulich, Sam Lampert, Jeremy Landau, Kate Letourneau, Miriam Mansury, Katie Marcot, Timothy Mooney, Rafael Munoz, Janice Pardue, Michael Parker, Robert Porter, Nathaniel Probert, Karthick Ramakrishnan, Veronica Roberts, Amanda Rothschild, Julia Schlozman, Ganesh Sitaraman, Dorothy Smith, Kathryn Smith, Martin Steinwand, Emily Thorson, Clay Tousey, and Jill Weidner.

11. As a result, we were able to find information about all but 164, or 1.4 percent, of the nearly 12,000 organizations in the 2001 directory. See Appendix 2.1 for the instructions given to coders to find information about the organizations listed. Reading those instructions, originally written in 2001, makes clear how far the Internet has come since then.

12. This emerged when the editor explained this change of procedure in response to our query about the decrease in the absolute number of corporations from the 1981 directory to the 1991 directory.

13. On the provisions of the LDA, see Salant (1995b, p. 3632). The editor indicated that the act had a substantial impact on her operation. She described having more or less started from scratch in putting together the 1996 directory.

14. Appropriate weights were applied to organizations that were placed in more than one category. Thus, the NMA is considered to be 0.5 professional association and 0.5 African American racial or ethnic group.

15. We were thus able to generate data about attempts to influence through the electoral process as well as through the direct expression of preferences. Unfortunately, we were unable to find an analogous source that would allow us to aggregate data about organizational activity in the executive branch.

16. If the information was not available on opensecrets.org, we also searched politicalmoneyline.org (now CQMoneyLine).

17. Because the *Washington Representatives* directory lists only those organizations that have an office in the Washington area or hire Washington-based consultants or counsel to represent them, many organizations that testified

in Congress were not listed in the directory. Such unlisted organizations were added to the database and coded into the appropriate category (or categories). Organizations not listed in the directory that made campaign donations through a PAC or filed amicus briefs were also added to the database and coded into categories. As a result, the *Washington Representatives* database includes more than 35,000 organizations.

18. We did not record political contributions made by political action committees associated with politicians.

19. Unfortunately, the idea for this data collection did not come to us until the spring of 2008. Even then, we were able to find Web sites for 78 percent of the organizations listed in the 2001 directory – ranging from 69 percent of the foreign organizations to 95 percent of the educational organizations listed in 2001 – or 83 percent of the 2001 organizations not known to be out of existence. Because their Web sites are used to inform the public about issues currently under consideration, we did not include state and local governments in this analysis.

References

Burns, N., K. L. Schlozman, and S. Verba (2001) *The Private Roots of Public Action: Gender, Equality and Political Participation* (Cambridge, MA: Harvard University Press).

Jordan, G., D. Halpin, and W. Maloney (2004) 'Defining Interests: Disambiguation and the Need for New Distinctions?', *British Journal of Politics and International Relations*, 6, 195–212.

Lowery, D., V. Gray, J. Anderson, and A. J. Newmark (2004) 'Collective Action and the Mobilization of Institutions', *Journal of Politics*, 66, 684–705.

Salant, J. D. (1995a) 'Senate Passes Tighter Rules on Registration, Disclosure', *Congressional Quarterly Weekly Report*, July 29, p. 2239.

Salant, J. D. (1995b) 'Highlights of Lobby Bill', *Congressional Quarterly Weekly Report*, December 2, p. 3632.

Salisbury, R. H. (1984) 'Interest Representation: The Dominance of Institutions', *American Political Science Review*, 78, 64–76.

Schattschneider, E. E. (1960) *Semi-Sovereign People* (New York: Holt, Rinehart and Winston).

Schlozman, K. L. and J. T. Tierney (1986) *Organized Interests and American Democracy* (New York: Harper & Row).

Strolovitch, D. Z. (2007) *Affirmative Advocacy: Race, Class, and Gender in Interest Group Politics* (Chicago: University of Chicago Press).

Verba, S., K. L. Schlozman, and H. E. Brady (1995) *Voice and Equality: Civic Voluntarism and American Politics* (Cambridge, MA: Harvard University Press).

3
Interest Organization Populations: The Demands of the Scale of Analysis and the Theoretical Purposes of Counting

David Lowery

The primary suggestion from this contribution to the discussion of the practice of counting populations of interest organizations is that we always need to be attentive to the boundaries of the population or populations being counted. What scale do we map at? On what basis do we define populations? Answering these questions is not easy for any number of reasons, including quite complex, if very practical, issues involving data availability. But perhaps the most important issues guiding these choices must concern the theoretical purposes to which the data are being put. Simply put, data on populations of interest organizations can, and are, used for a variety of very different purposes, ranging from testing theories of mobilization to testing theories of influence. For valid analysis, data on interest populations must be appropriately matched to the theoretical question at hand.

The study of communities of organized interests has developed very rapidly over the last decade and a half. Indeed, prior to 1995, populations of organized interests were not considered to be especially interesting. Rather, they were assumed to be simple tallies resulting from mobilization events whereby institutions became active in lobbying or they, along with individual citizens, joined groups or associations that lobbied (Truman 1951; Olson 1965). We now know that populations matter a great deal. They matter most immediately in terms of defining the severity of the collective action problems organizations face (Lowery and Gray 1995). We know as well that interest system density influences their mortality risks even after they overcome initial problems of collective action, the kinds and number of issues they lobby on (Lowery 2007; Lowery *et al*. 2010), and how they do so (Lowery *et al*. 2009). Perhaps of greatest interest, we now know that the diversity or bias found in interest systems is a complex result of variations in the density functions of different subsets or guilds of interest organizations rather than a simple product of wealth as power (Lowery *et al*. 2005). And at the end of the influence production process, we know that the density and diversity of interest communities can sometimes, but not always, influence the shape of public policy (Gray *et al*. 2007a, 2007b). Given these findings, it is not surprising that the study of interest communities as a distinct topic, albeit linked to both mobilization and influence, has now become an established part of the literature.

Nevertheless, this proliferation of studies of populations of organized interests is not without emerging conundrums. This chapter examines the practical problems of enumerating populations and how these relate to the theoretical purposes to which population data are applied, starting with the kinds of data now employed to study populations in the US and Europe. Basic issues of scale and boundaries are then discussed in light of the assumptions of ecological analysis. This is followed by a discussion of the different purposes for which population-level analysis might be used, linking these to those core assumptions underlying population-level analysis.

Population analysis in the US and Europe

As is well demonstrated by the contributions to this volume, contemporary analysis of interest organization populations is now often, although not exclusively, approached from a population ecology perspective. Population ecology theory originated as biologists sought to understand the density and diversity of species (Real and Brown 1991). Sociologists studying the density and diversity of organizations of all kinds (Hannan and Freeman 1989) later adopted it as a useful theoretical approach. Drawing from both sources, political scientists then applied the theory to the study of populations of organized interests (Gray and Lowery 1996a). This approach offers the two central insights that have proven to be influential in all of the fields to which the theory has been applied: that the density and diversity of populations of any kind are determined by more than the microlevel processes that govern the behavior of individual species or organizations and that it is environmental forces that are most telling in determining the density and diversity of populations. Both are expressed in the ecologist Paul Colinvaux's observation that

> the way in which an animal breeds has very little to do with how many of it there are. This is a very strange idea to someone new to it, and needs to be thought about carefully. *The reproductive effort makes no difference to the eventual size of the population....* The numbers that may live are set by the environment and these are quite independent of how fast a species makes babies. (1978, p. 12; emphasis in original)

Once this theoretical perspective is acknowledged, our attention almost automatically shifts to asking new questions about how the political and organizational environment determines how many and what kinds of interest organizations survive, questions that have rarely been asked before.

There are, of course, a number of precursors to population analysis of US organized interests.[1] In the absence of a broader sample and, more importantly, a population-level theory, none of these provided much in the way of a generalizable explanation of interest system population density and diversity. A true population-level analysis evolved only when a broader, more valid set of data about participation in lobbying was combined with a theory that addressed populations as populations rather than simply assuming that interest communities were merely a summation of mobilization events.

The data were provided by lobby registrations. In the US, quite strict and uniform lobby registration rules at the national and state levels provide researchers with a rich source of data with which to define lobbying communities. The states significantly overhauled their lobby registration rules during the late 1970s in response to political scandals earlier in the decade so that, by 1980 or so, a fairly uniform set of registration rules were in place such that their variation had little impact on registrations (Lowery and Gray 1997). Gray, Lowery, and their students have collected state registration data for 1980, 1990, and three years at the end of the 1990s during which the total number of registrations increased to more than 35,000. In contrast, the national government adopted rigorous lobbying registration rules only in 1995 (Baumgartner and Leech 2001), yielding data that remain, despite more than a decade's accumulation, largely unexploited.

However, data alone were not sufficient to constitute a population-level analysis.[2] Arguably, the appropriate data and theory came together only with Gray and Lowery's *The Population Ecology of Interest Representation*, which derived, as noted above, from the innovative work of Hannan and Freeman (1989) in organization sociology and more indirectly from population biology models designed to understand the density and diversity of species. Treating the states as islands, they employed a cross-sectional energy, stability, area (ESA) model similar to the island biogeography models used to understand the density and diversity of species. The model highlights how the environmental forces of policy uncertainty (energy) and competition with *similar* interest organizations (area) influence the density and diversity of lobbying populations. Later developments included, most notably, a time series version of the population ecology model by Nownes (2004) and Nownes and Lipinski (2005) of a sector or guild of interests – gay and lesbian organizations – that was far more comparable to the kinds of models used in organization ecology by focusing on periods of legitimation, growth, and density dependence in population growth (see Nownes, Chapter 5). Both types of model support the theory's central hypothesis of density dependence – that the births of new lobby organizations decline and their deaths increase as interest communities become more crowded. This analysis has been extended to develop a new organization ecology model of interest system diversity based on variations in the density response functions of different kinds of interest guilds (Lowery *et al.* 2005).

Other scholars have used niche theory from organization ecology (Gray and Lowery 1996b) to understand how similar interest organizations interact with each other in a crowded market for representation (e.g., Bosso 2005). And a number of scholars have used the cross-sectional state registration data to assess how the structure of lobby communities influences public policy. How has this work traveled to Europe? Not surprisingly, the kinds of data used in studies of interest populations vary markedly across systems. In the member states of the EU, which lack lobby registration comparable to the US case, researchers have used several alternative types of sources, ranging from commercial directories (Bennett 1999), to legally registered social partners (Visser and Wilts 2006), to memberships on consultation committees (Pappi and Henning 1999). Perhaps the most innovative of these efforts is Poppelaars' (2009) bottom-up construction of a census of the interest population in the Netherlands by applying successive filters to lists of mandatory registrations of *all* organizations within the country in order to extract a plausible count of political organizations. Nevertheless, it is unlikely that these efforts provide a census comparable to the US state or national registration lists based on actual lobbying (but see Halpin *et al.*, Chapter 6, on Scottish population data).

Despite ongoing suggestions about establishing a true registration system in the EU, no such system yet exists (Chabanet 2006). As a result, research on the population-level traits of the EU interest system is relatively new (Coen 1998, 2007; Grote and Lang 2003; Eising 2004; Wessels 2004; Broscheid and Coen 2007). And scholars of the EU have also relied on alternative sources of data purporting to provide some form of census of the EU interest system. Despite their limitations, they offer some advantages in comparison to data derived from lobby registrations, including better linking data to the institution being lobbied than is typically found in US registration data[3] and in at least one case (the Parliament door pass data) a temporally fine-grained level of resolution on the timing of lobbying.[4]

Yet there are important disadvantages associated with existing sources of data on EU lobbying and, by extension, lobbying in its member states where some of the same types of data are commonly used. The most important of these lies in how these various censuses of organized interests are constructed. The dominant source used by scholars and the only one providing a long and continuous time series is the list maintained by the European Commission and made available via CONECCS (Wessels 2004, p. 204; Eising and Kohler-Koch 2005, p. 18; Balme and Chabanet 2008, pp. 78–79). But it counts only EU umbrella associations, thereby excluding most lobby organizations, including individual firms and national associations (Berkhout and Lowery 2008). Indeed, the list of organizations on CONECCS is considerably smaller than that in any other source. Further, the CONECCS list is no longer available, since a new and quite different Register of Interest Representatives replaced it in 2008 (Berkhout and Lowery 2011).

Quite different in terms of temporal coverage, inclusive breadth, and registered information is the door pass register of the European Parliament. It reports the personal names and affiliations of everyone entering the Parliament's premises as a lobbyist as a result of the requirement, since 1996, that they have a special entry pass (Chabanet 2006, pp. 10, 21). But there were changes in implementation over its early years.[5] And more recently, a new expedited guest pass system counts far fewer lobbyists than did the original system. Given these problems, it is hardly surprising that the EP data have rarely been used (Bernhagen and Mitchell 2006). However, the EP door pass list is more comprehensive than any other EU source (Berkhout and Lowery 2008).

A final potential source of data on the EU interest community is provided by several commercial directories of EU lobby organizations (Landmarks 1990–; Euroconfidentiel 1999, 2002; Butt Philip 1991). Their coverage differs considerably, although all are more comprehensive than CONECCS, if more limited than the EP registry in defining the lobby population (Berkhout and Lowery 2008). The directories have, however, rarely been employed in scholarly research on the EU interest system. This is not surprising given that each uses its own methodology, seemingly changing those methods over time, and only Landmarks provides continuous coverage over a usefully long period (Berkhout and Lowery 2008). At best, scholars have created a patched-up design in which different sets of directories are used to construct a short time series of the interest population after adjusting for the different rules of inclusion used by each of these commercial sources (Berkhout and Lowery 2011).

Theory and population analysis

The kinds of data used to enumerate populations of interest organizations are, as we have seen, quite different in the US and European contexts, and we have until recently considered the two loci separately. In large part, this likely results from the very fact that we use such different kinds of data in different settings. The data remain so different that valid cross-jurisdictional analysis is probably a long way off (Lowery *et al.* 2008; but see Poppelaars 2009). However, some issues in population analysis are common to both settings, even if their import remains somewhat hidden until we begin to research comparatively across these institutional settings for population research. Two issues stand out.

First and perhaps the more important of these is that no one has yet thought through the logic of selecting the appropriate scale of analysis across interest guilds or sectors. As noted earlier, the initial organization ecology studies of the American states were a somewhat haphazard result of the right data appearing just as organization ecology theory was developing. As a result, coding decisions were often made in what might now seem an arbitrary manner. Defining interest sectors or guilds as organizations of similar or related interests, Gray and Lowery (1996a) initially employed a number of categories that made plausible sense (transportation, government, utilities, manufacturing, and so on), but changed these in later analyses when it seemed appropriate to do so. But they did not articulate a more complete logic underlying such selections, and such a logic should obviously be linked to the theoretical issues that are being addressed in the several types of population-level analysis that have now developed

There are certainly other categorizations available for analysis even at the highly aggregated level examined by Gray and Lowery (1996a). The most notable is that derived from Baumgartner and Jones' (1993) agendas project. Although the two are not strictly unrelated (Baumgartner *et al.* 2009), it would still seem necessary to further consider the appropriate scale of analysis in moving beyond either simple time series analyses of single guilds or simple cross-sectional models of guilds across states to pooled state–guild models (Gray *et al.* 2005). And both systems of categorization are essentially arbitrary in that they represent a slicing of interest systems into sectors or guilds by convenience or transitory intellectual interest rather than some deeper underlying rationale.[6] To date, little thought has been given to developing such a rationale. One is especially required for the EU and national-level analyses because of the necessary recourse to comparison across guilds – rather than comparisons within guilds across systems – given few other obvious within-system units of analysis capable of providing the variation needed for testing hypotheses.

A second major theoretical issue shared by scholars on both sides of the Atlantic is simply defining what a 'population' is. To date, driven by pragmatic concerns of finding any data to analyze, neither European nor American scholars have thought a great deal about this question. But it is unlikely that there exists any objective phenomenon that we can label 'the population' that can serve as the true focus of all such research. Simply put, the relevant population of study is likely to be different for different theoretical questions. As shown below, questions concerning how population size feeds back to influence mobilization processes must actually be concerned with two populations: the population of similar interest organizations that is drawn from a large population of similar potential members. When we turn to issues of influence in the political process, the relevant population might vary depending on the stage of the policy process. At the early stage of policy making, when advocates are seeking a champion within government to promote their causes, the relevant interest population may be all those organizations broadly on the left or the right of the ideological spectrum because they are all competing for the same official's time and energy (Hall and Wayman 1990). In contrast, at the end of the policy process, the relevant population might include organizations actively supporting *and* opposing a specific policy proposal (Heinz *et al.* 1993). (But see Chapter 5, where Nownes specifically distinguishes between proponents and opponents. Here the 'contest' is over constituency support rather than policy attention.) In all of these cases, the specific population of interest is defined with respect to a specific theoretical question, not a pre-existing categorization within an extant source of data. Further, these different 'populations' are plausibly, even inevitably, embedded within each other. There is, for example, a population of all organizations of a given type, such as that defined by the directories/ encyclopedias of organizations that are now more typically used by European scholars doing population-level analysis, and also a lobbying 'population' made up of those in the larger set who become politically mobilized, as is evident in the reliance of US scholars on lobby registration data. At times, such as in Nownes' (2004) study of populations of gay and lesbian organizations, the difference between these two populations is not likely to be great; most cause organizations do in fact lobby. But this is certainly not true of firms and other institutions, and it is not clear whether it is so for trade associations. And not only is neither data source intrinsically preferable for answering all theoretical questions; it remains to be fully understood how these different populations are theoretically and empirically nested within each other because scholars have rarely had the luxury of having data at all of these levels of analysis. For now, we use what data are available without fully assessing the assumptions we are then implicitly making about how these different 'populations' are related to each other.

In considering both types of problem in light of the different kinds of theoretical questions we ask, and before we try to assess the utility of current data sources with respect to different theoretical questions, it would seem useful to step back to consider some more fundamental assumptions underlying population-level analysis to use as guidelines for our matching of data and questions. At core, population or organization ecology models are related to competition for scarce resources needed to survive among interest organizations (Grote and Lang 2003; Lowery 2007), a point of departure broadly consistent with resource dependence theory (Pfeffer and Salancik 1978). Organizations compete with other organizations and either survive or do not. We will see that it is this competitive environment – 'the selective environment' in population ecology terms – that is most relevant for solving scale and boundary problems and, thereby, allowing us to validly match data to theoretical questions.

To this, organization ecology theory adds a specific interpretation of how organizations of all kinds compete with each other (Hannan and Freeman 1989). That is, niche theory, initially developed by biologist Evelyn Hutchinson (1957) to understand the diversity of biological species, looks at the relationship between a population of organisms thcrein and variables in the environment that bear on survival. In niche analysis, each resource in the environment that is potentially vital is conceptualized as an array. 'In this way,' noted Hutchinson, 'an n-dimensional hypervolume is defined, every point of which corresponds to a state in the environment which would permit the species S_1 to exist indefinitely' (1957, p. 416). The space so defined constitutes the 'fundamental niche' of the species, the space in which it might be able to survive. But given competition with similar species or similar organisms or similar organizations over space on shared resource arrays, the realized niche of most species is merely a portion of each resource array defining its fundamental niche. Borrowing from this biological insight, niche analyses have been usefully conducted on many kinds of organizations (Baum and Singh 1996), including organized interests (Wilson 1973; Browne 1990; Gray and Lowery 1996b; Bosso 2005; Lowery *et al.* 2010).

Further, organization ecology theory and empirical findings suggest that competition among similar interest organizations to establish viable realized niches operates more through competitive exclusion than through overt strife or conflict. That is, competitors engage less in direct conflict than in partitioning critical resource arrays. As Gause noted for biological species, 'as a result of competition two similar species scarcely ever occupy similar niches, but displace each other in such a manner that each takes possession of certain peculiar kinds of food and modes of life in which it has an advantage over its competition' (quoted in Real and Levin 1991, p. 180; see also Lack 1947). Similar results have long been observed for interest organizations in terms of the issues on which they lobby (Wilson 1973; Laumann and Knoke 1987; Browne 1990), although Gray and Lowery (1996b; Gray *et al.* 2004b) have suggested that competitive exclusion is more likely to occur on other resource arrays more central to interest organization survival, especially members and finances (see also Halpin and Jordan 2009).

Thus, an assumption of the pervasiveness of competition underlies organization ecology analysis, as does its attendant hypotheses about organizational niches and the process of competitive exclusion. Thinking about these concepts can help us to sort through the issues of defining relevant populations and the appropriate scale for their analysis. And they can help to assess the utility of the existing data sources discussed earlier.

Linking data to theoretical questions

To better match data and organization ecology theory, it is useful to look at the range of theoretical questions asked about the politics of interest representation. Research can be usefully divided into four distinct topics that Lowery and Gray (2004) have labeled the 'influence production process': (1) the initial mobilization then maintenance of an interest organization, (2) its entry into a population of sometimes similar and sometimes very different kinds of interest organizations, (3) its lobbying activities, and finally (4) the collective consequences of interest organizations for democratic politics. The second step in the influence production process – the study of the density and diversity of interest communities – constitutes the hard core of organization ecology analysis in which explaining these traits of populations is the object of analysis. In the remaining three topics, these population traits are independent variables that might influence variation in a dependent variable, whether it be the mobilization of an interest organization or its selection of a lobbying strategy. Indeed, one key feature of population ecology models is their insistence that these several sets of issues, usually treated separately within the literature, are inextricably related. Each of these stages is discussed below in light of issues noted earlier.

Organization mobilization and maintenance

The contribution of population-level analysis to the study of organization mobilization and maintenance inheres in identifying how both the number of organizations already existing and the availability of resources they commonly rely on for survival influence the birth and death rates of interest organizations – issues not commonly addressed in the traditional literature on mobilization and maintenance. Here, the focus of competition is first and foremost among very similar organizations for resources that they collectively rely on. Only environmental groups compete with each other for members among or finances from environmentalists. Industry groups opposed by environmentalists in the policy process have little direct bearing, therefore, on the mobilization and maintenance of environmental groups except insofar as they, like BP and the Gulf of Mexico oil spill of 2010, provide a ready rallying cry for recruiters. But the boundary of the relevant population might be expanded somewhat if we shift our attention to another vital resource array. For example, several different kinds of left-leaning social groups, including environmental groups, may rely on a few major donors for their financing. In this case, all such groups would define the relevant selective environment. Therefore, the appropriate scale of analysis, and thus the setting of the boundary of the population under study, depends on identifying those who are competing or potentially competing for common resources required for organizational survival.

Given this, it would be very inappropriate in a deep theoretical sense to use data on the mobilization rates and death rates of the overall population of interest organizations as more than an approximation of the underlying processes actually at work. Thus, Gray and Lowery (1995; Lowery *et al.* 2010) assess the demographic consequences of their biogeography-based ESA model (Gray and Lowery 1996a) on relatively tightly defined subpopulations wherein competition can be plausibly assumed. Similarly, Nownes (2004) and Nownes and Lipinski (2005) conducted their path-breaking time series analysis of only one: the small subpopulation made up of gay and lesbian organizations. And qualitative work on mobilization and maintenance that can be, at least retrospectively, identified as ecological in orientation has focused on small sets of environmental and agriculture organizations (Rothenberg 1992; Bosso 2005). In all of these analyses, the population of interest is defined quite narrowly so as to plausibly link competition for common resources and the specification through competitive exclusion of realized niches.[7]

This is the primary reason that our inattention to carefully defining the scale of our analysis is so important. Indeed, it matters on issues of mobilization perhaps more than on any other topic we examine within the population ecology approach. At present, the broadly coded categories using, for example, the agendas project coding scheme (Baumgartner and Jones 1993) are just too highly aggregated for effective research on the mobilization and maintenance consequences of niche competition and competitive exclusion. In this regard, European scholars actually have some advantage in not having ready access to the all too seductive lists of lobby registrations. The temptation to rely on someone else's coding scheme to define the boundaries of the subpopulation for study is easier to resist if no such data and coding scheme exist. And European scholars have a deep tradition – albeit too rooted in corporatist theory – of looking at subsets of similar interest organizations. Indeed, it might be very useful to return to the hundreds of qualitative studies of corporatism in the German transport sector and their like with Bosso's (2005) organization ecology analysis of environmental groups in the United States in mind. Reanalyzing their findings from an organization ecology perspective using meta-analysis of the type employed by Wolf (1993) would seem a very useful project.

The density and diversity of interest communities

As a consequence of these problems, it is difficult to fully test some of the core propositions of population ecology density and diversity models in a European Union context. Simply put, population-level analysis requires comparisons of populations. While, as we will see, population-related issues might be studied using the data sources described above, the units of analysis in the core density and diversity models of organization ecology are whole populations where a single community under selection pressure is studied over time in the manner in which Nownes (2004) analyzed gay and lesbian organizations, or several populations or multiple populations are studied in the manner in which Lowery and Gray (1995) analyzed US state interest communities using an analog of island biogeography. Neither is available for scholars attempting to understand the EU interest system. The only time series of sufficient length is provided by CONECCS. But it provides a tiny count in comparison to the other sources given its exclusion of both national associations and individual firms. And there is no comparable government to compare the EU with in cross-sectional analyses without running serious risks of specification error by failing to take account of substantial differences in institutions (Lowery *et al.* 2008). In a heroic attempt to compare something, EU scholars have used interest guilds or sectors as units of analysis (Broscheid and Coen 2007; Messer *et al.* 2011). Unfortunately, this necessarily assumes that all of the sectors are similarly responsive to the supply and demand forces specified in the ESA model, something that is likely to be only proximally true (Gray *et al.* 2005; Leech *et al.* 2005; Lowery *et al.* 2005). Thus, the EU case is very difficult to analyze in terms of the hard core of organization ecology analysis.

At present, there seems to be no ready solution to this problem. This is especially the case in terms of studying the overall diversity of the interest community, since such studies require looking at variation across the density functions of multiple guilds over space or time. Given a lack of comparable institutional comparisons with the EU and the lack of a stable time series encompassing many different interest guilds, we are left with temporal snapshots of the composition of the EU (or national) interest community that, while providing some descriptive evidence on the diversity outcomes of the underlying density processes, are not capable of allowing us to examine those processes in anything like a direct manner. For now, it seems that our best alternative is to look at density processes underlying specific interest guilds over time in the manner adopted for gay and lesbian organizations in the United States by Nownes (2004) and Nownes and Lipinski (2005) on the basis of a careful piecing together of their histories from the several European data sources now available (and discussed earlier).

Lobbying by interest organizations

It seems fair to say that despite the traditional importance of mobilization in interest group research and the growing importance of population-level analysis, most students of interest representation are ultimately interested in lobbying influence. With respect to our interest in the scale of population analysis, two issues become prominent when we consider lobbying and its influence on public policy. Both issues derive from the emphasis of population ecology theory on the nature of competition found in specific settings in which policy is made and the specific times at which it is made. In other words, the definition of allies and enemies is not static but changes over time and space. And both issues are equally applicable to and similarly problematic for studies of interest organization influence in the United States and in Europe.

First, the stage of the policy process matters a great deal (Hall and Wayman 1990). Simply put, interest organizations need different things at different points in the policy process. And these different vital resources bring them into competition with other interest organizations. At the beginning of the policy process, as noted earlier, they need a champion to argue their cause. This will likely bring them into competition with other interest organizations that have very different substantive interests (e.g., labor unions and welfare organizations) and that are not part of the selective environment operating at the level of mobilization, but share a general left–right orientation. Indeed, competitors at the mobilization stage may now become allies. At later stages of the policy process, the selective environment changes again, so that competitors when seeking a champion may become allies. At the final stage of the policy process, the critical resource may be a legislator's vote. At this stage, the selective environment will include opponents of the policy proposal (e.g., some or all business interests) and allies who might have been opponents when seeking a champion. Thus, specifying allies and enemies varies across and even within the stages of the policy process. This necessarily complicates how organizations interact.

An opponent at one stage of the process may become an ally at another. But more to the point, there are no natural allies or enemies that we can draw from our pre-existing delineations of interest guilds. Rather, the allies and enemies that define a selective environment must be identified *in situ* with respect to a critical resource required at a given time and place, and our empirical specifications must be defended with respect to that specific selective environment.

Second, just as there are no natural allies and enemies across the stages of the policy process, seemingly similar policies themselves may differ greatly in terms of how they influence competition among interest organizations. Take, for example, three sets of health policies considered by the American states over recent years: pharmaceutical assistance programs (Gray *et al.* 2007a), managed care regulation (Gray *et al.* 2007b), and steps toward universal care requirements (Gray *et al.* 2010). All were broadly considered proposals of the 'left' and were opposed by the 'right', and many analyses of such policy battles (Johnson and Broder 1996), including those in Europe (de Gooijer 2007), assessed the resulting battles in rather simple terms of corporate interests versus citizens and health interests. But closer examination indicates that corporate interests do not always wear black hats and citizens' groups and health professionals do not inevitably dress in white. These traditional roles certainly emerged in the case of steps toward universal coverage. But in the case of managed care regulations, nearly the opposite was true. Further, even corporate interests are far from homogeneous. In the pharmaceutical assistance case, for example, general corporate interests promoted reform while drug companies opposed it, and both were influential, if in opposing ways, when these laws were later modified. That is, determining who the good guys are depends crucially on the specific issue at hand. Again, the main point of this is that the specification of our policy influence models cannot emerge automatically from our prior delineation of interest guilds, but must be defended with respect to specific policy proposals.

The consequences of interest organization populations

There is, of course, a long tradition of going beyond the analysis of the fate of specific policy proposals to assessing the overall influence of interest organizations on democratic governance, with claims ranging from those that view interest organizations as a vital element of democratic governance to those that view their influence as pernicious. While this is clearly an important topic with profound implications, population ecology research suggests that any such claims are almost entirely without empirical foundation. Simply put, to make such a claim, one must first have a plausible description of the entire composition and structure of an interest community over time and/or across space. And then one must have a plausible measure of the overall direction of policy over time and/or across space. We have precious little of either.

In regard to the first, we have seen in the discussion of the second stage of the influence production process that the very good data on Washington lobby registrations remain fallow. And we have seen that developing good temporal or cross-national descriptions of interest organization populations in Europe remains problematic because of the lack of a valid census of lobbying organizations. At best, we have patched-up designs for the EU that give us some sense of how its interest community has changed over time (Berkhout and Lowery 2011), but only at very high levels of aggregation. And as with the case of the US national population, it is not clear what we would validly compare EU policy with. And while the excellent time series developed by Nownes (2004) is crucial for analyzing the development of a specific interest guild over time, it tells us little about the interest community as a whole. To date, the best data available for this purpose are the successive snapshots of US state interest populations developed by Gray and Lowery (1996a). Such data allow us to compare how different configurations of interest systems influence overall policy in different settings that are plausibly comparable. The point is simply that to analyze the overall consequences of interest populations on overall policy, we need to validly compare the structures of whole populations.

And even if such data were available, they would have to be matched to a valid sample of policy outcomes or an overall measure of policy direction. In terms of specific policies, the findings of scholars are heterogeneous in the extreme. Sometimes organized interests are found to be influential and sometimes not (Baumgartner and Leech 1998). But even if this evidence were one-sided, the policies studied hardly constitute anything like a sample. Indeed, it is difficult to imagine what such a sample would look like or how it might be constructed. At best, we have a few general measures of policy direction built on indices of a limited number of policies that are assumed to be representative of the overall direction of public policy at the American state level (Erikson *et al.* 1993). These indices have been usefully connected to the cross-sectional characterizations of interest communities in the American states (Gray *et al.* 2004a; Monogan *et al.* 2009) to constitute what is perhaps the best assessment now available of the overall influence of interest organization populations. But even this work remains limited to a static snapshot and tells us little about how changing configurations of interest organizations influence overall public policy. Indeed, what is ultimately required to address the grandest questions about the impact of populations of organized interests on democratic governance is to incorporate population-level data into existing models of policy making such as that provided by Erikson *et al.*'s macro-policy model (2002). But before that is done, we need to collect data on whole interest populations.

The future of population analysis

We have seen that there remain many problems in the analysis of interest organization populations. Data problems remain perhaps the most obvious limitation to further work. But to some considerable degree, such problems can be addressed through hard work and clever mining of current resources for empirical analysis. But before we undertake such work, it is perhaps even more important to think about the theories and hypotheses guiding population-level analysis. We have seen that population-level analysis, whether of the core hypotheses highlighting the density and diversity of interest communities or of how different configurations of interest systems bear on mobilization and influence, is most fundamentally based on an assessment of competition among interest organizations. And the nature of such competition changes as we move through the stages of the influence production process and through different policies. Thus, a fuller and deeper consideration of the selective environment of interest organizations in specific settings is required to tell us what data to collect and how to include them in the models we specify. There is nothing in the data we collect *per se* that can tell us whether they are at the appropriate scale of analysis or encompass the most meaningful selective environment in which interests operate. That is a job for theory.

Such caution should not be taken as undue pessimism. Population-level analysis remains a very promising theoretical tool with which to link the several stages of the influence process to each other and to the broadest and most important questions about democratic governance. Rather, the caution suggests that we are still at the very beginning of population-level research. We really have only a tiny thimbleful of data and have only begun to exploit the thinnest layer of population theory (Renshaw 1993). And before we put in the hard work of gathering more data and building our empirical specifications, it would seem prudent to think more deeply about what we are studying and why. Again, there is nothing in the data *per se* that constitutes a meaningful population outside of theoretical specification of the selective environment of interest organizations in a specific time and place. Such theoretical specification will tell us what data to collect so that they are at an appropriate scale and scope to answer the questions about the representation of interests.

Finally, I have suggested at several points that the analysis of populations of interest organizations need not be confined to the use of complete or full population data. It is important that this not be read to suggest that we abandon the study of full populations of organized interests in the face of the scale and cost of such work. Such studies remain the gold standard of population-level analysis and represent its most unique contribution to the study of interest representation. Rather, the attention given here to the utility of smaller-scale analysis of organization niches and even individual organizations is based on the opportunities such studies can provide for scholars to conduct useful research from a population perspective even in the face of such severe data constraints. Even stronger, the importance of population-level work ultimately inheres, as we have seen, in how population-level processes influence the births and deaths of specific organizations and how they conduct their influence activities. Without mapping these influences by conducting both macro- and microlevel studies, population ecology studies risk becoming a type of sterile demography of little consequence. Population-level studies are required at all levels and scales of analysis, especially in terms of how these different levels and scales of analysis are related to each other.

Notes

1. For example, directories of professional associations and counts of firms with Washington offices have long been used to assess the diversity or bias of the Washington interest community (e.g., Schlozman and Tierney 1986). But this work has been largely descriptive, leaving the heavy theoretical lifting to rather quick cites of Olson (1965) and assuming that mere presence equated to influence. Other scholars, most notably Heinz *et al.* (1993), examined the interest communities surrounding several major issues addressed by Congress. But while notable for its rigor and insights, this analysis is arguably not representative of lobbying as a whole since we now know that most lobbied issues never make it onto political agendas (Berry *et al.* 2009). And studies of densities of political action committees (PACs) across business sectors in the US (e.g., Grier *et al.* 1994), again relying largely on Olson, purported to

measure lobbying when, in fact, PACs are a lobbying tactic used by relatively few organizations (Gray and Lowery 1997).

2. Indeed, there were a number of false starts even when appropriate data were available. In their initial analyses of density (Lowery and Gray 1993) and diversity (Gray and Lowery 1993), for example, Gray and Lowery relied on *ad hoc* Olsonian mobilization explanations. Conversely, Hunter *et al.* (1991) hinted at the right theory – organization ecology – in 1991, but applied it to the wrong data, trying to explain not number of lobby registrations by organizations but number of lobbyists. While an important issue, this mismatched theory and level of analysis.

3. The key advantage of data on participation on consultation committees of the Commission or the Directorate-General of Trade is that they clearly identify the venue of participation, something that is rare in the US case (but see Yackee 2006). In contrast, interest organizations in the US are expected to register with the legislature irrespective of the institution that is lobbied. Thus, it may not always be possible to distinguish using US lobby registration data which institution is being lobbied. Although research suggests that most interest organizations in the United States tend to lobby across the full range of political institutions (Gais and Walker 1991), the evidence supporting this supposition is based largely on surveys of organized interests rather than on objective measures of actual lobbying. Moreover, even if US interest organizations lobby widely across institutions, it is not at all clear that interest organizations in the EU do so (Beyers 2004; Beyers and Kerremans 2004; Eising 2005).

4. The European Parliament door pass data provide finely detailed counts over time, enabling monthly analysis of the comings and goings of lobbyists (Berkhout and Lowery 2011). In contrast, all of the US registration data are annual or semiannual, a time interval too crude to allow for precise interpretation of whether, for example, policy agendas lag, lead, or are coterminous with lobbying (Lowery *et al.* 2004).

5. This includes application of the annual expiration rule and the identification of interest organizations.

6. For example, women's groups were counted separately in the original Gray and Lowery (1996a) analysis because a decade earlier Virginia Gray had first gathered data on state-level lobbying by women's groups for an entirely different kind of project. Its separate inclusion was a simple legacy of prior research.

7. This does not mean, of course, that looking at higher levels of aggregation is always wrong or useless. Virginia Gray and I have on many occasions looked at the birth and death consequences of density and diversity using the entire list of lobbying organizations or large subsets thereof in the American states (Gray and Lowery 2001a, 2001b). But these aggregations are at least one step removed from the processes of competition that underlie demographic process. Thus, their validity rests on a strong assumption that the economies of scale of mobilization are reasonably common across very different kinds of interest organizations, something that we know is unlikely from studies of the diversity of interest communities and how diversity is a function of different growth rates among different lobbying guilds. Indeed, the organization ecology understanding of the underlying process shaping the diversity

of interest communities, as discussed below, rests most fundamentally on the assumption that there are indeed different economies of scale underlying the mobilization of different kinds of interest organizations (Lowery *et al.* 2005). Thus, more aggregated levels of analysis run a very serious risk of committing an ecological fallacy if theoretical and empirical interpretation is not sufficiently cautious and limited.

References

Balme, R. and D. Chabanet (2008) *European Governance and Democracy* (Lanham, MD: Rowman & Littlefield).

Baum, J. A. C. and J. V. Singh (1996) 'Dynamics of Organizational Responses to Competition', *Social Forces*, 74, 1261–97.

Baumgartner, F. R. and B. D. Jones (1993) *Agendas and Instability in American Politics* (Chicago: University of Chicago Press).

Baumgartner, F. R. and B. L. Leech (1998) *Basic Interest* (Princeton, NJ: Princeton University Press).

Baumgartner, F. R. and B. L. Leech (2001) 'Interest Niches and Policy Bandwagons: Patterns of Interest Group Involvement in National Politics', *Journal of Politics*, 63, 1191–1213.

Baumgartner, F. R., V. Gray, and D. Lowery (2009) 'Congressional Influence on State Lobbying Activity', *Political Research Quarterly*, 2, 552–67.

Bennett, R. J. (1999) 'Business Routes of Influence in Brussels: Exploring the Choice of Direct Representation', *Political Studies*, 47(2), 240–57.

Berkhout, J. and D. Lowery (2008) 'Counting Organized Interests in the E.U.: A Comparison of Data Sources', *Journal of European Public Policy*, 15(4), 489–513.

Berkhout, J. and D. Lowery (2011) 'Short-Term Volatility in the EU Interest Community', *Journal of European Public Policy*, 18(1), 1–16.

Bernhagen, P. and N. J. Mitchell (2006) 'Global Corporations and Lobbying in the European Union', paper presented at the 64th Annual National Conference of the Midwest Political Science Association, Chicago.

Berry, J. M., F. Baumgartner, M. Hojnacki, B. L. Leech, and D. C. Kimball (2009) *Lobbying and Policy Change: Who Wins, Who Loses, and Why* (Chicago: University of Chicago Press).

Beyers, J. (2004) 'Voice and Access: Political Practices of European Interest Associations', *European Union Politics*, 5, 211–40.

Beyers, J. and B. Kerremans (2004) 'Bureaucrats, Politicians, and Societal Interests: How Is European Policy Making Politicized?', *Comparative Political Studies*, 37(10), 1119–50.

Bosso, C. J. (2005) *Environment, Inc.* (Lawrence: University of Kansas Press).

Broscheid, A. and D. Coen (2007) 'Lobbying Activity and Fora Creation in the European Union: Empirically Exploring the Nature of the Policy Good', *Journal of European Public Policy*, 14(3), 346–65.

Browne, W. P. (1990), 'Organized Interests and Their Issue Niches: A Search for Pluralism in a Policy Domain', *Journal of Politics*, 52(2), 477–509.

Butt Philip, A. (1991) *Directory of Pressure Groups in the European Community*, (Harlow, UK: Longman).

Chabanet, D. (2006) 'The Regulation of Interest Groups in the European Union', pp. Work Package A1: Report (October 9, 2006). CONNEX Research Group 4.

Coen, D. (1998) 'The European Business Interest and the Nation State: Large-Firm Lobbying in the European Union and Member States', *Journal of Public Policy*, 18, 75–100.

Coen, D. (2007) 'Empirical and Theoretical Studies in European Union Lobbying', *Journal of European Public Policy*, 14(3), 333–45.

Colinvaux, P. (1978) *Why Big Fierce Animals Are Rare: An Ecologist's Perspective* (Princeton, NJ: Princeton University Press).

Eising, R. (2004) 'Multilevel Governance and Business Interests in the European Union', *Governance*, 17, 211–45.

Eising, R. (2005) 'The Access of Business Interests to European Union Institutions: Notes towards a Theory', *Working Paper No. 29*, Centre for European Studies, Oslo.

Eising, R. and B. Kohler-Koch (2005) 'Einleitung: Interessenpolitik im europäischen Mehrebenensystem', in R. Eising and B. Kohler-Koch (eds.) *Interessenpolitik in Europa* (Baden-Baden: Nomos).

Erikson, R. S., G. C. Wright, and J. P. McIver (1993) *Statehouse Democracy* (New York: Cambridge University Press).

Erikson, R. S., M. B. MacKuen, and J. A. Stimson (2002) *The Macro Polity* (New York: Cambridge University Press).

Euroconfidentiel (1999) *Directory of 9300 Trade and Professional Associations in the European Union*, 4th edn. (Genval, Belgium: Euroconfidentiel).

Euroconfidentiel (2002) *Directory of 12500 Trade and Professional Associations in the European Union 2002–2003*, 5th edn. (Genval, Belgium: Euroconfidentiel).

Gais, T. L. and J. L. Walker (1991) 'Pathways to Influence in American Politics', in J. L. Walker (ed.) *Mobilizing Interest Groups in America: Patrons, Professions, and Social Movements* (Ann Arbor: University of Michigan Press).

de Gooijer, W. (2007) *Trends in EU Health Care Systems* (Amsterdam: Springer).

Gray, V. and D. Lowery (1993) 'The Diversity of State Interest Group Systems', *Political Research Quarterly*, 46, 81–97.

Gray, V. and D. Lowery (1995) 'The Demography of Interest Organization Communities: Institutions, Associations, and Membership Groups', *American Politics Quarterly*, 23, 3–32.

Gray, V. and D. Lowery (1996a) *The Population Ecology of Interest Representation* (Ann Arbor: University of Michigan Press).

Gray, V. and D. Lowery (1996b) 'A Niche Theory of Interest Representation', *Journal of Politics*, 59, 91–111.

Gray, V. and D. Lowery (1997) 'Reconceptualizing PAC Formation: It's Not a Collective Action Problem, and It May Be an Arms Race', *American Politics Quarterly*, 25(3), 319–46.

Gray, V. and D. Lowery (2001a) 'The Expression of Density Dependence in State Communities of Organized Interest', *American Politics Research*, 29(4), 374–91.

Gray, V. and D. Lowery (2001b) 'The Institutionalization of State Communities of Organized Interests', *Political Research Quarterly*, 54(2), 265–84.

Gray, V., D. Lowery, M. Fellowes, and A. McAtee (2004a) 'Public Opinion, Public Policy, and Organized Interests in the American States', *Political Research Quarterly*, 57(3), 411–20.

Gray, V., D. Lowery, and J. Wolak (2004b) 'Demographic Opportunities, Collective Action, Competitive Exclusion, and the Crowded Room: Lobbying Forms among Institutions', *State Politics and Policy Quarterly*, 4(1), 18–54.

Gray, V., D. Lowery, M. Fellowes, and J. Anderson (2005) 'Understanding the Demand-Side of Lobbying: Interest System Energy in the American States', *American Politics Research*, 33(1), 404–34.

Gray, V., D. Lowery, and E. Godwin (2007a) 'Public Preferences and Organized Interests in Health Policy: State Pharmacy Assistance Programs as Innovations', *Journal of Health Politics, Policy, and Law*, 32(1), 89–129.

Gray, V., D. Lowery, and E. Godwin (2007b) 'The Political Management of Managed Care: Explaining Variations in State HMO Regulations', *Journal of Health Politics, Policy, and Law*, 32(3), 457–95.

Gray, V., D. Lowery, E. Godwin, and J. Monogan (2010) 'Incrementing toward Nowhere: Universal Health Care Coverage in the States', *Publius*, 40(1), 82–113.

Grier, K. B., M. C. Munger, and B. E. Roberts (1994) 'The Determinants of Industry Political Activity, 1978–1986', *American Political Science Review*, 88(4), 911–26.

Grote, J. R. and A. Lang (2003) 'Europeanization and the Organizational Change in National Trade Associations: An Organizational Ecology Perspective', in K. Featherstone and C. M. Radaelli (eds.) *The Politics of Europeanization* (Oxford: Oxford University Press).

Hall, R. D. and F. W. Wayman (1990) 'Buying Time: Moneyed Interests and Mobilization of Bias in Congressional Committees', *American Political Science Review*, 84, 797–820.

Halpin, D. and G. Jordan (2009) 'Interpreting Environments: Interest Group Response to Population Ecology Pressures', *British Journal of Political Science*, 39(2), 243–65.

Hannan, M. T. and J. Freeman (1989) *Organization Ecology* (Cambridge, MA: Harvard University Press).

Heinz, J. P., E. O. Laumann, R. L. Nelson, and R. Salisbury (1993) *The Hollow Core* (Cambridge, MA: Harvard University Press).

Hunter, K. G., L. A. Wilson, and G. G. Brunk (1991) 'Social Complexity and Interest-Group Lobbying in the American States', *Journal of Politics*, 53(2), 488–503.

Hutchinson, G. E. (1957) 'Concluding Remarks', *Population Studies: Animal Ecology and Demography. Cold Spring Harbor Symposia on Quantitative Biology*, 22, 415–27.

Johnson, H. and D. S. Broder (1996) *The System: The American Way of Politics at the Breaking Point* (Boston: Little, Brown).

Lack, D. (1947) *Darwin's Finches* (Cambridge: Cambridge University Press).

Landmarks (1990–) *The European Public Affairs Directory* various editions (Brussels: Landmarks).

Laumann, E. O. and D. Knoke (1987) *The Organizational State: Social Choice in National Policy Domains* (Madison: University of Wisconsin Press).

Leech, B. L., F. R. Baumgartner, T. La Pira, and N. A. Semanko (2005) 'Drawing Lobbyists to Washington: Government Activity and Interest-Group Mobilization', *Political Research Quarterly*, 58, 19–30.

Lowery, D. (2007) 'Why Do Organized Interests Lobby? A Multi-Goal, Multi-Context Theory of Lobbying', *Polity*, 39(1), 29–54.

Lowery, D. and V. Gray (1993) 'The Density of State Interest Group Systems', *Journal of Politics*, 55(1), 191–206.

Lowery, D. and V. Gray (1995) 'The Population Ecology of Gucci Gulch, or the Natural Regulation of Interest Group Numbers in the American States', *American Journal of Political Science*, 39, 1–29.

Lowery, D. and V. Gray (1997) 'How Some Rules Just Don't Matter: The Regulation of Lobbyists', *Public Choice*, 91, 139–47.

Lowery, D. and V. Gray (2004) 'A Neopluralist Perspective on Research on Organized Interests', *Political Research Quarterly*, 57, 163–75.

Lowery, D., V. Gray, M. Fellowes, and J. Anderson (2004) 'Living in the Moment: Lags, Leads, and the Link between Legislative Agendas and Interest Advocacy', *Social Science Quarterly*, 85(2), 463–77.

Lowery, D., V. Gray, and M. Fellowes (2005) 'Sisyphus Meets the Borg: Economic Scale and the Inequalities in Interest Representation', *Journal of Theoretical Politics*, 17(1), 41–74.

Lowery, D., C. Poppelaars, and J. Berkhout (2008) 'A Bridge Too Far: The Limits of Comparative Research on Interest Representation' *Journal of European Public Policy*, 31(6), 1231–54.

Lowery, D., V. Gray, J. Benz, M. Deason, J. Kirkland, and J. Sykes (2009) 'Understanding the Relationship between Health PACs and Health Lobbying in the American States', *Publius*, 29, 70–94.

Lowery, D., V. Gray, J. Kirkland, and J. Harden (2010) 'Generalist Interest Organizations and Interest System Density: A Test of the Competitive Exclusion Hypotheses', paper presented at the annual meeting of the American Political Science Association, Washington, DC, September.

Messer, A., J. Berkhout, and D. Lowery (2011) 'The Density of the EU Interest System: A Test of the ESA Model', *British Journal of Political Science*, 41(1), 161–90.

Monogan, J., V. Gray, and D. Lowery (2009) 'Organized Interests, Public Opinion, and Policy Congruence in Initiative and Noninitiative States', *State Politics and Policy Quarterly*, 9(3), 304–24.

Nownes, A. J. (2004) 'The Population Ecology of Interest Group Formation: Mobilizing for Gay and Lesbian Rights in the United States, 1950–98', *British Journal of Political Science*, 34(1), 49–67.

Nownes, A. J. and D. Lipinski (2005) 'The Population Ecology of Interest Group Death: Gay and Lesbian Rights Interest Groups in the United States, 1945–98', *British Journal of Political Science*, 35, 303–19.

Olson, M. (1965) *The Logic of Collective Action* (Cambridge, MA: Harvard University Press).

Pappi, F. U. and C. H. C. A. Henning (1999) 'The Organisation of Influence on the EC's Common Agricultural Policy: A Network Approach', *European Journal of Political Research*, 36, 257–81.

Pfeffer, J. and G. R. Salancik (1978) *The External Control of Organizations* (New York: Harper & Row).

Poppelaars, C. (2009) *Steering a Course between Friends and Foes: Why Bureaucrats Interact with Interest Groups* (Delft, Netherlands: Eburon).

Real, L. and J. H. Brown (1991) *Foundations of Modern Ecology* (Chicago: University of Chicago Press).

Real, L. and S. A. Levin (1991) 'Theoretical Advances: The Role of Theory in the Rise of Modern Ecology', in L. Real and J. H. Brown (eds.) *Foundations of Modern Ecology* (Chicago: University of Chicago Press).

Renshaw, E. (1993) *Modelling Biological Populations in Space and Time* (New York: Cambridge University Press).

Rothenberg, L. (1992) *Linking Citizens to Government* (New York: Cambridge University Press).

Schlozman, K. L. and J. T. Tierney (1986) *Organized Interests and American Democracy* (New York: Harper & Row).

Truman, D. B. (1951) *The Governmental Process* (New York: Alfred A. Knopf).

Visser, J. and A. Wilts (2006) 'Reaching Out and Fitting In: Dutch Business Associations at Home (and) in Europe', in W. Streeck, J. R. Grote, V. Schneider, and J. Visser (eds.) *Governing Interests: Business Associations Facing Internationalization* (London: Routledge).

Wessels, B. (2004) 'Contestation Potential of Interest Groups in the European Union: Emergence, Structure, and Political Alliances', in G. Marks and M. R. Steenbergen (eds.) *European Integration and Political Conflict* (Cambridge: Cambridge University Press).

Wilson, J. Q. (1973) *Political Organizations* (New York: Basic Books).

Wolf, P. J. (1993) 'A Case Survey of Bureaucratic Effectiveness in U.S. Cabinet Agencies: Preliminary Results', *Journal of Public Administration Research and Theory*, 3(2), 161–81.

Yackee, S. W. (2006) 'Sweet-Talking the Fourth Branch: Assessing the Influence of Interest Group Comments on Federal Agency Rulemaking', *Journal of Public Administration Research and Theory*, 26, 103–24.

4
The Changing Contours of British Representation: Pluralism in Practice

Grant Jordan and Jamie Greenan

> Americans of all ages, all stations in life, and all types of disposition are forever forming associations. There are not only commercial and industrial associations...but others of a thousand different types – religious, moral, serious, futile, very general and limited, immensely large and very minute. ... Nothing, in my view, deserves more attention than the intellectual and moral associations in America. (Tocqueville, quoted in Putnam 2000, p. 48)

Like the rest of this volume, this chapter assumes that a focus on the proliferation of associations, as Tocqueville suggested in his Preface to *Democracy in America* in 1835, is a focus on something central in practicing democracies: 'The voluntary association of the citizens might then take the place of the individual authority of the nobles, and the community would be protected from tyranny and license.' This chapter has two parts. The first section, following on from Chapter 1, discusses the variety of available options with regard to capturing the phenomenon and the choices that have to be made in deciding what to count in this field. The second section reports on a specific counting exercise that reflects particular definitions. The data link up group entries in the successive issues of the *Directory of British Associations* to establish continuity of associational histories and thus allow exploration of population change over time.[1]

Deciding what to count: complaints with a history

Complaints about an absence of scholarly UK interest group research findings on numbers are not new. More than 30 years ago Grant and

Marsh observed that 'there has been relatively little work on interest groups generally and economic interest groups particularly' (1977, p. 4). They identified a number of possible reasons, including a displacement effect: the 'growth of research into political attitudes and voting behaviour' taking attention away from interest groups. In the US Schlozman and Tierney anticipated more recent complaints about the neglect of groups: 'Political scientists have been admirably sensitive to various modifications in the conduct of our politics... [but] they have paid less attention to the realm of pressure group activity' (1983, p. 351). Lowery and Gray noted that time series data would be particularly useful and pointed to the difficulties in going beyond nontrivial conclusions 'from one-shot lists of organizations' (2004, p. 5; see also Walker 1983). The work on which this chapter is based certainly does not address all of these gaps, but it tries to map the trends over time and to do so in a definition-aware manner with explicit links to other work.[2]

Toward a sense of scale in pluralist competition

This chapter reports on a scoping study which attempted to give a sense of scale to a phenomenon typically discussed only in terms of generalizations about 'more' or 'less'.[3] By using associational numbers it tried to map (what was assumed to be) the growth in group numbers. This information was intended to illuminate the representativeness, or otherwise, of the group population and thereby contribute some basic information to discussions of British democracy. While groups are commonly seen as vital in working democracies, information about overall patterns of mobilization is even thinner than case study material.

The principal underlying motivation for studying groups is the possible link to democracy. Despite traditional suspicions, groups seem to be democratically useful: as Bealey (1988, p. 189) said, governments appear to find it difficult not to be involved with interest group activity. Despite concern about the adverse implications of self-interested and sectional claims throughout much of the history of political thought, Dahl (1984, p. 235) noted that one of the features of totalitarian regimes is that groups are routinely restrained and suppressed. It seems that the suppression of democracy is likely to involve preventing an open and free group system. Berry noted that interest groups constantly push government to enact policies that benefit small constituencies at the expense of the general public. Yet, he said, 'If the government does not allow people to pursue their self-interest, it takes away their political freedom' (1984, p. 1). Walker pointed out that the apparently tenuous

links between citizens and their representatives are replaced by group
links:

> Legislators may not communicate often with each individual voter,
> but they are in contact, almost every day, with professional advo-
> cates who claim to speak for the elderly, manufacturers of plastic
> pipe, teachers in the public schools, or some other specialized seg-
> ment of the public. (1991, p. 19)

Walker conceded that while groups might be an imperfect democratic
tool, the competitive group system was desirable in a 'warts and all'
sense:

> Despite its shortcomings as a sensitive register of the passions and
> desires of the American public, however, the interest-group system
> does allow for the expression of concern about emerging new prob-
> lems, such as the growing menace of air pollution or the rising
> aspirations of black Americans for political equality.... The interest-
> group system provides a mechanism in an increasingly complex
> society through which emerging issues and ideas can be offered
> up as possible new items on the national political agenda. (1991,
> p. 13)

Yet, if this group activity is an important element in democratic processes, there remains little quantitative material on, or scholarly discussion about, the overall levels of such activity or the organizations that
engage in it.

As sketched above, there are frequent claims and assumptions that
groups are useful elements in the democratic mix. Knoke, in the US,
noted that associational vitality determines democratic health and that
'associations enjoy a privileged position in various theories of mass
society ... they are crucial mechanisms for social integration, bastions of
democracy' (1986, p. 7). Schlozman (2010, p. 425) discussed the shape of
the organized interest group as a modern reflection of Schattschneider's
classic question about the biases in the pluralist heaven, but until
the current generation of research reflected in this volume there was
more speculation about than illumination of actual scale and types.
Certainly the assumption of a simple link between group fecundity and
democratic health would be naïve, but this chapter is in a preliminary
way trying to establish some broad configurations that can be refined
to allow for types of groups, fields of policy, and so on (see Hooghe and

Stolle 2003). A simple equation 'more groups = more democracy' is too crude, but the basic premise driving a focus on group activity is that diversity is a democratic good. There has been a broad acceptance in the literature that there is *some* linkage between democracy and group proliferation. To advance these discussions, the project underpinning this chapter attempted to identify the scale, and trends of change, in the (UK) group world.

Part of the attraction of addressing the existing lack of group data is recording *completeness* in the political map, but in recent years filling this empirical gap has been more core to political science than simple 'tidiness'. If interest groups have an important role in governance arrangements, the number and types of associations or groups are important. To date, such basic information is lacking.

Parties, previously seen as vital in descriptions of political life, are increasingly challenged as democratic institutions by single-issue movements and interest groups. And both associational democracy and social capital discussions reinforce associational importance: groups, it appears, now warrant more, rather than less, attention. However, the shift in focus to studying groups implies research problems. Parties tend to have organizational longevity, and there is a continuous data record. The group field typically lacks pre-existing data that permit us to get a sense of the degree of change. Party politics data and electoral results emerge for analysis at limited academic cost, but group studies tend to require *ad hoc* construction. There are operationalization problems in any effort in this area. For example, when is a new group new? When Fields in Trust replaced the National Playing Fields Association, was this a new group or a relabeling of a group with antecedents? If the Scottish Ramblers split from Ramblers UK,[4] is that two new groups or one group with continuity and a new example? Would the start-up date for an independent Scottish Ramblers be 2009 or 1935?[5] Students of political parties have similar problems, but these relate mainly to the characteristics of fringe parties (which are seldom studied).

The longstanding research imbalance weighted in favor of party/voting studies is clear. Walker (1983) suggested this might reflect a normative belief within the profession that parties are particularly valuable instruments in a democracy or that it might reflect a reluctance to abandon academic 'sunk costs'. Any conclusion, however, that more work in the associational world is necessary means increasing research in an area where there are fewer data and greater uncertainty than in electoral and party fields.

The significance of governmental consultation: national associations as policy participants

There are two broad, even caricatured, conceptions of how practicing democracies respond to public views and how groups interact democratically with government. On the one hand there is a majoritarian expectation that governments gain legitimacy from electoral endorsement and then introduce manifesto-based programs. On the other hand there is a belief in a consensual style that sees democracy as essentially a process of government securing consent from affected interests. In general, this chapter, and some other chapters in this volume, assume that the associations counted are of political science relevance because they have *potential* (as a minimum) to have a role in the consent-building process. Those entities recorded in the *Directory of British Associations* (*DBA*),[6] on which this exercise is based, are (largely[7]) those national bodies of the sort involved in governmental consultation exercises. (In fact, the directory counts all broadly national bodies, but one theme of this chapter is that in practice 'all' is not very different from 'all participating'.) The scale of such consultation is indicated by governmental routinization of a requirement for such procedures in all policy making – irrespective of which party is in control in Westminster.[8] While formal consultation may often be cosmetic, those who are simply dismissive of the overall processes ignore detailed academic work – and the willingness of groups to engage in successive exercises – and fail to understand the importance of consensus in British policy making. The significance of consultation by government is underestimated by those who accept Lijphart's majoritarian image of top-down, party-led British policy making. It is facile to discount political activity on this scale because some groups lose out on some occasions (inevitable in competitive politics) or because governments sometimes indulge in tokenistic processes: such conclusions are about cases not a system.

The argument that group consultation is important and deserves quantitative attention does not assume that governments always start with a blank sheet of paper and then try to find group preferences and act on them. Of course governments have preferences based on their ideology and experience of problems. In the UK policy-making practices *require* formal consultation, but this formality reflects the fact that there are cultural *expectations* of governing through consent. In addition, there is simply too much knowledge about the feasibility of implementing proposals to ignore external views on them. Consultation is practiced not just to follow the rules, but because it often is functionally beneficial.

A subsidiary argument is thus that even if groups have no discernible impact on the drafting of policy or in refining published policy, there is a democratic importance to the 'dance' of exchanging views between groups and official policy makers. This is part of the legitimation of policy (Luhmann 1969). Current conventional political science builds up expectations that individual citizens in deliberative local forums can have meaningful influence, yet wants to downplay and disregard interventions by organizations with membership numbers, professional research skills, and policy expertise. This is the triumph of hope over realism.

The sheer volume of organizations recorded in this chapter is probably inconsistent with naïve corporatist conclusions. Determined corporatists could argue that this account of organizational proliferation and confusion does not distinguish between those who are mobilized and those mobilized to have policy influence: that this proliferation is concealing the much narrower contacts of significance. It could thus be argued that a hidden hand is concealed by the thousands of interactions between governments and groups. But the pluralist position is that the complexity *is* the system not a veil concealing it.

The British policy process is accepted here as largely based on exchanges between elements of government and relevant groups. If such contact is all window dressing rather than evidence of real group influence, as skeptics suggest, it is fooling the campaigning groups themselves who continue to make efforts to engage. Obviously the participation in the policy process of large numbers of diverse groups does not prove the existence of effective pluralism, but it suggests it cannot be ruled out and that there is a need for more detailed study of the impact of these activities. The significance of this huge volume of activity associated with this large population of groups should not be disregarded simply because of unproven *a priori* assumptions that it does not count. The significance of consultation should not be tested against unrealistic expectations of frequent direct impact: a system that respects consultation is also open to pre-legislative changes that reduce obvious consultation concessions.

The UK system – in the pluralist interpretation – is thus open to groups who want to participate, and accordingly it is meaningful to try to capture all national and high-profile regional organizations that are part of that interaction. In summary this chapter argues that there are large numbers of national-level groups and that the variation among types appears to be increasing.

As this exercise is about recording the full range of national associations, we look now at what might be anticipated by skeptics to be the powerless periphery of the group population and not major economic forces. To test the idea of a purely cosmetic consultative system the following quotations deliberately pick up views from the sort of noneconomic groups that are often seen as excluded. The scale of involvement in consultation in the UK means few groups are not involved, and the repeated engagement of noneconomic groups suggests they find value in the exercises.

An arbitrarily selected example such as the Absorbent Hygiene Products Manufacturers Association is not so peripheral to politics as might be assumed; it has a central expertise in terms of sustainability arguments, services for care of the elderly, and recycling at the British and European levels. For example, on its Web site the director said:

> Disposable nappies are compatible with all prevalent forms of waste management, and the AHPMA welcomes DEFRA's Waste Implementation Programme funding for new waste technologies. This will move the UK away from its overdependence on landfill, and enable us to reach and maintain landfill reduction targets. (Accessed December 2008)

This is a 'political' statement if not partisan. Similarly, the National Association of Women's Clubs (NAWC) may not be a key interest group by conventional thinking, but its Web site shows that it does have a self-consciously political dimension: NAWC acts as 'an intermediary with Government Departments regarding resolutions debated at the Annual General Conference'. Almost all associations listed in the *DBA* would be invited to give advice on some issue – not simply through open invitations but through specific invitations to particular organizations. Thus, for example, the Web site of the Royal Society of Edinburgh says, 'The RSE is frequently asked to comment on proposals prepared by Government departments, Committees of Inquiry, Parliamentary committees and other public bodies.'

So while it is often claimed that there are barriers in the UK to effective access by social or campaigning groups, evidence to the contrary is plentiful. The Power Inquiry was a largely reformist project about extending democracy in the UK. The volume of its report covering campaign groups in 2006 did find some complaints of lack of access, but despite a broadly critical stance the project did not sustain the charge of cosmetic consultation. The Power Inquiry research cited interview data that undermined the idea that campaigning groups are totally marginalized in the consultative process. The quotations below show that campaigning groups – which might be viewed as the less credible consultees – see themselves as engaged in the broad process of governing. The British process may involve a large number of trade and professional groups, but the Power Inquiry did not sustain a privileged access perspective. Instead, it echoed Berry's (1999) US data demonstrating the volume of citizen group representation in congressional processes. While some of the groups the Power Inquiry interviewed naturally reported that they did not get everything their own way, they were at least part of the process. By definition, not all groups can succeed, as they are in competition, and campaign groups seemed realistic about this. Martyn Williams of Friends of the Earth said:

> With ministers... well you might get the Environment Department on side, but not Trade and Industry. Government is being lobbied by counter pressure on many things that we are fighting for. ... if it [government] can upset both of us it thinks it must be about the right place, in the middle, so it's those sorts of things. (p. 37)

The Campaign for Real Ale asserted, 'we face a huge challenge to get government departments to recognize our legitimacy and listen to what we say... [but] if we ask an MP [member of Parliament] to act on our behalf, we will get a meeting' (p. 36). Friends of the Earth said that occasionally governments talk because the campaigning pressure has built up but that the evidence also showed they were called in for window dressing to allow the government to say it was talking to Friends of the Earth.

The Catholic Agency for Overseas Development said:

> we are a single issue group and the government is bombarded with messages from other single-issue groups and the government has to decide the priority which it gives to competing demands... and it is the government's job to trade off these demands. One recognizes, perhaps not in public, that we will not always get everything we ask for. (p. 38)

Jill Johnstone of the National Consumer Council noted, 'I work quite closely with American colleagues and they don't have the same entrée that we do in the UK. They have to shout on the outside... while we have the opportunity to be on the inside as well.' Alison Dean of the YMCA suggested that 'the voluntary sector has actually probably increased its power and influence within the last 5/10 years, particularly the last

5 years. ... So I think politically we do have quite a strong voice' (p. 40). These comments suggest a realism among group professionals that access implies opportunities to comment, not a guarantee that the government will accept all advice.

A report by ICT Foresight (2006, p. 7), supported by the Hansard Society and NCVO Third Sector Foresight, on *Campaigning and Consultation* endorsed the view from within the voluntary sector that consultation was an important policy opportunity for groups, not a charade: 'VCOs [voluntary and community organizations] are key intermediaries in the relationship between the state and citizens. ... Voluntary and community organizations are often integral to such consultation processes.' The report saw new technologies as opening up ways to involve individuals in making the group case.

A trite academic conclusion that – without investigation – rules out the possibility that such groups are integrated into meaningful governance exchanges might want to discount this activity, but that seems premature. There is at least potential here for political impact. Indeed, if one accepts *in principle* the distinction between 'political' and 'non-political' groups, the challenge in practice is to find organizations that pass a test as associations that are not engaged under some everyday circumstance in particular political processes. In other words, the associations listed in the *DBA* are (generally) seen as authoritative representatives of their policy niche.

Coverage choices: counting policy-active or comprehensive, social capital organizations?

As argued in Chapter 1, the 'population' in interest group studies is definition-dependent – more, one suspects, than in most fields. There is an elasticity about terms such as 'association', 'pressure group', and 'interest group' that is not simply a difference between technical political science and more popular use, but also reflects major variations in scope in different academic interpretations. As Halpin and colleagues show, different arenas are associated with very different patterns: group types appear in different proportions in different political settings. In other words, in practice very different populations have been identified in different exercises, and even within exercises. Recording large numbers of cases is itself a practical research problem, but (as is a central theme in this volume) deciding what to count is an even bigger issue. Definitional consensus is needed for consistent counting. *Post hoc* comparison of loosely analogous concepts is defensible only as a last-resort strategy. It is perhaps ironic that it is the empirical urge to count that in fact often drives researchers to consider concepts with some precision.

This chapter reinforces the early proposition in this volume that there are two principal perspectives underpinning different approaches to counting. Here they are set out as the *social capital/comprehensive* and the *policy-active* focuses. These imply very different population scales, but as noted above the differences may in practice be less significant than initially appears to be the case. The 'policy-active' notion essentially wants to find out who are holding the smoking guns in politics: which groups are in the policy battle. The broader comprehensive option used here (loosely co-termed a 'social capital' orientation) includes (apparently) nonpolitical organizations. In this latter perspective, eligibility for inclusion as an association is essentially compositional: all organizations that aggregate are relevant. Critics of this operationalization would say that many such organizations are not policy-influencing (i.e., political), but there are three main rejoinders. First, there is the idea that almost all organizations seem to have the potential to be pulled into politics in a response mode. Second, the social capital assumption is that all organizations have educative functions potentially relevant to political activity while not being directly political. Third, joining a collective body is an identity statement that might become politicized.

In this context 'comprehensive' or 'social capital' essentially means all nationally organized multimember organizations, and 'policy-active' means those organizations intervening in the policy process, but the argument is that almost all of the former could, on occasion, be in the second category. The data in this chapter are gathered from a (limited) social capital/comprehensive perspective; however, in practice they connect to the policy-active account, as realistically inclusion means a body has to be prominent enough to be on the radar of the *Directory*, which implies a media profile that suggests some policy capacity.

An implicit argument for the social capital approach was famously advanced by Tocqueville in *Democracy in America*:

> In democratic countries knowledge of how to combine is the mother of all other forms of knowledge; on its progress depends that of all the others. ... So one may think of political associations as great free schools to which all citizens come to be taught the general theory of association. (1969, p. 193)

Following Tocqueville, and anticipating Putnam, Knoke said that associations transform nonpolitical organizational involvements into political participation through several related processes. He argued:

> Association membership broadens one's sphere of interests and concerns, so that public affairs and political issues become more salient to the individual. It brings one into contact with many diverse people, and the resulting social relationships draw the individual into a wide range of new activities, including politics. It gives one training and experience in social interaction and leadership skills that are valuable in the political sphere. It provides one with multiple channels through which he or she can act to exert influence on politicians and the political system. (1986, p. 8)

This broad social-capital-friendly interpretation – that an association is a group of members cooperating for a shared purpose (perhaps, but not necessarily, with a political dimension) – accepts that one of the consequences of group membership is that an apolitical group membership may have spillover political ramifications. This pushes research to include in its scope organizations not primarily established for political purposes. Approaching the exercise of measurement with such a broad definition would seem to have the potential to generate far more cases than an approach that requires actual political intervention before inclusion. But in a sense all associations in the social capital orientation are regarded as at least potentially politically active. Thus the Web site of the Border Terrier Club carries a draft letter from the Kennel Club for members to send to MPs arguing against pedigree breeding being seen as detrimental to dog welfare. If an organization exists in a formal way, it is part way to being available to act as a policy-influencing body.

In the social capital approach, quantification attempts to list all formally organized, member-based organizations – and at all levels. (The exercise reported on in this chapter did not attempt the 'all levels' goal and hence is a partial social capital approach.) If all local as well as national, informal as well as formal, 'apolitical' (in practice, perhaps, occasionally political) organizations are relevant, is it wholly practical to capture this population by research? Despite the potential attractiveness of the results if they could be obtained, multilevel counting of comprehensively defined organizations appears unrealistically ambitious considering the limited progress on much more modest agendas. The limited (national-level) social capital scope here may be all that is feasible. This comment reflects not just a recognition of the problems in handling hundreds of thousands of cases, but concerns about definitions and rules of inclusion when less formal requirements are made of the constituent organizations.

An alternative approach to counting (using a policy-active definition) is exhibited by the most recent major US data set (Schlozman *et al.* 2008) and reported on by Schlozman in this volume (Chapter 2). For Schlozman *et al.* it is political representation in Washington that triggers inclusion. This approach uncovered more than 27,000 organizations with a presence in national politics listed in the 1981, 1991, 2001, or 2006 *Washington Representatives* directories. Unlike the US and UK directories used here, the work by Schlozman *et al.* is explicitly confined to the policy-active,[9] but in including businesses acting on their own account this may actually be a 'pressure participant' census (Jordan *et al.* 2004) rather than associational. The Schlozman *et al.* (2008) approach looks for explicit political engagement, but the assumption in our study was that all organizations have at least the *potential* for political relevance in a system that relies upon consultation of affected interests. First, then, the claim is that these associations are proxies for interest groups and give insight into interest group trends. But, second, we assert that politically marginal associations are themselves democratically relevant in social capital terms. They are worth studying *per se*, not simply as proxies.

In summary, the coverage of many different (similar-sounding) research projects is simply variable – normally making cumulative findings impossible. For example, Schlozman and Tierney (1986, p. 10) exclude church groups whose members work together to raise money for a new chapel as being apolitical, but they do accept organizations such as General Motors whose primary purpose is manufacturing and profits, but which have a tangential and perhaps occasional political focus. The directory used in this UK research would exclude the church group because it is subnational and exclude the car company as there are perfectly good other categories (e.g., firms) for such cases, but it would include any collective (but national-level only) association even if the political dimension were only remote. Both approaches are valid, but they give different results.

The directory-based lists of associations of the sort used in this study in the UK and by Jordan *et al.* in the US (Chapter 7) are thus subject to two contradictory criticisms. One is that in their comprehensiveness they potentially capture too much of the politically trivial at the cost of political 'meat' (that is, they are too wide and prefer the comprehensive idea to the pressure participant idea); the other criticism is that they are biased toward formal, national, and bureaucratized organizations (that is, they are too restricted). These associational lists can be criticized. The point here is to emphasize that the frequent calls for better data about groups need detail. A large number of different populations can be identified as providing 'group numbers'.

National level or multilevel?

As set out in Chapter 1, one possible consequence of going beyond a national-level focus is an overwhelming number of cases. The first edition of the *Directory of British Associations* itself suggested (probably too conservatively) that if all *local* societies were included, the volume would contain 250,000 entries as opposed to the approximately 5,000–6,000 actually recorded as the national-level population. In line with the reservation about social capital approaches above, on practical grounds this exercise does not attempt to capture the multilevel total of all UK associations. The sheer quantity of cases means it is difficult to count even at the national level; realistically, the challenge is near impossible in any comprehensive and multilevel sense.

Good reasons can be advanced for pursuing any of the following combinations of level and breadth:

- national and comprehensive,
- national and policy-active,
- multilevel and comprehensive, or
- multilevel and policy-active.

The data in this chapter essentially pursue the first category – the national and comprehensive (but large regional players are also included). The chapter tries to provide a rough handle on such topics as how many *major national* groups there are, whether there are more or fewer than before, and which fields are growing or shrinking.

The available British data: (largely) national and comprehensive

The foregoing discussion to clarify what could be counted was required to make the point that an ambition to map associations or interest groups or pressure groups, and so on, raises numerous practical issues over exactly what it would be ideal to collect – and possible to collect reliably. This section focuses on the pattern found in the UK in the

Directory of British Associations. Each of the 20 print editions used is a major reference book with around 600 pages of text. In addition, there are several CD-based issues, of which 2009 is edition 7. The 2005 text version, for example, lists about 7,000 organizations. It uses a pragmatic definition:

> national associations, societies, institutes and similar organizations... which have a voluntary membership. Regional and local organizations concerned with important industries and trades... local chambers of commerce and county agricultural, historical, natural history and similar organizations which are the principal sources of information and contacts in their areas. (p. vii)

So the *DBA* data are firmly oriented to national-level bodies, although in practice important regional bodies are also included.

The main reason for using these national-level data are their availability, but it is also important to note the practicality: the national level is simply more manageable. The focus on membership-based collective action organizations automatically excludes (among others) governmental institutions and corporations that would be included in a wider pressure-participant-type categorization, but it is wider than a strict policy-active concept. In practice, rather than being an extreme, the *Directory* data lie between the two broad approaches established earlier. In generating a commercially useful list of organizations, the *DBA* approximates to a politically relevant population that may impact national policy making. By limiting inclusion to formal, national organizations with established office bearers and formal status and addresses, and so on, the associational list captures both collective action organizations that are regularly involved in the political process and an approximate list of those collective action bodies that *might* be involved in the specialist niches and interstices of national-level consultative politics.

An indicator that the directory used *is* reasonably reliable is that it has satisfied its market and has publishing stability; that is, a preliminary pointer to accuracy is its commercial survival. Other indicators of reliability include tests against press coverage. Thus when the 'Farepak' prepaid hamper crisis hit Christmas shoppers in the UK in 2006 (a huge consumer story when a company folded and customer savings were lost), the relevant association (the Hamper Industry Trade Association) was already listed in the *Directory*. Of course, it did not anticipate flash groups such as Unfairpak, which emerged as a consumer advice and lobbying organization. Published directories will inevitably underestimate the ephemeral.

As noted earlier in connection with the importance of consultation, the broad argument here is that policy making in the UK typically involves low-key exchanges between civil servants and organizations with limited breadth of interest but authoritative status in their niche. Specific examples often seem trivial – to the unaffected. Thus in the case just raised, the Hamper Industry Trade Association could be dismissed as marginal to politics, but it did dominate British headlines for several weeks in 2006. It is the sort of niche organization that would be part of routine consumer policy making. This 'importance of the particular' is unlike the political party area, where the number of significant cases may be larger than often assumed, but the total would be in the scores rather than the thousands. There is no tradition of studying *all* parties as a category. Various rules – such as 'likely to participate in government' – allow pruning. In the interest group field the inability to forecast agendas makes exclusion dangerous.

Basic associational demographics

While published research focuses on the mega-groups with the largest memberships, the data suggest that nearly 40 percent of UK national associations have between 100 and 999 members; 30 percent have 10–99; and 10 percent have fewer than 10 (Table 4.1). To put it another way, less than 5 percent of associations have 10,000 members or more: studies of large groups are studies of exceptions. The high-volume, membership-churning, mail-order type of group is unusual – another case of the academic community perhaps focusing on the exception rather than the norm. Skocpol's research on larger membership bodies over time was described in Chapter 1. This was a useful device to get good coverage of most participation by individuals, but of course few organizations would meet the 1 percent of the population threshold.

Table 4.1   Distribution of UK associations by membership size, 2009

Membership	Number of associations	%
1–9	558	9.5
10–99	1,708	29.1
100–999	2,294	39.1
1,000–9,999	1,019	17.4
10,000–99,999	230	3.9
100,000–999,999	55	0.9
1,000,000+	9	0.2
Summed total	5,873	–
Group count	7,755	–

In the *DBA*, groups can claim individual or firm members (or both); 78 percent had individual members and 41 percent had firm members; 19 percent reported both; 59 percent had only individual members and 22 percent had only firm members (Table 4.2; Figure 4.1). It is clear that individual membership organizations are the commonest currency in the associational universe.

Table 4.2   Group membership composition of UK associations

Membership type	Number of associations	%
Individual	3,278	78
Individual only	2,491	59
Firm	1,705	41
Firm only	918	22
Both	787	19
All reported	4,196	100
Total groups	7,755	–

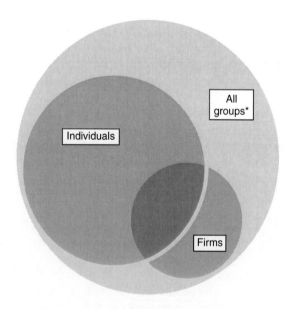

Figure 4.1   Group membership composition of UK associations, 2006
*'All groups' includes groups which did not report membership type.

The expected biases?

The initial broad contours of representation are recorded in Figure 4.2.[10] A preliminary look confirms a proliferation of business and trade groups that is usually read as a bias toward business. However, while many of the bodies involved in consultation are trade, this may be a measure of governmental impact on business rather than trade group dominance. Salisbury noted that 'groups have come to Washington out of need and dependence rather than because they have influence' (1990, p. 229).

Trade/employer associations and professional bodies dominate numerically. However, with hindsight, it is clear that powerful interests might prosper without multiple (and hence perhaps fragmented) representation. Certainly, the data over time reported below suggest that the conventional wisdom of reading strength and bias from proliferation might be questionable. As numbers in these categories are apparently declining (as recorded in numerous studies), the conventional wisdom implies these interests must be less powerful. This is unlikely.

Patterns over time: explosion?

In the absence of a real metric about what is going on in group populations, commentators have tended to offer an *impression* of low-level stability, followed by an organizational *explosion* during the 1960s. This conventional wisdom is as clear as any in political science. For example, Baumgartner and Leech wrote, 'Political scientists writing since the turn of the [20th] century have repeatedly noted the vast proliferation

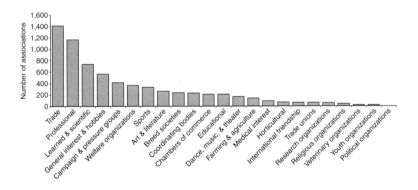

Figure 4.2   Fields of interest of UK associations, 2006

Note: These categories are those applied by the publishers of the *Directory of Business Associations*; the data were also recoded to be compatible with the Agendas project.

of interest groups in Washington, DC, and in recent decades it has become common to refer to the interest group "explosion" of the late 1960s and early 1970s' (2001, p. 1191). (This topic is further discussed in Chapter 7.)

Unlike the US results (see Chapter 7), and in stark contrast to the finding in the 'explosion' literature, the British situation gives the *appearance* of remarkable stability over time. While 'explosion' is a reasonably valid summary in the US, it is far less so in Britain. In the case of Britain there is very limited net growth, as shown by observations in 1970, 1992, and 2005. The UK figure shows sectoral change, but limited overall expansion (Table 4.3; Figure 4.3).

As shown in Chapter 7, while Britain and the US show very different rates of overall growth, initial discomfort with these conflicting results was replaced by acceptance that the UK data about *reductions* in some categories (leading to overall 'stability') are compatible with other important evidence. For example, the Certification Officer's *Annual Report 2008–9* (which is the official UK record of trade unions and employers' associations) reports:

> Continuing the trend which has now been uninterrupted since 1983, the total number of trade unions and employers' associations has again decreased over the most recent reporting period. In 1983 there were 502 trade unions and 375 employers' associations. At the end of this reporting year there were 184 trade unions and 133 employers' associations.

Table 4.3 Total number of associations reported in the *Directory of British Associations*, 1970–2009

Year (edition)	Number of associations
Printed directory versions (after amending)	
1970 (3rd edition)	6,663
1992 (11th edition)	7,359
2006 (17th edition)	6,894
Unamended versions	
2006 (CD6)	7,755
2009 (CD7)	8,399

Note: These totals are those after duplications were deleted (e.g., former names). This means that the times series figures are lower than those in the individual volumes. The totals from the CDs are in the same ballpark at higher levels as they are not subject to the exclusion process. For this reason, while there is apparently a slight increase in 2009, it would shrink if 2009 were integrated back into the larger data set.

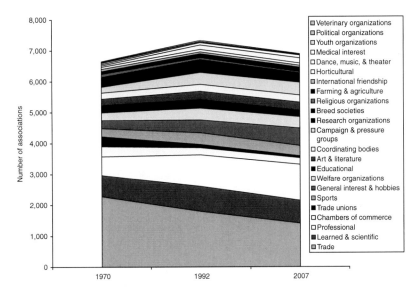

Figure 4.3   Change in number of UK associations, by sector, 1970–2007

An example of definitional problems is that one of those unions listed as defunct is Amicus, which merged with the Transport and General Workers Union as the mega-union Unite. Is a merger the same as a termination?

The planning peaks?

The general topic of this chapter is the trends in numbers. One unexpected observation from Figure 4.4 is the spiking of group births in 1914–20 and 1945–50. This suggests associational proliferation in a planned economy. Plotting a separate line for trade and employment groups only – in comparison with a line combining all other group types – shows that trade groups were particularly likely to appear around wartime. From the perspective of 1970 (that is, including only groups which had survived until 1970), the birth rate of trade and business bodies peaked during the wars, while for other categories the peak came five years later (during postwar reconstruction). This is phenomenon is evident in both periods of world war, and while the trend was unanticipated before the research process, with hindsight it seems credible.

This suggests that one factor determining overall population might be government needs in terms of policy development and administration.

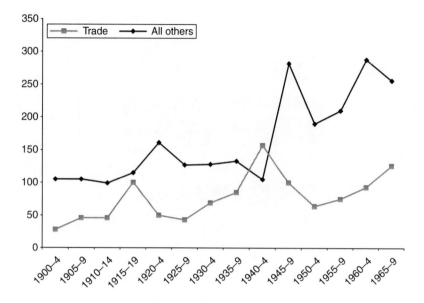

Figure 4.4   Births of UK trade associations compared with other types of association, 1900–1969

Note: Wartime birth rates as seen from 1970; trade groups against all other group types. The figures include only associations that were still in existence in 1970.

But this is a small growth factor in the overall scheme: the population is not the consequence of one variable but is the net result of pressures of growth and shrinkage.

The changing composition of the total: growth versus decline tendencies

While the UK group population has remained steady, rather than exploding as (possibly) anticipated, 'stability' is in fact the product of group demise and creation roughly balancing each other. Figure 4.5 shows that the composition has changed substantially by policy area and over time. Furthermore, there is often a busy 'revolving door' at the individual organization level. A number that is consistent over time often masks turnover at the level of individual cases. (See the discussion of chambers of commerce in Chapter 7.)

While trade/employer groups are the biggest category, they are easily the biggest loser in terms of volume. This matches Baumgartner's conclusion for the US (2005, p. 6; see also Schlozman *et al.* 2008, p. 1).

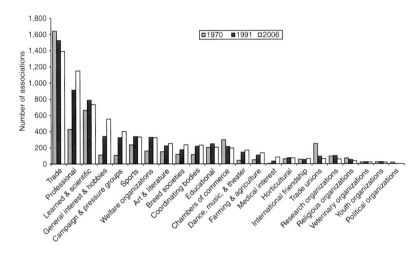

Figure 4.5 Changing numbers of UK associations, by field of interest, 1970–2006

Note: Total numbers: 1970 = 6,664; 1991 = 7,359; 2006 = 6,894.

While a fifth (20 percent) of UK associations in 2006 were trade/employer groups, this was down from a third (34 percent) in 1970. The collapse in trade union volumes was even more spectacular in percentage than in absolute terms. The data here imply that the relationship between group numbers and group influence requires further consideration. Berry noted (1999, p. 4) that the enthusiasm political scientists have shown for documenting the advantages of business has not been matched by any inclination to study ways in which the bias might be decreasing over time.

The key dynamic is the contrast between the descending 'skyscrapers' for trade, and the ascending numbers for professional bodies. These are the two biggest categories, but they reflect very different life histories: decline and expansion. Trade/employer groups reduced from 2,280 to 1,411 between 1970 and 2005/6, but they remain the largest category. Can fewer groups signal increased influence? Figure 4.6 shows the same data as a percentage of the total populations; it indicates how even the diminished trade category is very important.

While they remain a large part of the total, trade/employer groups have fallen by 13.1 percent of the total. This basic finding undermines the assumption that business dominates the political system because it dominates in terms of representation. If the original assumption that

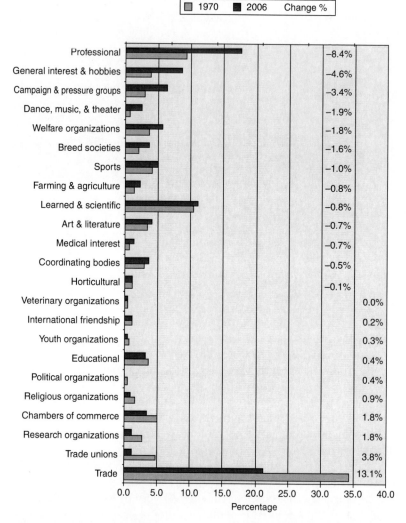

Figure 4.6 Change in field of interest categories of UK associations as a percentage of total, 1970–2006

large group numbers implied large political resources were correct, then we would be in an era of dwindling business influence as numbers reduce. But common sense suggests there might be a disconnect between number and influence; business might be powerful despite organizational proliferation rather than because of it.

Cross-referencing to other sources confirms the major trends in the *DBA* of reduction in business and trade groups. The Certification Office recorded a decline of 70 trade unions between 2006 and 2009 alone (Web site, January 1, 2010). The official record lists 163 unions as of December 31, 2009 – much higher than the 63 recorded in Figure 4.6; however, this list included many organizations that would not have been easily recognized as (national) unions in the directory in terms of their coding. For example, it included the Association of Somerset Inseminators, the Aegeon UK Staff Association, the Balfour Beatty Group Staff Association, the Currys Supply Chain Staff Association, the Chartered Society of Physiotherapy, the Diageo Staff Association, 10 regional units of the National Union of Mineworkers, and the Shield Guarding Association. The fact that the Certification Office list is longer does not reflect on the more narrowly defined *DBA* information. Neither is 'more' accurate; the two are different.

Moreover, the relevant statistic might not be organizational numbers, but membership numbers. If trade unions are weaker it is because of their failure to mobilize members, not their failure to maintain organizational diversity. The Certification Officer *Annual Report 2008–9* stated that 'The total recorded membership of around 7.6 million compares with a peak of 13.2 million in 1979' (www.statistics.gov.uk/CCI/nugget.asp?ID=4).

As early as 1968 the Donovan Royal Commission on Trade Unions and Employers' Associations was recording associational reduction in these sectors in the UK, with recommendations for future 'culling'. It said, 'At the beginning of the present century there were 1323 trade unions. ... The number has steadily decreased since then. ... At the end of 1966 there were 574 trade unions' (1968, p. 7). It is important to note that the culls were recommended to increase effectiveness, not to reduce influence. In relation to employers' associations it suggested that groups should combine employer association and trade association roles: 'There is a strong case for amalgamations among smaller associations. ... Many small associations lack the resources to provide effective services to their members' (1968, p. 200). One effect of these pressures was that May *et al.* (1998, p. 263) reported that although the Devlin Report of 1972 had identified 2,500 trade associations, their studies could identify only 1,300 in the 1990s.

In understanding the declines in trade groups and trade unions, it is clear that the contours of the UK interest group system have been affected by government policy as well as by the groups affecting policy. The clearest example of associational system management by government is perhaps seen in the efforts of Michael Heseltine as President of the Board of Trade in the early 1990s. He wanted to reduce the number of trade groups, but with a view to enhancing their power. The premise was that fewer were more influential. He told the CBI in 1993 that business influence was undermined because

> Many trade associations simply do not have the resources they need to be effective because of a fragmentation in coverage, because key companies are not members, or because the industry is not prepared to provide the funds they require. (Quoted in May *et al.* 1998, p. 261)

He wanted simplification of the associational pattern so that civil servants would recognize a business interest and not be faced with conflicting demands that could be ignored.

The fall in the recorded number of trade associations and unions in the UK thus 'feels' right – reflecting pressure from government to increase lobbying efficiency and amalgamation pressures within organizations to decrease organizational costs. The fall recorded is real rather than a collection artifact. With hindsight, and with an appreciation of the changes in the economy, looking at the 1965 directory there is no surprise that some groups did not survive through to 2006 – for example,

- Amalgamated Society of Journeymen Felt Hatters and Allied Workers (not to be confused with the Amalgamated Society of Journeymen Breakers-Up of Clog Blocks)[11]
- Boot and Shoe Stiffener Manufacturers Association
- British Cast Iron Pressure Pipe Association
- British Coking Industry Association
- British Steamship Owners Association

Such organization names signal interests that would diminish over the next four decades. Yet the demise of associations is not simply about dead economic interests. Some groups may have amalgamated to pursue political interests more effectively or to deliver services more cost-effectively. Few political analysts devote their attention to those aspects of social, technological, and economic life that are withering away. Growth seems more interesting. This is one reason for the continued identification of 'explosions'. However, death and change are as important in a full mapping. A typical example from the more or less weekly email record from the Certification Officer of changes in the area stated:

MERGERS 1 January 2011

Staff Union Dunfermline Building Society to Nationwide Group Staff

The Assistant Certification Officer registered the Instrument of Transfer in relation to the merger by transfer of engagement on 1 January 2011.

LISTINGS

17 January 2011 The Independent Pilots Federation has change its name to the Independent Pilots Association.

10 January 2011 The National Hairdressers' Federation changed its name to the National Hairdressers' Federation Ltd. The British Glove Association has been removed from the list of Employers' Association held by the Certification Officer as it ceased to exist as a result of being dissolved.

This may read like the chaff of organizational life, but the cumulative effect makes the task of tracking overall populations not simply time-consuming, but a matter of opinion rather than certainty. Some calls are inevitably personal opinion.

The data set has four other main points of interest:

1. There was a doubling of general interest and hobby societies between 1970 and 2005 (though from a low base). It can be speculated that the Internet reduced the organizational costs for such groups and facilitated communication among those with shared interests.
2. Like other business groups, chambers of commerce saw substantial reductions, and this fits in with a well-established trend of chambers merging for economies of scale. Again the base numbers are relatively low. (There may be more effective competitors, such as the Federation of Small Businesses. Some new-entry organizations, such as Business over Breakfast, are commercial service franchises rather than membership controlled. Again such new organizational forms raise inclusion issues in counting exercises.)
3. There was an unexpected (and not well-explained) increase in the number of professional organizations from 606 to 1,167.
4. Except for these specific large change categories, the other elements were strikingly static in terms of both raw numbers and percentages.

The expanding fields of interest in the UK are less concentrated than those in decline, but the top three categories more than doubled between 1970 and 2006 and grew by 15.2 percent as a share of the total (professional groups, general interest and hobby, campaigning). This represents strong growth (if scarcely an explosion):

	1970	2006
Professional	606	1,167
General interest	259	565
Campaigning	191	414
Total	1,046	2,146

One explanation for the widespread assumption that there has been a UK group population explosion may be an overgeneralization from such subfields. There are indeed areas of expansion, and in some sources they are seen as being emblematic of overall position rather than exceptional. (Because of their focus political scientists may be particularly prone to extrapolating from campaigning group increases to the whole field.)

Government liaison: more of the same?

One disconformity in this volume is between data collections that are broad (social capital) and those that focus on organizations directly engaged in political influence. However, this chapter has suggested that the stories of these different measures may well be pointing in similar directions. On the suggestion of one of the authors, the *DBA* introduced a question in the early 1990s that allowed groups to signal as one of their concerns 'Liaison with government'. That gives a subpopulation of about one third that include this as one of their roles (Figure 4.7). In other words, this is a subpopulation of groups that self-define a direct political role. This provides a way to compare the more politicized organizations and those that are simply potentially political. Analysis of this subpopulation reveals a need to reinforce some tendencies rather than requiring a wholly new interpretation. The trends to dominance by business are, not unexpectedly, even clearer, but there is nonetheless a diversity even within that subpopulation.

The small diamonds allow us to distinguish between fields of interest where government liaison is more common that nonliaison (e.g., trade) and the range of other fields where most groups did not assign themselves a government liaison role. Figure 4.8 shows that a neat half of the government liaison associations are trade and professional (more if chambers of commerce are added) but that a wide range of other organizations are also mobilized.

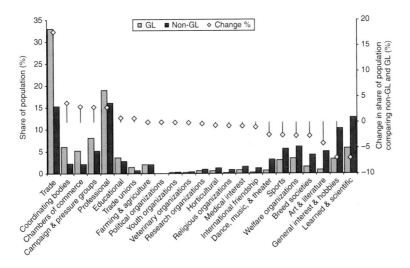

Figure 4.7   UK associations identifying a government liaison (GL) role, 2006

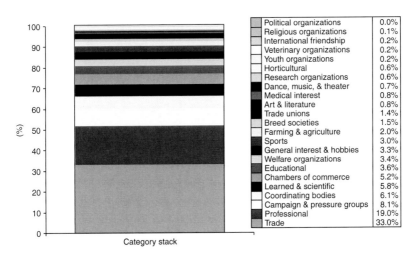

Political organizations	0.0%
Religious organizations	0.1%
International friendship	0.2%
Veterinary organizations	0.2%
Youth organizations	0.2%
Horticultural	0.6%
Research organizations	0.6%
Dance, music, & theater	0.7%
Medical interest	0.8%
Art & literature	0.8%
Trade unions	1.4%
Breed societies	1.5%
Farming & agriculture	2.0%
Sports	3.0%
General interest & hobbies	3.3%
Welfare organizations	3.4%
Educational	3.6%
Chambers of commerce	5.2%
Learned & scientific	5.8%
Coordinating bodies	6.1%
Campaign & pressure groups	8.1%
Professional	19.0%
Trade	33.0%

Figure 4.8   Government liaison in UK by associational field of interest, 2006

Conclusion

An initial expectation of an expanding or exploding associational world in the UK appears to have been wrong on several grounds. Certainly there is diversity and proliferation, as might be anticipated from a pre-liminary pluralist perspective, but there is no ongoing explosion – and indeed there are strong trends toward national-level takeover of regional and local structures and merging of national-level examples. The idea of explosion and expansion has to be amended by recognizing group termination as well as creation. The implication is that decline can be as legitimately expected as explosion. The population ecology literature (see Chapters 3 and 5) suppresses expectations of unlimited group expansion: continuous growth is impossible as groups ultimately are competing for organizational resources – and government attention.

Within systems, pressures work in contrary directions to both bolster and suppress growth. Thus, because the UK has a consultative policy-making culture, government has supported the emergence of some groups as policy interlocutors, but more recently, and more powerfully as a factor, it has been encouraging a simplification of the map. At the very least, counting the number of business representative organizations is now revealed to be a not very satisfactory indicator of influence. Those who persist with the simple interpretation that 'more groups = more power' would be forced to acknowledge they are watching the decline of business power. However, '*vigorous* representation' (to use the Schlozman *et al.* 2008 term) may in fact be inversely related to number. From first principles, it might be argued that the openness of the British consultation system provides a climate for group growth, but in practice this tendency is contradicted by governmental attempts to simplify the chaos of crowded sectors and by group appreciation that single views might be more influential. While the preliminary idea might be that 'more is better', reduced numbers might (perversely perhaps) indicate more effective organizations.

Growth or decline depends on the balance between conflicting trends. The data show that some sorts of association are increasing their numbers, and others sharply declining. The changes confirm Truman's basic notion of changing economic structures. There is massive turnover as traditional, regionally based manufacturing declines (e.g., the cloth manufacturing that propped up large numbers of regional trade and trade union associations). Some interests are simply unfashionable (e.g., temperance) or economically superseded (e.g., radio valves); this leads to (eventual) termination. New interests emerge (e.g., mobile telephones), and the trend toward the service economy has sustained a striking expansion in professional groups. Undoubtedly the proliferation of professional groups is congruent with the discussion in Schlozman *et al.* (2008), which stresses that some potential group constituencies simply lack resources that would permit mobilization – unlike professional constituencies. The shrinkages in part reflect changes in economic and social structures, but they also seem to indicate mergers for intra-organizational reasons of efficiencies of scale and in pursuit of enhanced influence. Easier communication has reduced the organizational costs of national-level groups' relations with dispersed members, and micro-niches may be easier to organize, but the expansionary pressures are limited by government looking to simplify patterns of links and seeking credible 'partners' in society.

Unlike the US pattern, the UK experience cannot be simply summarized as 'group explosion'; the two countries face similar conflicting tendencies, but the balance of these pulls is different. In the US too there are number-reduction factors such as economies of scale, the search for political credibility, the decline of industrial sectors, and the ease of national mobilization through new technology, but these are offset by greater numbers of new interests being mobilized, perhaps sustained by easier securing of resources from supporters by new organizational tactics such as on-street, face-to-face recruitment. The initial question about whether a national interest group system is growing or declining needs to be replaced by investigating the balance of the growth and reduction pressures.

Overall the British data over time show a different profile from the US one (see Chapter 7). The overall UK profile (Figure 4.3) shows remarkable stability, or apparently does so. The qualification 'apparently' is key: in two different ways the British population is not stable. First, its dynamic changes in opposite directions have been self-balancing – in a coincidental way. Second, in a way not stressed in this chapter, there is churning of individual organizations. The contrast between the US and the UK implied by Figure 4.3 is not growth versus stability, but growth in the US compared with growth in the UK which is accompanied by greater group termination. The conclusion is that the US and UK differences represent the difference not between growth and stability but between growth restricted in a limited way by death (US) compared with growth more substantially reduced by death (UK). Growth is moderated by mortality, merger, and takeover.

With hindsight, this British pattern makes sense: the areas of reduction are not random, but concentrated where other information tells us they should have been expected. The UK picture seemed to show surprising consistency of scale over time, but this conclusion is primarily about stressing the distinction between overall constancy in totals and stability at the individual level. While the pattern of data differs from that of comparable US data, the differences appear to be real and comprehensible. However, most notably, both systems show clear reductions in the number of business interests. While this need not indicate a reduction of business power, the corollary is that it squashes the conventional wisdom that the number of associations is an indicator of business power.

The main conclusion proposed here is a warning about misinterpreting the striking data that appear to show US growth versus British stagnation. Growth and decline in Britain generate an *illusion* of stability. This is an artifact of a coincidental balance between growth and death. It does not reflect continuity, but the outcome of dynamic change.

This chapter started with the premise that more associations suggested a healthier democracy. The basic data show that in the US there are indeed more groups, that in the UK there are more of some important types of groups such as campaigning organizations, and that overall in the UK there is greater diversity, with fewer peaks of apparent dominance in the contours of representation. But rather than leading to a confident judgment about democratic enhancement, this preliminary picture suggests the need for a second generation of data. To what extent do these associations really have the intra-organizational qualities (e.g., face-to-face engagement) that are assumed to give beneficial experiences? To what extent is the policy participation of some organizations tokenistic rather than pivotal (Halpin 2011)? To what extent are fewer (more coordinated) organizations more powerful than a proliferation? While having broad overall data is an important step forward, ironically it also suggests the importance of other types of studies.

Notes

We would like to thank Dr. Liu Yang for her contribution in constructing the data set, and Herschel Thomas III for his assistance in coding. While the discussion centers on the UK, the data (to be precise) refer to British associations and associations in Ireland. Preliminary screening suggested there was nothing distinctive about the Irish data.

1. Using established directories saves some research effort, but it does not deliver 'costless' data. Although the directories have been published since 1965, these data start in 1970 (to 2006) to allow the directory the opportunity to evolve consistency of practice in recording data. The most recent numbers cited are from the latest edition at the time of writing (2009). They confirm overall trends, but the data are not integrated into the time series and we simply report overall totals. While this is a 'population of convenience' and might be criticized as such, it has the major advantage that it avoids having to try to retrospectively build past populations.
2. Both the US and UK data were coded to a common frame to allow direct comparison of group types and trends.

3. RES-000-22-1959 'Group metrics: Scoping the scale, types and trends of UK interest group numbers'.
4. Cameron McNeish, vice president of Ramblers Scotland, aired this idea in a blog in July 2009: 'Ramblers members [should] sit tight, bear with us during this difficult time, and look forward to a time when Ramblers Scotland won't be dictated to by a bunch of individuals who know very little about the workings of devolution and who don't seem to understand that Scotland is a nation in its own right, with a different government and different laws.'
5. The 1931 National Council of Ramblers' Federation changed its name in 1935 to the Ramblers' Association. It was rebranded as The Ramblers in 2009.
6. The *Directory* is published by CBD Research Ltd., Beckenham, Kent (www.cbdresearch.com). The authors are very grateful for the cooperation of CBD Research.
7. Some important regional bodies are included.
8. See www.cabinetoffice.gov.uk/regulation/consultation/policy_review/index.asp. It is possible that the scale of the departmental budget cuts in 2010 will at least temporarily suspend the usual 'logic of negotiation' between departments and client groups. However, the National Council for Voluntary Youth Services said on its Web site, 'Recognising the wealth of experience within the voluntary sector in delivering services on the frontline, often in the most disadvantaged areas, the Cabinet Office has issued an open offer to our sector to offer ideas on how the sector can deliver more efficient services' (July 2010).
9. The argument in this chapter, of course, is that this difference is less dramatic than it first appears.
10. Associations could record multiple responses, but including subsidiary reported categories of interest affected the relative distributions of group types by less than 1 percent in any given category.
11. See www.unionancestors.co.uk

References

Baumgartner, F. (2005) 'The Growth and Diversity of US Associations, 1956–2004: Analyzing Trends using the *Encyclopaedia of Associations*', working paper. Available at www.unc.edu/~fbaum/papers.htm.
Baumgartner, F. and B. Leech (2001) 'Interest Niches and Policy Bandwagons', *Journal of Politics*, 63, 1191–1213.
Bealey, F. (1988) *Democracy in the Contemporary State* (Oxford: Oxford University Press).
Berry, J. (1984) *The Interest Group Society* (Boston: Little, Brown).
Berry, J. (1999) 'The Rise of Citizen Groups', in T. Skocpol and M. Fiorina (eds.) *Civic Engagement and American Democracy* (Washington, DC: Brookings Institution Press).
Dahl, R. A. (1984) 'Polyarchy, Pluralism, and Scale', *Scandinavian Political Studies*, 7(4), 225–40.
Donovan Royal Commission (1968) *Report of the Royal Commission on Trade Unions and Employers' Associations*, Cmnd 3623 (London: HMSO).

Grant, W. and D. Marsh (1977) *The Confederation of British Industry* (London: Hodder and Stoughton).

Halpin, D. (2011) 'Organized Interests and Cascades of Attention: Unpacking Policy Bandwagon Dynamics', *Governance*, 24(2), 205–30.

Hooghe, M. and D. Stolle (2003) *Generating Social Capital: Civil Society and Institutions in Comparative Perspective* (Basingstoke, UK: Palgrave Macmillan).

ICT Foresight (2006) *Campaigning and Consultation in the Age of Participatory Media* (London: Hansard Society and NCVO Third Sector Foresight).

Jordan, G., D. Halpin, and W. Maloney (2004) 'Defining Interests: Disambiguation and the Need for New Distinctions', *British Journal of Politics and International Relations*, 6, 195–218.

Knoke, D. (1986) 'Associations and Interest Groups', *American Journal of Sociology*, 12, 1–21.

Lowery, D. and V. Gray (2004) 'Bias in the Heavenly Chorus', *Journal of Theoretical Politics*, 16, 5–30.

Luhmann, N. (1969) *Legitimation durch Verfahren* (Neuwied/Berlin: Luchterhand).

May, T., J. McHugh, and T. Taylor (1998) 'Business Representation in the UK since 1979', *Political Studies*, 46, 260–75.

Putnam, R. (2000) *Bowling Alone* (New York: Simon & Schuster).

Salisbury, R. (1990) 'The Paradox of Interest Groups in Washington', in A. King (ed.) *The New American Political System*, 2nd edn. (Washington, DC: AEI).

Schlozman, K. (2010) 'Who Sings in the Heavenly Chorus?', in J. Berry (ed.) *The Oxford Handbook of American Political Parties and Interest Groups* (Oxford: Oxford University Press).

Schlozman, K. and J. Tierney (1983) 'More of the Same: Washington Pressure Group Activity in a Decade of Change', *Journal of Politics*, 45, 351–77.

Schlozman, K. and J. Tierney (1986) *Organized Interests and American Democracy* (New York: Harper & Row).

Schlozman, K., S. Verba, H. Brady, P. Jones, and T. Burch (2008) 'Who Sings in the Heavenly Chorus?', paper presented at the annual meeting of the American Political Science Association, Boston, August.

de Tocqueville, A. (1969) *Democracy in America* (New York: Doubleday).

Walker, J. L. (1983) 'The Origins and Maintenance of Interest Groups in America', *American Political Science Review*, 77, 390–406.

Walker, J. L. (1991) *Mobilizing Interest Groups in America: Patrons, Professions, and Social Movements* (Ann Arbor: University of Michigan Press).

5
Numbers in a Niche: A Practitioner's Guide to Mapping Gay and Lesbian Groups in the US

Anthony J. Nownes

In the mid-1990s I had an idea. Like so many others I have had over the years, it was inspired by Jack Walker's 1983 article 'The Origins and Maintenance of Interest Groups in America'. The thought occurred to me that perhaps *age* was a crucial determinant of the extent to which citizen groups rely upon institutional patrons (e.g., corporations, the government, private foundations) for monetary support. Specifically, I hypothesized (and still believe, incidentally) that older groups rely less upon patronage than younger groups. To test this hypothesis, I set out to map a single interest group sector (rather than compare groups across sectors)[1] and then determine the extent to which each group within the sector relied upon institutional patronage in a given year. The plan was to use tax forms and annual reports, hoping to find a negative correlation between age and extent of reliance upon institutional patrons. The sector selected was the population of nationally active gay and/or lesbian rights interest groups in the United States. This choice was driven by the sector's manageable size – big enough to allow comparisons, but small enough to make data gathering reasonable. Some sectors – the environmental group sector comes to mind – were too big to study; gathering data on so many groups would take too long. Several others – the sector of pro-gun groups, for example – appeared to be too small to allow comparisons. After the National Rifle Association (NRA) there are very few nationally active groups.

Thus in 1998 began a data-collecting odyssey that lasted several years. By the end of 2001, I had what I considered a comprehensive list of groups in the population of interest: gay and/or lesbian rights interest groups in the United States. If I had known it would take three years to complete the list I would not have started in the first place. But once I got started I could not stop. I became obsessed; everywhere I went I looked for the names of homosexual rights interest groups. I saw gay rights activists in my sleep.

I never managed to do the patronage project I initially envisioned, but the effort was a good investment. I veered off course in 2000, influenced by Virginia Gray and David Lowery. In the midst of collecting the data, I decided that rather than comparing groups on the basis of their reliance on patronage, I would use the data to test notions gleaned from Gray and Lowery's work, which spoke to population-level rather than group-level phenomena. This generated two rewarding publications (Nownes 2004; Nownes and Lipinski 2005).

The task of mapping the population of gay and/or lesbian rights interest groups was arduous. However, when I decided to map a different population – the population of nationally active transgender groups in the United States – things were much easier because I had learned a number of lessons (see Nownes 2010). This is not to say the task was effortless. It wasn't. Gathering population-level data is very difficult. This chapter elaborates on the difficulties inherent in mapping interest group sectors – that is, in putting together population lists – to help population researchers overcome these problems.

Some of this advice may not be particularly useful to scholars studying populations of organizations outside the United States (either transnational organizations or organizations operating solely in a single country other than the US). My references to volumes that list and describe organizations in the US will be of no direct use to non-US scholars. I hope, however, that some of my more general suggestions (about, for example, defining the population under study carefully) will be useful for the study of group populations outside the United States. Moreover, another chapter in this volume (Lowery, Chapter 3) contains information on how to gather data on populations of groups outside the United States (specifically, in the EU).

Population ecology and the study of interest groups

Why anyone would ever want to gather population-level interest group data perhaps needs clarification and justification. Discussion of group formation and maintenance must begin with Mancur Olson's *Logic of Collective Action* (1965). Olson's primary argument is that group formation and survival are unlikely as long as the collective benefits of group participation are available to free-riders. This insight is at the heart of incentive theory, which is the dominant lens through which interest group scholars study group mobilization and maintenance. Incentive theory holds that both group mobilization and group survival are a function of a successful exchange between a group leader (who offers benefits to supporters) and group members (individuals) or patrons (who offer support in exchange for these benefits). Numerous scholars have used the basic incentive theory framework to study group development. Among the most important are Robert Salisbury (1969), who emphasized the role of entrepreneurship in group development, and Jack Walker, Jr. (1983), who emphasized the role of patronage. However, the core of incentive theory is Olson's question of why an individual would join in an effort where group success is independent of his or her contribution.

One of the implications of incentive theory is that groups can change as the environment around them changes. If a group's ability to form and survive is a function of a leader's ability to offer incentives to members and patrons, then the leader can tinker with the group's incentive structure if the group begins to falter. Another implication of incentive theory is that we can learn what we need to know by looking at the inner life of groups themselves rather than at the environment in which groups operate. Indeed, it is a matter of faith among interest group scholars that incentive theory is a necessary corrective to the pluralist notions of David Truman (1951), who in his study of group formation and survival focused almost exclusively on the group and its governmental target, taking the membership as 'natural'. But what if a narrow focus on members and leaders and incentives and patrons causes us to miss a great deal of the action concerning group formation and survival? Such questions are far from rhetorical. They were asked (and answered) in the 1990s by Gray and Lowery, who began to use a population ecology (PE) approach to the study of interest groups. This approach, which took shape in the 1970s, is complex and variegated.

At the core of the PE approach is the idea that organizations are characterized by structural inertia. In other words, groups do not change much over time (Carroll 1988). Because this is the case, selection rather than group-level adaptation and change is 'the driving force of long-term change' in the organizational universe (Hannan and Carroll 1995, p. 23). Because organizational selection is a population-level phenomenon, PE theorists tend to study group populations rather than individual groups. In the end, what this means is that to test many of the notions derived from PE theories and to work within a PE framework, one must gather population-level data.

In short, gathering population-level data is necessary if we are fully to test PE theories and hypotheses about group formation and survival. (In Chapter 3 of this volume, David Lowery describes in more detail the various questions that can be addressed using the PE approach, and which thus necessitate the gathering of population-level data.)

Defining your population

The next task for this chapter is to explain how I assembled the population list used in my studies of gay and/or lesbian rights groups in the United States. This discussion is aimed at revealing wise practices when engaging in such an enterprise. The first step in formulating a population list is defining the population of interest. As noted in other chapters in this volume, this is easier said than done. Lowery (Chapter 3) notes that political scientists using the PE approach have not paid a great deal of attention to defining what a population is. He also notes that precisely how we (should) define a population is determined primarily by the theoretical questions at hand.

The term 'population' in this chapter is not a synonym for 'total', as perhaps it is used by Jordan *et al.* (Chapter 7) in referring to an 'associational population'. In my case I was testing a theory (the theory of density dependence) that had been tested extensively by sociologists and business scholars working within the PE approach. Before defining my specific population, I adopted the prevalent definition of an organizational population. Generally, scholars who test density dependence theory define an organizational population as a set of organizations that share a '*common dependence on the material and social environment*' in which they operate (Hannan and Freeman 1988, p. 9; emphasis in original). In the specialist literature a set of groups is a population if the groups within the set 'have a common standing with respect to the processes of interest' and if 'members are affected similarly by changes in the environment' (Hannan and Freeman 1988, p. 9).

Is there an easy way to operationalize concepts such as 'common dependence', 'material environment', 'social environment', 'common standing', or 'processes of interest'? Probably not. But the common PE assumption that organizational survival is a function of environmental conditions pushes us in the direction of defining an organizational population as a set of groups that we can reasonably expect to rely upon the same supporters for human and financial capital. My test of whether a specific group was part of the population was 'Is it reasonable to conclude that this group relies upon the same pool of real and potential supporters for resources that other groups in the population rely upon?'

It is important to note that when it comes to testing density dependence theory, there is a difference between an interest group *population* and an interest group *community*. Borrowing from biology, an interest group population can be thought of as a set of groups of one type (or species if you like) that exist together in some defined geographic area. An interest group community, in contrast, is a set of all the groups that live in a particular area, and comprises many interest group populations.

Density dependence theory is based on assumptions about resource competition between like-groups. Thus, distinguishing between an interest group population and an interest group community was essential. Studying *either* interest group communities *or* interest group populations is difficult, but either way the research strategies will differ.

Define the population as specifically as possible

Defining the population as specifically and thoroughly as possible is absolutely crucial to this sort of work. In my study of homosexual rights interest groups, I defined the population as 'the set of politically active organizations that lobby at the national level and advocate for public policy favourable to homosexual men and women in the United States' (Nownes 2004, p. 59). I experimented with other definitions, but none were precise enough. To be included in the population for my purposes, a group had to be (or have been) (1) politically active, (2) active in *national* politics (rather than solely state or local politics), (3) active solely or primarily on the issue of gay and/or lesbian rights, (4) active on the 'pro' side of the homosexual rights issue, and (5) active in the United States. Each aspect of the selected definition was crucial for both practical and theoretical reasons.

Practically speaking, defining the population as precisely as possible makes identifying members of the population much easier. For example, if I found a group that worked only at the state or local level (for example, the Gay Youth Alliance of San Diego, the Illinois Gay and Lesbian Task Force, and Outright Vermont) I excluded it from my study. Similarly, a group that served only as a support group for homosexuals (such as Gay AA) and did not engage in any policy advocacy activities was excluded from consideration. Accordingly, precision in definition makes life easier when data are collected.

A conjectural counterexample helps make this point. Imagine that we wanted to study the population of environmental groups in the US, and we defined the population rather lazily as 'groups interested in environmental change'. This definition is obviously problematic because it might lead us to include groups that did not belong to the same genus. Take, for example, a group called Citizens for the Environment. The group (which appears no longer to exist) was founded in 1990 as an offshoot of the conservative Citizens for a Sound Economy. The group promoted 'free market' solutions to environmental problems, and actively lobbied *against* virtually all environmental laws and regulations. Including this group in the population of 'environmental groups' makes sense only if you define that term to include any understanding of the issue. Defining the population more precisely would, of course, lead us to exclude this group.

Perhaps more important than the practical considerations that require a precise definition of the population are the theoretical considerations. Many of the theories and notions of population ecology – density dependence theory, for example – simply cannot be tested properly unless the population is defined closely. If I had decided to test density dependence theory against data on the population of 'organizations interested in gay and lesbian rights in the United States', I would have ended up with a population list that included groups that actively work *against* gay and lesbian rights (such as the Christian Action Network). Including groups like this would be problematic, for groups such as the Christian Action Network do *not* compete for resources with the Human Rights Campaign or the National Gay and Lesbian Task Force. In fact, the supporters of Christian Action Network are among the least likely supporters of these groups.

Define the terms within your definition

After defining the population as precisely as possible, it is important to take great care in defining the terms used *within* that definition. To recap: to be included in the population I was studying, a group had to be (or have been) (1) politically active, (2) active in *national* politics, (3) active solely or primarily on the issue of gay and/or lesbian rights, (4) active on the 'pro' side of the homosexual rights issue, and (5) active in the United States. First, I had to define what I meant by 'political activity'. Drawing upon the existing interest group literature, I defined the term very broadly to mean virtually any activity designed to influence government decisions. Second, I defined 'national politics' as advocacy efforts at the national government level. Third, 'active solely or primarily' on gay and/or lesbian rights was something of a judgment call, as the terms are somewhat subjective. I used this part of the definition more to exclude than to include groups. If I found a group that was very active on gay and/or lesbian rights but also very active on other issues (such as the American Civil Liberties Union), it did not fit the definition and was thus not part of the population. Fourth, 'active on the "pro" side' of the issue was taken simply to mean advocating for expanded rights for homosexuals rather than fewer rights. Finally, 'active in the United States' was self-explanatory, and groups that aimed their efforts primarily at non-US governments or international bodies were excluded.

Specify a time period

Finally, after defining the population, it is important to specify the time period of the study. Whenever possible, the beginning of 'the observation window' (the time period you are examining) 'should be set as close as possible to the population's inception' (Carroll and Hannan 1999, p. 165). In other words, if you are studying nationally active American homosexual rights interest groups and you find that the first such group was founded in 1945, then the period under study should start in 1945 (rather than, say, 1955).[2] Of course, sometimes it is simply not possible to get good data on the early history of a population, especially if this early history took place decades (or centuries) ago. But, as a rule of thumb, you should try to start as early in a population's history as possible. When it comes to choosing an endpoint, this should be as close as possible to the population's endpoint if it has one. My chosen population was alive and well, so I chose an endpoint on the basis of the last year for which I had good data.

Summary

The first step in gathering population-level data is defining the population in question. This definition needs to be precise and straightforward. Moreover, the composite parts of the definition must be adequately defined so that data gathering is possible. Once a population has been specified and defined, it is time to collect data. And in my case, this meant putting together a population list. Defining a population is not all that difficult. Using the definition to identify members of the population, however, is exceedingly difficult and time-consuming. Fortunately, it is also tremendously rewarding.

Building the population list

The first step in building a population list, of course, was to find out whether a version already existed. Sometimes one does. For example, after I published my two articles on gay and lesbian rights groups, several people contacted me and asked for my list. I was happy to share it, and I hope it made their lives easier. I have since compiled a population list of transgender interest groups in the United States. So if anyone needs this population list, their work is done! However, more often than not a complete and accurate population list does not exist. This is the case especially when the population in question is old – that is, contains (or contained) groups that were formed many decades (or perhaps centuries) ago. In such cases, you must start from scratch. In this section, on the basis of my own experience, I will try to offer a few helpful hints.

Start with the *Encyclopedia of Associations*

My first piece of advice is this: start with the *Encyclopedia of Associations*.[3] The *Encyclopedia* is an annual volume (but has not always been) that lists voluntary associations in the United States. Each volume contains background information on thousands of organizations. Each entry (which describes a single organization) includes a founding year, membership size, staff size, and mission for the year in question (in some cases, some of this information is missing). The *Encyclopedia* relies upon organizations themselves to provide the information it reports. In other words, the information for each group is self-reported once the staff of the *Encyclopedia* (which is now published by Gale/Cengage Learning) locate the group (or the group requests that the *Encyclopedia* include it).

For my project, I examined the *Encyclopedia* for every year that it was published. I began by looking in each volume's index for the words 'gay', 'homosexual', 'homophile' (which is an archaic term but was used a great deal during the 1950s and 1960s), and 'lesbian'. The *Encyclopedia*'s index is a good one, and under these terms I found the names of groups and the pages on which I could learn more about each group. I looked at all the groups listed under these headings in all the volumes of the *Encyclopedia*, and created a preliminary master list of groups. The *Encyclopedia* allowed me to find the names of many of the most active and prominent groups in the population – groups such as Human Rights Campaign, Log Cabin Republicans, the National Gay and Lesbian Task Force, and Parents, Families, and Friends of Lesbians and Gays.

Some students and scholars of interest groups tend to use the term 'nonprofit organization' rather cavalierly, implying that it applies only to the types of groups we normally associate with the 'third' sector – for example, arts organizations, charitable organizations, educational organizations, museums, service organizations, and 'public interest' groups. In reality, the nonprofit world contains numerous labor unions, professional associations, think tanks, trade associations, and other types of groups that we normally do not call 'nonprofits'. Fortunately the *Encyclopedia* contains entries for these groups as well as 'traditional' nonprofits, and thus is a good source of information on groups of all kinds, not just citizen groups. If I had limited myself to traditional citizen groups or 'nonprofits', I would have missed a number of groups, including the Association for Gay, Lesbian, and Bisexual Issues in Counseling, the Association of Gay, Lesbian, and Bisexual People in Medicine, the Association of Gay and Lesbian Psychologists, and Lesbian and Gay Associated Engineers and Scientists.

The *Encyclopedia* is not perfect

Unfortunately, my advice to start with the *Encyclopedia* is not foolproof. I say this for several reasons. First, the *Encyclopedia* is not helpful if you are studying a population of for-profit entities (e.g., business firms). It is now the conventional wisdom among interest group scholars that business firms make up a large part of the universe of organized interests active in the United States (and elsewhere). So if you want to study the population of, say, politically active automakers or pharmaceutical companies or book publishers, the *Encyclopedia* will be of little help. To study populations of business firms a good strategy is to start with industry directories – that is, periodic directories that contain information on firms within a given industry. These directories are often relatively easy to locate. Many industries are also covered in volumes similar to the *Encyclopedia of Associations*. As for groups of business firms, the *Encyclopedia* is helpful, as it does (as I mentioned earlier) contain listings for trade and professional organizations. A good supplement to the *Encyclopedia* if you are studying such groups is the *National Trade and Professional Associations Directory of the United States*, which has been published periodically since 1965.[4]

An additional problem with the *Encyclopedia of Associations* is underinclusion. The *Encyclopedia* is a good source, but in every population I have examined – either thoroughly or casually – it has overlooked groups. Many of the volume's oversights are due to the associations themselves rather than the *Encyclopedia*'s staffers, but the fact remains that the *Encyclopedia* is often (and probably always) incomplete in its listings. In other words, for virtually any population you can think of, the *Encyclopedia* misses some organizations. The *Encyclopedia*, I have found, is particularly deficient when it comes to small and/or ephemeral organizations. This is especially troubling for population-level analyses, because at the beginning of any population's history these sorts of groups may predominate. There is also a problem of over-inclusion. This occurs when the *Encyclopedia* for a particular year contains listings for organizations that no longer exist.

Use multiple sources

In short, when you are building a population list of nonprofit organizations, *starting* with the *Encyclopedia of Associations* is a good idea, but *stopping* with the *Encyclopedia* is not, so my next piece of advice is to use multiple sources. Using the *Encyclopedia of Associations*, I crafted a preliminary population list. Crafting my initial master list took a very long time. With my preliminary population list in hand, I turned to the Internet to try to identify any organizations I may have missed in my initial analysis. Specifically, my next step was to search for the names of LGBT organizations using Google. I searched on numerous words and phrases, including 'gay', 'gay rights', 'gay rights advocacy', 'gay rights groups', 'gay rights movement', 'homophile', 'homosexual', 'lesbian', 'lesbian rights groups', and 'LGBT advocacy'. This exercise led me to thousands of Internet pages, news articles, and blog entries, some of which contained the names of groups. Most of the groups I identified during this process were already on my master list, but I also discovered the names of several groups I had missed.

After the Google search, I turned to the *New York Times*. I looked at every volume of the *New York Times Index* for the years 1950–2002. In the index, I looked under terms such as 'gay', 'homophile', 'homosexual', and 'lesbian' for articles that might reference specific interest groups. If I found a reference to an article that looked promising (that is, looked as if it might mention the name of a specific homosexual rights interest group), I found that article on microfilm (or online) and read it, searching for the names of groups I may have missed in my previous searches. *New York Times* articles from the 1950s and 1960s were particularly helpful, as they contained the names of several early and ephemeral gay and lesbian rights groups that the *Encyclopedia* had missed and that I had not encountered elsewhere.

Next, I looked at books. I searched for books on LGBT history, looking for references to groups. This method yielded the names of a few more groups that I had not identified elsewhere. There are a number of excellent historical accounts of gay and/or lesbian politics in the United States, including Barry D. Adam's *The Rise of a Gay and Lesbian Movement* (1995), Margaret Cruikshank's *The Gay and Lesbian Liberation Movement*

(1992), and Mark Thompson's *Long Road to Freedom: The Advocate History of the Gay and Lesbian Movement* (1994). Whatever population you choose, however, there are likely historical accounts that can help.

I also relied heavily upon scholarly journals and popular magazine and newspaper articles. To locate articles I consulted a number of databases. Of all the databases I used, I found the expansive Factiva database the most helpful. It provides access to articles, photographs, and transcripts from literally tens of thousands of sources. It provides access to articles in more than 20 languages and from more than 150 countries. To locate articles on gay and/or lesbian politics, I searched on the same terms I had used on Google. These searches took me to thousands of individual articles which I then perused for the names of specific interest groups. Most of the groups I came across during this process were already on my list, but some were not. There are other databases, to be sure, but Factiva offers incredible coverage.

Finally, I relied to some extent on people as sources. The population of gay and/or lesbian rights groups in the United States is not particularly old – it dates back to the mid-1940s. This makes it easier to study than some other populations for many reasons, one of which is that many of the people involved in the early days of the movement for gay and/or lesbian rights are still alive. In studying populations it is most difficult to find information on ephemeral groups and groups that form early in a population's history. People are most useful for identifying these groups. Reading thousands of printed pages and Web sites on gay and lesbian politics, I learned the names of hundreds of gay and lesbian activists. I called or (more often) emailed some of them. I was especially interested in making contact with people who were involved in the pioneering gay and/or lesbian rights organizations of the 1950s and 1960s. In some cases, I sent along my list and asked, 'Can you see any groups that I left out?' In other cases, I asked, 'Can you tell me which groups you think were most important in the 1950s?' In still other cases, I asked about specific groups. (I will say more about this later.) The point here is that people involved in the movement you are studying are often good sources of information. I drew on these people extensively as sources of information, and several gay rights activists mentioned groups that I had overlooked.

Before moving on I should say a few words about sources that I should have utilized but did not. Specifically, I should have visited historical archives. For example, I wish I had had the money to visit the ONE National Gay and Lesbian Archives in Los Angeles, the GLBT Historical Society in San Francisco, and several other archives. I did, however, speak to some people affiliated with archives over the telephone, and they were very helpful. Whatever population you choose, be sure to see whether there are historical archives that you can visit.

Unfortunately, I did not keep good enough notes during the data-gathering process to calculate exactly how many groups I identified using the *Encyclopedia* and how many I identified using other sources. I would estimate, however, that I identified approximately 60 percent of all the groups on my population list using the *Encyclopedia* and 40 percent using other sources. This is a pretty good track record for the *Encyclopedia*, but it shows the need to consult multiple sources.

Did each of the groups on my list fit my definition?

Each time I located a group that I thought might be part of my population, I asked, 'Does this group truly belong on my population list?' To answer this question, I had to gather substantial information about each group – (again) information that would help me determine whether a group was or is politically active, nationally active, active primarily on homosexual rights, active on the 'pro' side of the issue, and active in the United States. In some cases, I gathered the information at the same time I located the group. For example, upon first encountering the National Gay and Lesbian Task Force in the *Encyclopedia of Associations*, I had enough information just from the entry to determine that the group was indeed part of my population. In other cases, I located a group – for example, the Council on Religion and the Homosexual – and initially did not have the requisite information to make a determination. In such cases, I put the group on my list and only later sought to determine for certain whether it belonged on the final population list.

To make a final determination about each group I relied primarily upon the same sources I relied upon to identify groups. For example, I relied heavily upon the *Encyclopedia of Associations*. Again, each entry in the *Encyclopedia* contains a great deal of information about the group in question. The *Encyclopedia* was especially helpful in determining which groups were nationally active, active on homosexual rights, and active in the United States. The *New York Times* was also helpful, especially for determining whether a group was or is nationally active and politically active. The articles and publications in Factiva also were helpful, as were historical accounts (mostly books) and organizational Web sites. Virtually every group I identified that was still alive had its own Web site. Typically a group's Web site contains a great deal of information about the group's activities, its mission, and its stance on homosexual rights. Generally, if I had any doubts about an extant group, the group's

Web site settled the issue once and for all. Nevertheless, there were groups about which I had lingering doubts. In these cases, I made telephone calls and sent emails (if I could locate people associated with the groups). For example, if I found a group and was unsure about whether it engaged in any political activity, I might email a group staff member and ask about the group's activities.

Summary

Building a population list is difficult. But it is not impossible. The *Encyclopedia of Associations* is a vital source of information, and it is a good place to start identifying members of your population. Coming up with a complete and accurate population list requires the use of multiple sources. Among the sources I used were the Factiva database, historical treatments of gay and lesbian politics, the Internet, the *New York Times*, popular articles, scholarly articles, and individuals active in gay and

Table 5.1 Sources useful in identifying members of the target population

Source	Comments
The Encyclopedia of Associations: National Organizations of the U.S.	This monster annual volume contains listings and information on hundreds of thousands of organizations operating in the United States
Factiva database	This online database, available at many college and university libraries, collects articles and reports from a massive array of more than 8,000 newspapers and magazines
New York Times Index	The annual *New York Times Index* can direct you to articles that may contain the names of groups in the population you are studying
Books	Whatever population you are studying, chances are there is a book (or many books) about it – probably a historical treatment. Such books can be very useful for finding members of a population and learning more about them
People	People involved in organizations can be valuable sources of information about their organizations and others within the population you are studying
Organizational Web sites	Many organizations (especially large or successful ones) have their own Web sites, and these sites often contain valuable information for the population ecology researcher

lesbian politics. Triangulation is necessary and appropriate. For each group I initially identified, I had to make a determination as to whether it belonged on my final population list. To make this determination, I relied upon group Web sites and the same sources I relied upon to identify groups. Table 5.1 summarizes some of what I have written in this section, listing some of the sources upon which I relied most heavily.

Determining dates of vital events

Because I was testing the theory of density dependence in my work, I had to determine when each group on my population list was formed and when each group on the list died (if it did indeed die). Other PE theories and hypotheses also require determination of the dates of vital events, so in this section I explain how I sought to determine birth and death dates.

Founding dates

The *Encyclopedia of Associations* contained founding dates for most of the organizations I initially identified, and this was a good start. My experience suggests that the *Encyclopedia* does a very good job of nailing down founding dates for most of the groups it lists. Nonetheless, in each case I sought verification. Moreover, for a few groups on my list – groups that I identified from sources other than the *Encyclopedia* – I did not have a founding date. To verify or locate a founding date for each extant group I went to its Web site. Most groups' sites had a brief 'History' or 'Information' or 'Background' section that provided a founding date. If a group's Web site gave a date different than the *Encyclopedia* or some other source (such as a newspaper article or scholarly journal article), I trusted the group's Web site. After all, the group should know when it was founded! If a group was still in existence and neither other sources nor the group's Web site provided a founding date, I contacted the organization directly via email and asked a staff member to provide me with a founding date. If this did not yield results, I telephoned. The *Encyclopedia* and group Web sites combined enabled me to locate or verify the founding dates of approximately 90 percent of the organizations on my population list.

Some cases, however, were vexing. For example, a few of the groups that I found in the *Encyclopedia* were defunct, and thus contacting them to verify a founding date was impossible. Many of these defunct groups were listed in one or more editions of the *Encyclopedia*, and thus at least I had a place to start. But again, I wanted to verify the founding date for each group. For groups that I identified in the *Encyclopedia* that were defunct, I relied upon historical accounts and activists. By 'historical accounts', I mean books and articles. Books were especially useful. Some defunct groups on my population list, of course, never showed up in the *Encyclopedia of Associations*. In these cases, I had to rely upon other sources to locate the founding date. I consulted historical accounts, Internet pages of interest to gay and/or lesbian rights activists, and (whenever possible) people. Again, the most problematic cases were ephemeral groups and groups founded early in the population's history. For some of these groups it took considerable time and detective work to determine a founding date. But in virtually every case, I was confident about the date I settled upon.

Disbanding dates

As for disbanding dates, most cases were easy because most of the groups in the population did not disband. However, many did. To get an initial idea of when a group disbanded, I again started with the *Encyclopedia of Associations* and ascertained the year in which the group in question stopped appearing. But I quickly discovered that each volume of the *Encyclopedia* contains entries for groups that disbanded long before. So although I did consult the *Encyclopedia* when trying to determine disbanding dates, I did not rely upon the *Encyclopedia*. In some cases – again, primarily those of trailblazing early groups and ephemeral groups – I relied upon mainstream historical accounts (e.g., books and Web sites of interest to gay and/or lesbian rights activists) to discover disbanding dates. In other cases, primarily those of relatively obscure groups, I scoured newspapers and magazines for articles that might reference them (again, most of them located through Factiva). I also tried to locate people associated with each defunct group to ask them directly when their group died. For example, during my research on disbanding dates I came across an article on the Gay and Lesbian Democrats of America that mentioned the group's spokesperson at the time. The article did not, however, mention either the founding date or the disbanding date (which, of course, it could not have, because at the time the article was written the group was alive and well). I entered the name of the group's leader into Google and located him within three minutes. I emailed and asked him to tell me when the group was formed and when it disbanded. He happily supplied me with the information.

Of all the information I gathered, disbanding dates were the most difficult to locate and verify. Moreover, surprising though it might sound, 'disbanding' is not a straightforward concept. For example, the

Mattachine Society operated as a federation from 1950 (its founding) until 1961, but then basically fell apart. Nonetheless, there were still local Mattachine Societies operating in various cities across the country. In this case (and a few others) I chose the date that the organization basically stopped operating as a national group as the disbanding date.

Summary

For much research using a PE framework, determining the dates of vital events for each group within the population is crucial. The same sources used to identify groups can be used to determine the dates of vital events. By way of general advice, I would again urge PE researchers to use multiple sources. People associated with groups are especially useful in determining the dates of vital events, but the usual sources – the historical accounts, the Internet, and scholarly and popular articles – are also very useful.

Pitfalls

Research of any kind is open to pitfalls. But population-level research, I believe, is more open to pitfalls than many other types of research. In this penultimate section, I will mention two (of no doubt many) pitfalls.

Name changes

One thing that any population-level researcher needs to be aware of is that many interest groups – especially groups with long histories – undergo numerous name changes during their organizational 'careers'. Name changes make it particularly difficult to track the history of specific organizations and to track the trajectory of a population of groups. Name changes also make it difficult to determine whether and when specific groups drop out of the population you are studying. An example can illustrate what I mean. The National Center for Lesbian Rights (NCLR) is a public interest law firm that was founded in 1977. However, the organization was founded under a different name: the Lesbian Rights Project (LRP). The group did not change its name to the National Center for Lesbian Rights until 1989. If I had not been careful, I would have recorded both the NCLR and the LRP on my population list. I would have concluded that one group (the LRP) was founded in 1977 and died in 1989, and that another group (the NCLR) was founded in 1989 and was still alive at the end of the period under study. Needless to say, these conclusions would have been problematic for my data analysis.

For every group on my population list, I did all the research I needed to do to make sure I recorded any and all name changes. In most cases, I did this simply by contacting the group itself and asking someone 'in the know' whether its name had changed since the inception of the group. This was impossible for defunct groups, and it did not work for a number of extant groups. Thus, I was also careful to scan the usual sources – particularly the *Encyclopedia of Associations* (many entries in which actually contain information on name changes). Historical accounts were also very useful. Ultimately, it is always necessary to be aware of the fact that many groups undergo name changes. Moreover, the older the group, the more likely it is to have undergone one or more name changes. Clearly such puzzles can be resolved in niche studies, but more general studies perhaps have to use less time-intensive methods.

Mistakes

After studying two national interest group populations, I have reached the conclusion that it is virtually impossible to build a population list that does not contain mistakes. I am certain that under-inclusion was a problem for me. In other words, I am certain I missed at least a few groups. As much as I tried, I am sure that there were some groups that slipped through the cracks – especially (again) older and ephemeral groups. Is there any way to remedy this problem? Probably not. About all you can do is try really hard. I am less certain about over-inclusion; I cannot be sure I did not include a group or two that did not belong. Finally, there are problems in determining the dates of vital events. Again, all you can do is try your hardest to find as much information as you can.

If you are seeking perfection – that is, if you want to build a foolproof, definitive, perfect population list – then PE research such as I am describing here is not for you. There is too much involved in mapping a population to expect perfection. I took solace in the fact that my population list was the best there was. I also felt good about the fact that any mistakes were oversights and were stochastic in nature.

Summary

PE scholars conduct population-level research on interest groups. Conducting population-level research essentially means gathering population-level data, which means putting together a population list – a list of all the groups in a specific population for the entire period you are studying. In my case, the list also contained the founding and disband-ing (or merger) dates for each group. In this chapter I have attempted to provide some advice for PE researchers.

My general advice can be summarized as follows. First, start with the *Encyclopedia of Associations*. It is a good source. Second, use multiple sources. The *Encyclopedia* is good, but it is not perfect. Finally, be pre-pared to spend a lot of time gathering data. It took me a very long time to build my population list. In the end, I think that you will find build-ing a population list enormously satisfying. Building my population list taught me a great deal about interest groups and the people who work for them. I often use examples from the population of gay and/or lesbian rights interest groups in the United States in the courses I teach, and gathering population-level data gave me an appreciation of the dynamics of interest group politics – dynamics that can be overlooked when studying a cross-section of groups or a single group.

Notes

1. At the time I figured that this was the only reasonable way to test my idea, because it would control for cross-sectoral differences in reliance upon insti-tutional patronage.
2. In my first study of nationally active American homosexual rights groups I looked at the period 1950–1998 because I did not have good data on the period 1945–1950. I remedied this problem in my second study.
3. Here is the citation for the most recent edition: *Encyclopedia of Associations: National Organizations of the U.S. 2010*, edition 49 (Detroit, MI: Gale/Cengage Learning, 2010).
4. Here is the citation for the latest edition: *National Trade and Professional Associations Directory of the United States, 2011* (Bethesda, MD: Columbia Books, 2011).

References

Adam, B. D. (1995) *The Rise of a Gay and Lesbian Movement*, rev. edn. (New York: Twayne).
Carroll, G. R. (1988) 'Organizational Ecology in Theoretical Perspective', in G. R. Carroll (ed.) *Ecological Models of Organizations* (Cambridge, MA: Ballinger).
Carroll, G. R. and M. T. Hannan (1999) *The Demography of Corporations and Industries* (Princeton, NJ: Princeton University Press).
Cruikshank, M. (1992) *The Gay and Lesbian Liberation Movement* (New York: Routledge).
Hannan, M. T. and G. R. Carroll (1995) 'An Introduction to Organizational Ecology', in G. R. Carroll and M. T. Hannan (eds.) *Organizations in Industry: Strategy, Structure, and Selection* (New York: Oxford University Press).

Hannan, M. T. and J. Freeman (1988) 'Density Dependence in the Growth of Organizational Populations', in G. R. Carroll (ed.) *Ecological Models of Organizations* (Cambridge, MA: Ballinger).

Nownes, A. J. (2004) 'The Population Ecology of Interest Group Formation: Mobilizing for Gay and Lesbian Rights in the United States, 1950–98', *British Journal of Political Science*, 34, 49–67.

Nownes, A. J. (2010) 'Density-Dependent Dynamics in the Population of Transgender Interest Groups in the United States, 1964–2005', *Social Science Quarterly*, 91, 689–703.

Nownes, A. J. and D. Lipinski (2005) 'The Population Ecology of Interest Group Death: Gay and Lesbian Rights Interest Groups in the United States, 1945–98', *British Journal of Political Science*, 35, 303–19.

Olson, M. (1965) *The Logic of Collective Action: Public Goods and the Theory of Groups* (Cambridge, MA: Harvard University Press).

Salisbury, R. (1969) 'An Exchange Theory of Interest Groups', *Midwest Journal of Political Science*, 13, 1–32.

Thompson, M. (1994) *Long Road to Freedom: The Advocate History of the Gay and Lesbian Movement* (New York: St. Martin's).

Truman, D. B. (1951) *The Governmental Process: Political Interests and Public Opinion* (New York: Alfred A. Knopf).

Walker, J. L. (1983) 'The Origins and Maintenance of Interest Groups in America', *American Political Science Review*, 77, 390–406.

6
Multiple Arenas, Multiple Populations: Counting Organized Interests in Scottish Public Policy

Darren Halpin, Graeme Baxter, and Iain MacLeod

The basic premise of this book is that counting populations of organized interests is a worthwhile activity. The opening chapter – not to mention many of the contributions – provides numerous persuasive reasons. In this chapter, all this is taken for granted, and it pursues some of the challenges inherent in actually counting populations. It starts with what seems at face value to be a single perfectly reasonable and achievable aspiration in relation to data on organized interest populations – namely, to be able to say something authoritative about the basic size and composition of the politically active organized interest system. This is a deceptively difficult task.

As observed in Chapter 1, perhaps the core reason for concerning ourselves with counting organized interest populations is that it allows us to draw conclusions about the size and diversity of the system. This prompts questions such as: How large is the organized interest system? Are business interests numerically dominant participants in public policy? How important are citizen groups in the organized interest system? No doubt, these are just the types of aims or outcomes that scholars frequently place high on their research applications. And, as deliverables, they don't seem too lofty. In fact, one might expect them to be within the grasp of the average researcher endowed with sufficient time and resources. But, as will become evident, such simple aims are easily thwarted – not so much because the data are harder to collect than in other areas of the social sciences (although this is an issue), but because the underlying phenomenon – an organized interest *population* – itself is slippery.

This chapter recounts efforts to achieve this (apparently) simple research ambition with respect to the level of organized interest activity in consultations about Scottish public policy. It utilizes several related data sets generated on organized interests in Scottish public policy as a context to explore these broader issues. Not only are the actual data presented, but the chapter takes some time to retrace and make explicit the decisions made about what to count and why. The intention is to provoke questions about counting populations and interpreting findings. The purpose of this chapter is neither to offer a straitjacket for future practice nor to dissuade those who might be considering inserting the same tools in their own research application. Rather, the intention is to raise important issues concerning the choices to be made about collecting data and the implications these have for how we conceive of organized interest populations.

Addressing these points means in part following the lead of Robert Salisbury, who is perhaps the most important source for those seeking some precision on what sorts of pressure participants are empirically present in different policy arenas. Salisbury (1984) is widely cited on the strength of one innovative concept: 'institutions'. This chapter argues that equally important, yet mostly neglected, is his stress on the 'diverse array' of pressure participants and his proposition that the proportions of different types of participants will vary across different policy arenas.

More than a handful?

The aspiration to construct an *authoritative* account of systems of organized interests is not new. James Q. Wilson, framed in the US context, provides a good sense of the general problem:

> when I was an undergraduate taking my first course in American government, answering an exam question about interest representation was easy: all you had to do was remember seven names – the Chamber of Commerce, the National Association of Manufacturers, the AFK, the CIO, the Farm Bureau Federation, the American Legion, and the American Medical Association. Although none of these has disappeared, today no one would take you seriously if you tried to understand the exercise of influence with reference to seven, or even seventy, groups. (1995, p. xx)

Few if any would quarrel with this sentiment, regardless of national system. It is not hard to list out the 'key players' in any given policy area. And most of these players – like those on Wilson's list – would likely fit the description of an interest group. But few people would accept such a list as a satisfactory summary population or map of the organized interest system.

It is easy to point out the unsatisfactory nature of any list such as that produced by Wilson in his undergraduate essays. The harder question is: Where do we place the boundary around a more realistic (and expanded) population? At least two obvious issues emerge. First, if listing off a handful of national, large, longstanding, membership-based, and politically dedicated interest group organizations is insufficient, then what? Do we satisfy ourselves with a longer list of the same *type* of interest group organizations? Or do we cast a broader net? If we look at broad interest representation, then surely Salisbury (1984) is right to suggest that 'institutions', and not simply interest groups, will be important players. A second, and related, issue is how we might detect the existence of such an *organized interest* population. Where do we look? We might utilize directories and the like to catalog systematically groups that are in existence at any one time. Or we could look at policy engagement by organizations in specific policy arenas. Is the aspiration to list those organizations 'ever ready' to engage in policy issues generally? Or do we accept that the population concept is most useful when pegged to specific policy arenas (or even issues)?

There is no right or wrong answer to such questions; the point is that choices have consequences. As discussed in Chapter 1, two broad approaches are evident. Some studies use directories and the like to identify a population: if an organization is in the directory, then it is in the population. Perhaps the most commonly used directories of this type are *Washington Representatives* and the *Encyclopedia of Associations*, both covering the US. The alternative is to track organizations as they actually *engage* in some policy-related activity: if an organization is active (e.g., registered to lobby), then it is part of the population. The most used approach has been to examine lobby-registration records from the US (both Washington and the states). Regardless of approach, for those of us engaged in counting populations, decisions need to be made.

This chapter starts by saying that in Scottish public policy, there are more than a handful of active interest groups. Students of Scottish politics have tended to adopt the tradition noted by Wilson: they list a few large interest groups, often including the Scottish Law Society, the Scottish British Medical Association (BMA), the Scottish Confederation of British Industry (CBI), the National Farmers Union of Scotland, the Scottish Chambers of Commerce, and the Scottish Council of Voluntary Organisations. But, as Wilson suggests, this shorthand seems now too simplistic. The challenge is to do better.

Of course, the population of organized interests or pressure participants is large. With some confidence it can be said that it is larger than it used to be – and surely bigger than the lists in undergraduate texts. But how large? A directory of groups or associations for Scotland might have been helpful, but none exists (although it does for the UK; see Chapter 4). So the only means of constructing a map of the organized interest population in Scotland is to utilize public policy sources and capture groups engaged in a form of political action. In this case, the decision was made to count *policy-active* organizations. Since the cast of the policy-active is far broader than strictly defined interest groups, the population that emerged can be more accurately labeled 'pressure participants'. Of course, this approach also necessitates a decision concerning the arena(s) where policy participation is to be observed and registered.

In search of an authoritative system account

If nothing else, counting populations of organized interests or pressure participants in a national or subnational setting ought to be able to produce an authoritative map of that system. Studies utilizing directories can also claim to provide just that, but the directories are usually decoupled from any specific policy arena: editors make a list of whom they deem to be in existence and (in addition, in some cases) policy-relevant. They are deemed 'policy-relevant' in a general sense, which makes any discussion of which policy arena they are active in redundant. But when one moves to *directly* counting policy engagement, the question arises of which arena to count.

As a scholarly enterprise, counting populations of organized interests is a resource-intensive activity. Moreover, the publication payoffs flow slowly, and the upfront investment is high. Thus, decisions about what to count and which sources to utilize are not insignificant concerns. It is understandably rare for the organized interest scholar to compare multiple arenas in the same polity. One obvious consequence is that results for a single arena are used to generalize to the broader polity. But what if the shape of the population differs across arenas? What are we to make of this, and how do we choose which arena to map?

In his influential article, Salisbury (1984) argued that group scholars had tended to implicitly assume that interest representation would occur *mostly* through the activities of membership-based organizations, through interest groups. He was concerned that this emphasis had led scholars to ignore the diversity of the system of organized interests. Much as Wilson explained, the 'old-school' view was that populations of organized interests were populations of interest groups. Salisbury argued, 'The American political universe, in fact, contains a considerably more diverse array of actors than these conventional headings suggest'. The omissions he had in mind were 'individual corporations, state and local governments, universities, think tanks, and most other *institutions* of the private sector' (1984, p. 64). He also mentioned elected officials, such as members of Congress. In making this argument, he was not claiming that interest groups were not numerically dominant in *all* arenas, just that they were not dominant in populations of organized interests engaging in public policy work (Salisbury himself eschews the term 'lobbying').

While Salisbury's 1984 article may be widely quoted for its memorable finding that institutions dominate Washington lobbying circles (and interest representation), his broader argument was that the mix of institutions and interest groups – the *complexion* of the population – varied across policy arenas within the US. He found that while interest groups constituted a fraction of the population as measured by *Washington Representatives*, they were a more dominant presence in congressional hearings and in media coverage. Put another way, institutions dominated the broad population of organized interests engaged 'somewhere' in policy work (as captured by *Washington Representatives*), but they became less prominent in *specific* arenas. His analysis of data from the *Washington Representatives* directory suggests that 'individual membership groups [interest groups] constitute only one-sixth of the community of agriculture interests...in Washington' (Salisbury 1984, p. 74): institutions dominate, in particular individual businesses. Yet his analysis of congressional hearings and then of national media coverage revealed a different pattern: groups became more numerically dominant in these arenas.

How can this be interpreted? Salisbury suggests, from a demand-side view, that congressional hearings and the media are 'more public and visible arenas' which require the prominent role of interest groups given their *legitimating* capacity. He also suggests that, from the supply side, institutions are more likely to be interested in 'quite small items of no interest to most groups...or the general public' and 'few of them [these issues] may have attracted the attention of the *New York Times* or congressional committee hearings' (1984, p. 75).[1] Whatever the rationale, the finding has implications for the selection of populations to count and the interpretation of the data that are produced. Indirectly, Salisbury highlights the vexing issue of which arena within a single given polity one ought to count.

This research takes up Salisbury's often overlooked observation that counting populations in different arenas of US political activity (in his case congressional and media arenas) nurtures *different* populations of active organizations. It asks how we might utilize this in planning and executing population studies, and it explores implications in considering how to construct an account for Scotland.

Choosing a (Scottish) policy arena

The decision in respect of Scotland started with a basic choice about data source. As described above, with no authoritative directory to utilize, there was no convenient alternative to counting the policy activity of organizations. The question then arose of which public policy activity to count.

When it comes to mapping organized interests as they actually mobilize in Scottish policy contexts, there are several alternative relevant arenas. The most obvious ones, where data are available in one form or another, are outlined in Table 6.1. For our purposes – mapping the incidence of mobilization by organized interests – it matters only that the broader community of organized interests *does* see these as important arenas and access points to engage in public policy. The question as to whether their activity in these arenas is actually influential and impacts policy outcomes is not strictly relevant here.

These alternatives *are* broadly relevant to most Western democracies. Yet, over time, specific national scholarly traditions and conventions emerge and tend to dominate. US practice, which has a comparatively

Table 6.1 Possible policy arenas for mapping organized interests

Arena	Policy activity/institution	Details
Administrative	Scottish government stakeholder groups	Government establishes routinized engagement with organized interests
Administrative	Scottish government consultations	Government seeks 'open' input on established policy questions
Legislative	Scottish Parliament committee hearings	Parliament seeks open input on issues of interest and proposed bills
Media	Scottish media	Media outlets provide reportage on policy issues

long tradition of counting populations, provides a useful illustration. When policy activity data are utilized, the orthodox US tradition has been to examine the mobilization of groups in the legislative arena: whether through evidence to congressional committees or via congressional lobby registers (see as prominent examples Gray and Lowery 1996/2000; Berry 1999; Baumgartner and Leech 2001). Large mapping studies of the bureaucratic arena are rare, even though there is some evidence that US groups may see the bureaucratic arena as just as important as (or more important than) the legislative arena (but see, e.g., Yackee and Yackee 2006). In this regard Salisbury (1990, his table 6.2) lists lobbyists' most frequent tasks as 'maintaining relations with government' (3.8%), 'informal contact with officials' (3.7%), 'monitoring proposed changes in rules and laws' (3.7%), and providing 'information to officials' (3.5%), but has 'testifying' to Congress (2.7%) lower. Two decades on there is still a tendency to privilege the legislative arena when compiling population data. Traditions combine with data availability to shape where scholars focus their energy.

Traditions, where possible, ought to be made explicit.[2] That being said, many non-US scholars would relish a situation where they could utilize established sources with the confidence that little opposition over their 'choice' would result. Yet, following Salisbury, the message here is that it may be worth pausing intermittently to ask whether alternatives are worthy of exploration, if only to reaffirm the ongoing value of the tradition.

Forging a (Scottish) research tradition?

The absence of any extensive population-based work on groups or organized interests in Scotland – or British political science generally – means that students of public policy need to make some basic choices.[3] It is, therefore, important to be explicit in offering up rationales for those choices.

The initial decision in this project was to map *an* administrative/ bureaucratic process with external participation. The primary data set here maps the mobilization of organized interests in the consultative process over a 25-year period utilizing government records (including Scottish Office records pre-devolution and Scottish Executive records post-devolution). What was the justification? There are good reasons why an *initial* focus on the bureaucratic arena is justified in Scotland. Jordan and Maloney explain that 'the bureaucratic arena will almost always hold more appeal for groups in a country like Britain, characterized by a highly centralized political system with an executive-dominated Parliament' (2001, p. 44). Apart from the fact that records of organizations responding to consultations were available to the research team,[4] government-launched consultation exercises were chosen specifically because there is a UK tradition of civil servants consulting with organized interests at all stages of the policy process (from agenda setting to implementation). While data have not previously been collected and analyzed systematically, it has been long asserted that the 'consultative' system involving organized interests and the bureaucracy (1) is important alongside the parliamentary system (McKenzie 1958; Rose 1984), (2) constitutes the British (and Scottish) 'policy style' (Richardson and Jordan 1979; Jordan and Richardson 1987; Cairney 2008), and (3) is the 'orthodox' UK public policy approach (Grant 2001). Others have highlighted the importance of consultations as core 'policy work' among UK civil servants (Page 2003; Page and Jenkins 2005).

Of course, there is a healthy level of scholarly caution at accepting the policy importance of consultation exercises (see, e.g., Cook 2002; Wilkinson 2004). Moreover, the use of lists derived from these government consultations is not unanimously accepted (see Cavanagh *et al.* 1995; but also Jordan *et al.* 1994; Jordan and Maloney 1995). The core concern is that using invitation lists serves as an indicator of access, which is relatively easy to achieve, but not of influence. The research reported here uses lists of respondents (not simply those groups invited to participate in a consultation), which measure actual group policy mobilization.[5] As such, we count those groups that are *mobilized to act* when offered access. No assertion is made that access equates to influence.

In summary, apart from data availability considerations, the choice to pursue consultations as the initial place to invest resources in mapping the Scottish 'organized interest system' was made because (1) the bureaucratic arena is likely to be *a* main focus for public policy activity in Scotland; (2) consultations are launched on most issues of Scottish public policy, which makes them a good basis for generalizing about policy life (insofar as this can be achieved at all);[6] and (3) they are very open in terms of access, which means that they catch the broadest population of organizations that are both organizationally alive and in some way engaged in public policy. These are positives from a research-design perspective. Clearly, if the question were about identifying the *most influential* or *key* actors, then a data source that was very open in relation to access would not be as helpful. It is horses for courses. Given the research aims, it matters only that organized interests can and do readily utilize consultations as an avenue through which to engage in Scottish public policy.

What is the shape of the Scottish map of 'organized interests' as captured by engagement in public policy consultations? Table 6.2 reports the types of participants engaged in consultations using pooled data for 1982–2007. It reports both overall activity (allowing multiple counts of each organization) and the number of discrete participants (single counts, the usual metric deployed in mapping studies). The data are coded in a variety of (more or less detailed) ways, but here the broad coding scheme adopted by Baumgartner and Leech (2001) is utilized. The table shows that 'Government' and 'Public institutions' constitute the majority of overall activity. When combined with 'Businesses', these three categories map (broadly) onto Salisbury's usage of the term 'institution'. In the Scottish consultations data, institutions so defined account for almost 70 percent of all actors active at least once in this 25-year period. This suggests that Salisbury's finding of institutional dominance in the US holds for Scotland, or at least for the administrative arena (more on this below).

Table 6.2 Composition and activity of mobilized policy participants, Scottish consultations data, 1982–2007[a]

Type of actor	Actors		Activity		Activity ratio (activity/actors)
	N	%	N	%	
Public institutions[b]	5,367	29.1	19,575	21.1	3.6
Nonprofits and citizen groups	3,850	20.9	14,904	16.0	3.9
Businesses	3,748	20.3	7,032	7.6	1.9
Government[c]	2,590	14.0	32,016	34.5	12.4
Trade associations[d]	1,116	6.0	5,819	6.3	5.2
Professional associations	1,026	5.6	7,721	8.3	7.5
Unions	73	0.4	845	0.9	11.6
Other	686	3.7	4,974[e]	5.4	7.3
Total	18,456	100.0	92,886	100.0	5.0

[a] Excluding individual citizens, who were all coded as a single actor.
[b] This category includes the operational elements of government, such as schools and hospitals.
[c] This category includes central government departments, local authorities, Parliament, and nondepartmental public bodies.
[d] This category includes all business associations.
[e] This figure includes anonymous responses (which could be organizations or individuals) and politicians.

The 'Government' activity mapped was overwhelmingly dominated by local authorities. In fact, a list of the most frequent actors reveals local authorities as constituting the entire top 20.[7] In relation to 'Public institutions' the dominant actors are schools, hospital boards, and the like. This map may come as something of a surprise to political scientists, but civil servants with whom it was discussed seemed to anticipate it. This underlines the value of confronting our scholarly assumptions with empirical maps. The common currency of the profession might just be wrong.

Comparing arenas

As discussed above, the primary data set counted the mobilization of organized interests in governmental consultation processes. But, following Salisbury, there was the nagging question of whether this picture might look different in other arenas. To this end, other data sets were developed to cover the legislative and media arenas (summarized in Table 6.3). This helped establish the consequences of adopting any particular measure in the future.

An obvious alternative for a primary data set is the population of organized interests/pressure participants engaged in the legislative arena. In the US, there is a long tradition of examining the population of interests giving evidence to congressional committees. In contrast, in the UK political system, where the executive can use its whipped

Table 6.3 Summary of data sets, by arena

Arena	Policy activity/ institution	Data set
Primary data set		
Administrative	Scottish government consultations	Collected for all issues (1982–2007)
Additional data sets		
Administrative	Scottish government stakeholder groups	Collected for agriculture, environment and rural affairs, and transport (as at 2009)
Legislative	Scottish Parliament committee hearings	Scottish Parliament committee data (1999–2007)
Media	Scottish media	Collected for agriculture, transport, education, and health policy (January to April 2006)

majority in the House of Commons to ensure safe passage of bills, parliamentary committees are generally viewed as marginal. In fact, we could find almost no empirical work on committees at Westminster (but see Jordan *et al.* 1984; Marsh 1986). The Scottish case, however, provides a rationale for considering that committee evidence giving might be an important arena, and that populations of organized interests in that arena might be worth counting. After devolution in 1999, the new Scottish Parliament was designed in such a way as to – at least on paper – better utilize committees. Scottish committees combine legislative work with inquiries, and they have the power to initiate bills. Thus, in principle, they have considerable powers; in fact, they are considered to have 'high' strength on existing comparative measures of committee strength (see Cairney 2006, p. 183).

To quantify participation in parliamentary committee work in the legislative process, a data set was created based upon the activities of the committees of the Scottish Parliament in Sessions One (1999–2003) and Two (2003–2007). The data set collated information from the Scottish Parliament's Web site,[8] including the Official Report, minutes of proceedings, and information on written and oral evidence (including digital copies or transcripts of evidence where possible). The data cover all of the Parliament's subject committees, although several of the mandatory committees were excluded from the analysis due to the internal nature of their remit.[9] The data set includes details of the individual organizations giving evidence and the type of evidence given (oral or written).

Table 6.4 compares the population of organizations giving evidence (orally and in writing) with those engaging in government consultations over the same time period (1999–2007).[10] Results for oral and written evidence are presented separately because limited time is provided for oral evidence, which is allowed only upon invitation of the committee (written evidence may be provided unsolicited). Thus, oral evidence might be seen to serve as somewhat of a proxy for those organized interests that are deemed most crucial to the issue at hand (see the similar discussion for the US congressional case in Berry 1999). Further, in Salisbury's terms, oral evidence giving could be considered a more 'public arena' than written evidence giving and engagement in government consultations. By this logic, public attention is more likely to be attracted to oral evidence than to written submissions.

Reading Table 6.4 from left to right, the most notable change in composition is an increase of government itself (broadly conceived) as a contributor of oral evidence to committees. This is perhaps best explained

Table 6.4 Composition of organized interest system, executive versus Parliament, 1999–2007

| | Consultations | | Parliamentary committee evidence | | | |
| | | | Written | | Oral | |
	N	%	N	%	N	%
Public institutions[a]	3,176	27.3	344	13.1	229	14.2
Nonprofits and citizen groups	2,755	23.7	824	31.3	451	28.0
Businesses	2,201	18.9	423	16.1	177	11.0
Government[b]	1,741	15.0	494	18.8	402	25.0
Trade associations[c]	767	6.6	196	7.4	118	7.3
Professional associations	607	5.2	206	7.8	119	7.4
Unions	44	0.4	27	1.0	26	1.6
Other[d]	353	3.0	117	4.4	89	5.5
Total	11,644	100.0	2,631	100.0	1,611	100.0

[a] This category includes the operational elements of government, such as schools and hospitals.
[b] This category includes central government departments, local authorities, Parliament, and nondepartmental public bodies.
[c] This category includes all business associations.
[d] This category includes anonymous responses (which could be organizations or individuals) and politicians.

by the fact that it is standard practice for committees to call the minister and civil servants in the team responsible for bill to preparation give oral evidence at the opening and closing of evidence taking in bill-related hearings.[11] It is also usual for these actors to provide written evidence to such hearings. Business and public institutions are less active in both written and oral evidence giving. Salisbury (1984) expected institutions to be less prominent in policy arenas where the focus was on legitimating (publicly) a policy. Notwithstanding the point about the custom of government evidence giving to parliamentary committees, we found that the proportion of the population accounted for by interest groups was larger in the legislative arena. And, as Berry (1999) found for the US congress, among groups the largest rise was in citizen groups. It is not as overwhelming an upswing in group activity as Salisbury noted for the US, but (with the exception of government) it does broadly track his finding of a drop in the dominance of institutions as arenas become more public.

To the above, data from two other arenas have been added. First, a different (less accessible) bureaucratic/administrative arena was covered, namely the population of organized interests participating in government-established stakeholder groups or forums. The limits on what information could be extracted from government by a Freedom of Information request mean that these data are available only for a narrow sliver of activity: the rural affairs and environment (incorporating agriculture) and the transport policy areas.[12] The raw data consisted of a list of participants in 15 stakeholder or advisory groups in the transport policy area and 19 in the rural affairs and environment area. The choice of policy area might be expected to influence the populations mapped; for instance, it is not unreasonable to anticipate that citizen or professional groups might be more dominant in a nonindustry sector (say, health or education). But that research has yet to done.

Finally, we also generated population data based on the profile of policy actors in the Scottish media. The media data were based on a search of the *Scotsman* and *Scotland on Sunday* newspapers and covered the period from January 2006 to April 2006.[13] The decision to concentrate on this narrow window on the media was purely pragmatic: it was simply too time-consuming to search more broadly.

As far as possible, we followed the approach used by Salisbury (1984), but it has to be said that Salisbury is not entirely clear in outlining his counting method. An organized interest was recorded as 'appearing' in the media arena when it was attributed a set of interests or views, either directly (by way of quotation) or indirectly (by way of attribution). Thus organizations were not counted if they were simply mentioned by way of incidental background in reportage. After the search was conducted as described and duplicates and articles unrelated to the search had been removed, 177 articles were identified. In all, 448 individual organizations/participants were mentioned in the relevant articles sampled. Of these, 237 are unique. It is worth noting that 69 of these actors did not appear in either the parliamentary or the consultation data – mostly because they were individuals contacted by the media for expert comment. Table 6.5 puts these two additional data sets alongside the data sets described above. To focus more closely on Salisbury's point about the balance of institutions to groups, rows are ordered so that 'institutions' are at the top and interest groups at the bottom.[14] So what does the comparison reveal?

In principle, media coverage ought to be the most public of arenas. Journalists seeking to cover a policy story will seek out authoritative actors and try to balance coverage by using input from two contending

Table 6.5 Populations by arena, unique actors

	Media (The Scotsman and Scotland on Sunday, 2006)		Parliamentary committee evidence (1999–2007)				Consultations (1999–2007)		Stakeholder groups (agriculture & transport)	
			Oral		Written					
	N	%	N	%	N	%	N	%	N	%
Public institutions[a]	22	9.3	229	14.2	344	13.1	3,176	27.3	1	0.9
Government[b]	32	13.5	402	25.0	494	18.8	1,741	15.0	56	49.6
Businesses	20	8.4	177	11.0	423	16.1	2,201	18.9	9	8.0
Nonprofits and citizen groups	37	15.6	451	28.0	824	31.3	2,755	23.7	18	15.9
Trade associations[c]	26	11.0	118	7.3	196	7.4	767	6.6	23	20.4
Professional associations	11	4.6	119	7.4	206	7.8	607	5.2	5	4.4
Unions	6	2.5	26	1.6	27	1.0	44	0.4	1	0.9
Other[d]	83	35.0	89	5.5	117	4.4	353	3.0	–	–
Total	237	100.0	1,611	100.0	2,631	100.0	11,644	100.0	113	100.0

[a] This category includes the operational elements of government, such as schools and hospitals.
[b] This category includes central government departments, local authorities, Parliament, and nondepartmental public bodies.
[c] This category includes all business associations.
[d] This category includes anonymous responses (which could be organizations or individuals) and politicians.

sides (see Woolley 2000 for a discussion of using media data in politics). The data in Table 6.5 show that the 'Other' category is almost one third of the media-based population. This category includes elected politicians, mostly Scottish ministers and members of the Scottish Parliament. Government agencies – typically 'departmental spokespersons' – are also part of the population and serve the same narrative function as politicians in media coverage. Apart from this set of actors, citizen groups and business associations dominate: in fact, with elected politicians removed, interest groups make up more than 50 percent of the population. To give an idea of the dominance by individual groups, in the 80 media articles on agriculture the National Farmers Union of Scotland appeared 36 times (even more often than the Minister for Agriculture). To summarize, analysis of media data generates a population of interest groups and politicians. It is perhaps closest to the 'group' population imagined in Wilson's undergraduate essays and reproduced as lists of 'usual suspects' in textbooks on Scottish politics: for example, National Farmers Union of Scotland, the Royal Society for the Protection of Birds (Scotland), the Tenant Farmers Association of Scotland, the Scottish Rural Property Business Association, and the Scottish Crofting Foundation.

At the other end of the spectrum, stakeholder groups are dominated by the same interest groups, but with politicians replaced by actors within government. The 'government' in stakeholder groups comprises almost exclusively nondepartmental public bodies, such as Historic Scotland, the Scottish Environmental Protection Agency, and Scottish Enterprise, and local authorities. Given that the emphasis of stakeholder groups is usually on legitimating policy among key players at the policy-formulation stage, while also solving subsequent implementation problems, the focus is understandably on membership groups and those institutions (mostly governmental) with a statutory interest in the policy area. Just as the media are keen to capture the views of groups claiming to represent sets of interests, government is interested in having such groups sitting on stakeholder forums. Thus, individual companies and public institutions (such as school boards, individual universities, or hospitals) are largely unsuitable parties to such forums.

A direct comparison with Salisbury's work is not easy because his data sources did not include politicians or government departments: as is clear, in the Scottish case – almost regardless of arena – the population is heavily influenced by such actors. Thus, it is hard to critically appraise his specific argument that the more public and visible arenas will foster populations with relatively low numbers of institutions.[15]

But if we were to remove government and public institutions from the data set, in which case it would better resemble Salisbury's populations, we would find that institutions (now simply businesses) would be most heavily represented in the organized interest populations in consultations and written evidence to Parliament and almost absent from populations in the media and stakeholder arenas. For the present purpose, however, we simply focus on his broader point that populations vary across arenas.

Following Salisbury's lead, this rough-and-ready comparison of arenas demonstrates that the choice of lens through which to view organized interest populations is crucial to what one finds. If one accepts the general proposition that there is value in looking at *actual* policy mobilization when mapping pressure participant (or even interest group) populations, this finding is no doubt interesting, but at the same time a little worrying. A viable mapping literature needs to discuss the relative value of mapping these arenas, and become confident in both the choices and their implications.

Overlapping populations

An obvious question is to what extent these arena-specific populations overlap. This matters because it goes to whether it is in fact sensible, empirically, to talk of a given political system having an organized interest system or population. Put another way, if one wants to talk in terms of a general population separate from a specific arena, it helps to qualify what type of population is actually engaged in a 'general' manner across arenas. We found no work comparing actual mobilization data across arenas. But previous work comparing database sources has consistently found low levels of overlap. Work on US nonprofit data comparing IRS, state incorporation, and telephone listings found that almost three quarters of all entries were found in only one database (Grønbjerg 2002). Work on the sources used to map the Brussels lobbying community found similarly low levels of overlap (Berkhout and Lowery 2008). On this basis, this research did not expect 100 percent overlap; nonetheless, 'commonsense' expectations anticipated a significant core of organized interests active across these arenas.

Clearly the data to hand are not similarly comprehensive across all arenas. The comprehensive nature of the parliamentary and consultations data means a direct comparison is possible and reasonable. Both arenas engage in a similarly full cross-section of public policy issues and they are equally open in relation to access. Simply aggregating data on both arenas generates a population of 14,745 organizations. The combined population for parliament and consultations together, after removing duplicates, totals 12,844 organizations. Comparing the two figures gives a ratio of 'total' to 'cleaned' data of 0.87; this hints that the overlap between data sets is low.

Table 6.6 sets out the relationship between the populations of organized interests across the two arenas (legislative and administrative) for the same time period (1999–2007). Of the combined population of organized interests, 76 percent were active only in the administrative arena and 9 percent in the legislative arena only. Given the larger overall population engaged in consultations, this difference in magnitude is to be expected. What is perhaps most interesting is that only 14.7 percent of organized interests were engaged in both arenas at least once during the same time window.

The limited nature of the media and stakeholder data means a detailed comparison is not useful. But a brief comparison yields an indicative picture of what might be revealed with better data. For instance, of the 237 unique actors mentioned in newspaper coverage almost one third had not appeared in either the parliament or the consultation data. As discussed above, this is mostly because they were individual members of Parliament or experts contacted by the media but not likely to make individual submissions to inquiries. In contrast, only 16 of the 113 actors engaged in the stakeholder groups mapped were *not* also participants in the parliamentary or administrative arenas. These were by and large community councils that were invited to participate in transport-related working groups. Compared with the figures in Table 6.6, this suggests that most actors participating in stakeholder groups are also engaged in consultations and parliamentary hearings. In contrast, the media tap into politicians and individual experts who might comment on issues but not engage separately in the public policy process.

Table 6.6 Populations across arenas, level of overlap, 1999–2007

Arena (data source)	N	%
Administrative (consultation data)	9,770	76.1
Legislative (committee hearings)	1,181	9.2
Overlap (appear in both arenas)	1,893	14.7
Total	12,844	100.0

The point this drives home is that, at least empirically, there is not much sense in talking of a general organized interest population. The specific political arena seems to be crucial in shaping the population. Not only is the overall complexion – the mix of organized interest types – different, but the *specific* organized interests themselves are often different.

Conclusions

Where does this leave us? The initial implication is the rather trite-sounding observation that the arena chosen has implications for what is counted. In this light, it would be expedient to opt for directory or aggregate (e.g., lobby registers) data sources that are *not* explicitly arena-specific. While this choice by the student of organized interest populations comes at the cost of specificity, it obviates the need to erect too robust a case with respect to defending what to count and where to look. But, as in the Scottish case, there may be no such source of data.

Above, the absence of British (and Scottish) mapping studies was noted, and it was argued that this most likely reflects both the absence of 'off-the-shelf' directories and the lack of a clear tradition with respect to which arena one ought to count organizational mobilization in. Against this benchmark, the intention was to make a modest contribution to (or to institute) a Scottish population-mapping tradition. As discussed, the need to collect data based on policy mobilization raises the subsequent question of which window on policy engagement to utilize. The initial choice to map policy consultation processes was based on three principles: pragmatism (the data were available and accessible), relevance (the consultation process is very open and would likely capture most politically active groups), and scholarly salience (at least some researchers suggest that the bureaucratic arena is a likely focal point for the engagement of organized interests in British politics). Similar justifications of approach are welcome, indeed necessary – to justify both stepping away from established orthodoxies and (especially) taking a first tentative step when no orthodoxies exist to follow.

As Salisbury noted some time ago, populations will likely differ across arenas. We found support for Salisbury's often overlooked observation that policy arenas nurture *different* populations of active organizations; specifically, institutions dominate some arenas and interest groups others. And, with several arena-based data sets to hand, this chapter has established that this is indeed the case (at least for Scotland). Not only is the general complexion of each arena-based population different, but the mix of individual organizations is different. There is a core of interest organizations that engage across arenas, but this core is swamped by the sheer volume of actors that do not. Thus, caution needs to be exercised in letting data from one arena *stand for* (probably differing) populations in other arenas. Moreover, this finding underscores the need for scholars – at least those who do not utilize directories – to be clear on their choice of arenas to map. Of course, there are traditions and orthodoxies that emerge with respect to what arena to collect data in. Where counting multiple arenas is not feasible, a case ought to be made for why one arena is more (or less) suitable as a window onto the composition of an underlying national (or subnational) population.

The broader question is whether it makes any empirical sense to talk as if a given polity had an underlying or standing population of organized interests. While it is not made explicit, the study of organized interest populations sometimes proceeds with an image of an ever-present universe of organizations ready to engage in policy. This may constitute a convenient picture in our heads, but this chapter suggests it might lack a strong empirical foundation. The analysis of the Scottish data above suggests that many organizations are engaged in just one arena. The same data analyzed elsewhere show that most organizations are engaged very intermittently over time (see Halpin 2011). Together, these results imply a core of well-engaged organizations – policy professionals – engaged across all arenas, accompanied by a very fluid, rarely engaged set of policy amateurs. When we talk about organized interest populations, it might also be useful to distinguish between an ever-presently engaged policy-dedicated core and an ephemerally engaged amateur periphery. The question is then to what extent we are concerned with mapping only the former or both.

While utilizing directory sources – where available – might obviate the type of discussion above by simply providing a list of organizations considered generally 'active' in public policy, there are advantages in choosing to collect data directly from observations of policy activity. For one, it is possible then to utilize the data to generate *direct* measures of the frequency and breadth of activity by specific actors (Baumgartner and Leech 2001; Halpin and Binderkrantz 2011). This style of data is able to open up longstanding questions about the pattern of organized interest mobilization that have hitherto been largely explored through sample surveys. Moreover, if mobilization data can be linked to specific issue contexts – rather than just a particular arena – this adds an extra dimension to scholarship. Thus, we suggest that moving beyond directories is worthwhile, but without diminishing the value of such study: multiple lenses seem a sensible strategy.

Inevitably in a chapter of this length many important questions are pushed to one side. For instance, left entirely untouched is the whole question of how one might account for the size and diversity of the organized interest population levels mapped (and changes over time). This question has occupied the minds of many, not least because it goes to the heart of discussions of bias or business dominance of organized interest systems (Lowery and Gray 2004; Schlozman 2010). A few points are worth noting. First, public policy data – such as used here – are by definition about mapping the net effect of choices to engage in policy, and not about organizational disbandment. These populations arise because specific organizations overcome a 'secondary' collective action problem (Baumgartner *et al.* 2011). Second, if, as Schattschneider (1960) suggests, conflict expansion is a key factor in stimulating the engagement of the otherwise disinterested, then we might look to processes of governmental agenda setting as crucial in shaping the contours of populations of the mobilized. While environmental factors such as constituency size and population density might be crucial in explaining birth and/or disbandment, one could imagine that agenda diversity or similar policy system variables might be more valuable in explaining the mobilization of the *already formed*. This might especially apply where populations include policy amateurs who are not heavily engaged in expert monitoring of policy and thus operate by secondary cues (Halpin 2011).

Notes

The bulk of the research reported here arose from the UK Economic and Social Research Council funded project 'The Mobilisation of Organised Interests in Policy Making: Access, Activity and Bias in the "Group System"' (RES-000-22-1932). The public consultations data were collected (and coded) with Graeme Baxter, and the data on the Scottish Parliament were collected with Iain Macleod. The media data were collected (and coded) with the very able assistance of Mads Bjerre Clausen (Aarhus University). Darren Halpin has been greatly assisted in his work by Herschel Thomas III (University of Texas at Austin), who has been working on other outputs from some of the same data sets. We wish to acknowledge the assistance of numerous staff of the Scottish government for providing access to data for this project.

1. This logic has been subject to some criticism (see Lowery *et al.* 2004).
2. It is well established that any deviation from 'established' methods of measuring a given concept will mean that any novel findings are easily dismissed (see the discussion in Schmitter 2008). There are costs associated with stepping outside conventions, and thus they foster inertial forces.

3. Of course, there have been some attempts to count groups in specific fields. See for instance the work of May *et al.* (1998, fn. 9) on UK trade associations.
4. Although we had to collect most of these archival records from document storage facilities – a very laborious process indeed.
5. Analysis has been conducted comparing invitation lists to responses in order to determine the relationship. From a representative sample of 173 consultations conducted during the 25-year period, it was discovered that, on average, just 32 percent of those invited to engage in a given consultation do in fact participate. In terms of the number of consultation responses, 77 percent came from invited organizations, which means that 23 percent of responses came from organizations who were not invited directly.
6. Consultations are launched at all stages of the policy process and seemingly on all relevant topics. In Scotland, of course, this is principally only on devolved matters.
7. For more details see Halpin and Thomas (forthcoming).
8. www.scottish.parliament.uk.
9. For the purposes of clarity, the committees excluded were Audit; Finance; Public Petitions; Standards, Procedures and Public Appointments; and Subordinate Legislation. Two mandatory committees (European and External Relations, and Equal Opportunities) were included as their respective remits are more public in scope.
10. The Scottish Parliament was established in 1999, so there are no data before this date.
11. Author interview with committee clerks, Edinburgh, 2009.
12. This is based on the direct experience of having lodged numerous Freedom of Information requests during late 2009 and early 2010.
13. The search was conducted using LexisNexis. The search terms were 'agriculture' or 'farm', 'education', 'health', and 'transport', all in combination with 'policy' and 'legislation'. The time period was chosen as it overlapped with the original data collection period, and it was not in an election period (which tends to dominate policy reportage).
14. We admittedly apply a rather crude measure. Some of the nonprofits in the 'Nonprofits and citizen groups' category could arguably be considered institutions: they could go into Salisbury's category 'Nonprofit private institutions'. But it is hard to detect this difference from organizational names and Web sites. And we did not have many obvious cases, and certainly not enough to justify a bespoke category that would not fit with dominant orthodoxies in the contemporary US mapping literature. In any event, such recoding would simply add to the finding of the dominance of institutions.
15. Although the fact that 'open' media and 'closed' stakeholder groups seem to have broadly similar populations suggests a modification to Salisbury's explanation for the prevailing population mix.

References

Baumgartner, F. and B. Leech (2001) 'Interest Niches and Policy Bandwagons: Patterns of Interest Group Involvement in National Politics', *Journal of Politics*, 63(4), 1191–1213.

Baumgartner, F., H. Larsen-Price, B. Leech, and P. Rutledge (2011) 'Congressional and Presidential Effects on the Demand for Lobbying', *Political Research Quarterly*, 64 (1), 3–16.

Berkhout, J. and D. Lowery (2008) 'Counting Organized Interests in the European Union: A Comparison of Data Sources', *Journal of European Public Policy*, 15(4), 489–513.

Berry, J. (1999) *The New Liberalism: The Rising Power of Citizen Groups* (Washington, DC: Brookings Institution Press).

Cairney, P. (2006) 'The Analysis of Scottish Parliament Committee Influence: Beyond Capacity and Structure in Comparing West European Legislatures', *European Journal of Political Research*, 45, 181–208.

Cairney, P. (2008) 'Has Devolution Changed the "British Policy Style"?', *British Politics*, 3, 350–72.

Cavanagh, M., D. Marsh, and M. Smith (1995) 'The Relationship between Policy Networks and Sectoral and Sub-sectoral Levels: A Response to Jordan, Maloney and McLaughlin', *Public Administration*, 73, 627–29.

Cook, D. (2002) 'Consultation for a Change? Engaging Users and Communities in the Policy Process', *Social Policy and Administration*, 36(5), 516–31.

Grant, W. (2001) 'Pressure Politics: From "Insider" Politics to Direct Action?', *Parliamentary Affairs*, 54(2), 337–48.

Gray, V. and D. Lowery (1996/2000) *The Population Ecology of Interest Representation: Lobbying Communities in the American States* (Ann Arbor: University of Michigan Press).

Grønbjerg, K. A. (2002), 'Evaluating Nonprofit Databases', *American Behavioral Scientist*, 45(11), 1741–77.

Halpin, D. (2011) 'Organized Interests and Cascades of Attention: Unpacking Policy Bandwagon Dynamics', *Governance*, 24(2), 205–30.

Halpin, D. and A. Binderkrantz (2011) 'Explaining Breadth of Policy Engagement: Patterns of Interest Group Mobilization in Public Policy', *Journal of European Public Policy*, 18(2), 201–19.

Halpin, D. and H. Thomas (forthcoming) 'Evaluating the Breadth of Policy Engagement by Organized Interests', *Public Administration*.

Jordan, G. and W. A. Maloney (1995) 'Policy Networks Expanded: A Comment on Cavanagh, Marsh and Smith', *Public Administration*, 73, 630–33.

Jordan, G. and W. A. Maloney (2001) 'Britain: Change and Continuity within the New Realities of British Politics', in C. Thomas (ed.) *Political Parties and Interest Groups: Shaping Democratic Governance* (Boulder, CO: Lynne Rienner).

Jordan, G. and J. Richardson (1987) *Government and Pressure Groups in Britain* (Oxford: Clarendon Press).

Jordan, G., J. Richardson, and G. Dudley (1984) 'Evidence to Parliamentary Committees as Access to the Policy Process' in D. Hill (ed.) *Parliamentary Select Committees in Action: A Symposium* (Strathclyde Papers in Government and Politics No. 24).

Jordan, G., W. A. Maloney, and M. McLaughlin (1994) 'Characterizing Agricultural Policy-Making', *Public Administration*, 72, 505–26.

Lowery, D. and V. Gray (2004) 'Bias in the Heavenly Chorus: Interests in Society and before Government', *Journal of Theoretical Politics*, 16(1), 5–29.

Lowery, D., V. Gray, J. Anderson, and A. Newmark (2004) 'Collective Action and the Mobilization of Institutions', *Journal of Politics*, 66(3), 684–705.

Marsh, I. (1986) *Policy Making in a Three Party System: Committees, Coalitions, and Parliament* (London: Methuen).

May, T. C., J. McHugh, and T. Taylor (1998) 'Business Representation in the UK since 1979: The Case of Trade Associations', *Political Studies*, 46, 260–75.

McKenzie, R. T. (1958) 'Parties, Pressure Groups and the British Political Process', *Political Quarterly*, 29(1), 5–16. Reprinted in R. Kimber and J. Richardson (eds.) *Pressure Groups in Britain* (London: Dent, 1974).

Page, E. C. (2003) 'The Civil Servant as Legislator: Law Making in British Administration', *Public Administration*, 81(4), 651–79.

Page, E. and B. Jenkins (2005) *Policy Bureaucracy: Government with a Cast of Thousands* (Oxford: Oxford University Press).

Richardson, J. J. and A. G. Jordan (1979) *Governing under Pressure* (Oxford: Martin Robertson).

Rose, R. (1984) *Do Parties Make a Difference?* 2nd edn. (London: Macmillan and Chatham).

Salisbury, R. H. (1984) 'Interest Representation: The Dominance of Interest Groups', *American Political Science Review*, 78(1), 64–78.

Salisbury, R. H. (1990) 'The Paradox of Interest Groups in Washington', in A. King (ed.) *New American Political System*, 2nd edn. (Washington, DC: AEI).

Schattschneider, E. E. (1960) *The Semi-Sovereign People* (New York: Holt, Reinhart, and Winston).

Schlozman, K. (2010) 'Who Sings in the Heavenly Chorus? The Shape of the Organized Interest System,' in J. Berry (ed.) *The Oxford Handbook of American Political Parties and Interest Groups* (Oxford: Oxford University Press).

Schmitter, P. (2008) 'The Design of Social and Political Research', in D. della Porta and M. Keating (eds.) *Approaches and Methodologies in the Social Sciences* (Cambridge: Cambridge University Press).

Wilkinson, M. (2004) 'Campaigning for Older People: A Case Study Approach to the Input of Voluntary and Community Organisations in the Policy Process', *Social Policy and Society*, 3(4), 343–52.

Wilson, J. Q. (1995) *Political Organizations*, rev. edn. (Princeton, NJ: Princeton University Press; originally published 1973).

Woolley, J. T. (2000) 'Using Media Based Data in Studies of Politics', *American Journal of Political Science*, 44(1), 156–73.

Yackee, J. and S. Yackee (2006) 'A Bias toward Business? Assessing Interest Group Influence on the Bureaucracy', *Journal of Politics*, 68, 128–39.

7
Tracking Interest Group Populations in the US and the UK

Grant Jordan, Frank R. Baumgartner, John D. McCarthy,
Shaun Bevan, and Jamie Greenan

Characterizing interest group population change in the US and the UK

Using the entries in the US-based *Encyclopedia of Associations* and the UK *Directory of British Associations*,[1] this chapter reviews the growth and development of the associational universe in two political systems. The cases have been coded according to two separate national typologies, but to aid comparison the UK data have been recoded to use the US system, which in turn uses categories from those in the Policy Agendas Project (www.policyagendas.org; www.policyagendas.org.uk). The chapter attempts to get a handle on the broad scale of the national associational populations in the UK and the US. The associational data are seen as a proxy for the respective national interest group systems. Beyond that, the projects have tried to map how the overall numbers are responding sector by sector to conflicting pressures of expansion and reduction. Overall the exercises sought to test the widespread assumptions that the interest group systems in each country were dense and complex – and becoming increasingly so on both counts. However, the chapter identifies two slightly different conventional wisdoms. One is about group-level explosion and the second is about variation by subcategory of the whole.

Though interest groups have usually been seen as important and numerous in Western polyarchies, indicators of scale rarely get beyond broad assertions of 'more' over time. In practice the search for a feel for such numbers is likely to generate different totals, but if there had been a simple way of establishing *the* answer, the question would have been resolved before now. There are no existing authoritative group totals for the UK and the US. This exercise seeks to at least offer orders of magnitude in the field, and to track changes in these systems over time.

Different definitions identify different populations, and any particular target can be counted by simpler or more sophisticated exercises. A variety of results is therefore predictable, and in assessing a result attention has to be paid to the collection methods and assumptions about any total. Studies of the scale of interest groups are of course following Walker, who noted that there were 'almost no comprehensive descriptions of the world of interest groups in America' (1983, p. 391). Berry noted, 'unfortunately for scholars studying interest groups, there is no standard data base to measure the population of lobbying organizations over time. ... Even measuring the participation of groups in a single year is difficult' (1999a, p. 18). Gray and Lowery (1996, p. 5) cite Salisbury (1994, p. 13) to call attention to the very real difficulties of measuring population-level properties across multiple populations; they quote Cigler, who made the point that 'In large measure, data availability has been the major determinant of the interest group politics agenda, framing both the questions we explore, *and the topics we avoid*' (1994, p. 29; emphasis added). This suggests that solving the rather basic challenge of tracking numbers is a precondition for more sophisticated analysis.

The fact that in many fields attempts to establish metrics initially lead to uncertainty was, for example, demonstrated in 19th-century geology when creationist readings suggested the planet was about 6,000 years old, but then Hutton suggested, to the contrary, huge time horizons with 'no vestige of a beginning,–no prospect of an end'. In turn Lord Kelvin disputed this and proposed an age of 10–100 million years. This result is now seen as seriously inaccurate, with a widely accepted current consensus in the ballpark of 4,000-plus million years, but even this wrong number confronted religious assumptions and, unlike Hutton, found a pattern of creation and decline. 'Wrong' numbers which develop the debate can be more useful than no numbers.

This chapter uses two directory-based data sets of associational numbers to allow approximation of the current scale of national-level association mobilization in the US and the UK and patterns of change over time. As noted the data are derived from the well-regarded US *Encyclopedia of Associations* and the UK's similarly well-accepted *Directory of British Associations*. The companies that compile these sources follow established protocols for inclusion of entries. For the US data there are four main observation points in the analysis (1975, 1985, 1995, and 2005), but the growth in the absolute size of the entire system is indicated in Figure 7.1 (below), which plots the number of associations listed in each of the 42 volumes from 1956 to 2006. The *Directory of British Associations* reports on approximately 7,000 groups listed in the volumes used for analysis: 1970, 1992, and 2005.[2] The directory has had 20 editions; each is a major reference book of 600 or so pages. In addition, there are CD-based issues, with edition seven in 2009. These are pragmatically defined and the directory includes

> national associations, societies, institutes and similar organizations...which have a voluntary membership. Regional and local organizations concerned with important industries and trades [are included]...as are local chambers of commerce and county agricultural, historical, natural history and similar organizations which are the principal sources of information and contacts in their areas.

So the data are firmly oriented toward national-level bodies, though in practice important regional bodies are also included.

As set out in Chapter 1, a range of legitimate and feasible counts can be made in this area. Similar benefits – and possible defects – can be identified for both directories used. An important factor in using these sources is that each edition was collated more or less annually in real time. Unless such pre-collected data are exploited, researchers interested in change over time have to try to recreate previous levels. Retrospectively generating past totals is obviously even trickier than collecting contemporary information. Access to past totals (collected in real time) is the most important reason for using pre-collected material.

There is also an opportunistic benefit of minimizing effort in making use of data collected by others, but that advantage should not be exaggerated as both the UK and US exercises traced the associations across time so that the life history of individual groups was available. With the scale of cases this is more time-consuming than it might appear, involving the need to resolve name changes, terminations, and so on. What constitutes a name change as opposed to termination and a successor organization is often difficult to ascertain.

The two directories are similar in seeking to list every major national association from trade associations to hobby groups. While this seems a 'natural' target – and the difficulties might be expected to be in execution – other exercises prefer to focus on other (equally 'natural') targets. Christiansen, for example, addresses 'interest groups that want to affect political and administrative processes and outputs' (Chapter 8). This is a more focused population than featured in this chapter, although in practice, as Christiansen records, the cases are not always easily categorized. He gives the following example: 'The Danish Society of Internal Medicine has as part of its purpose to advise the medical authorities about medical education in Denmark. Is this a sufficient "political purpose" to be part of the population?'

Many of the associations in the UK and US directories are, in essence, apolitical (although such groups may be dragged into political controversy), and other research tries to focus on a more narrowly defined constituency. However, it can be argued that the broad sense used here is of political science interest because it represents the pool of national-level associational organizations relevant in policy consultation and advocacy. Unlike the work of Christiansen (Chapter 8) or of Schlozman (Chapter 2), who sought to capture the organizations physically represented in Washington and overtly seeking policy influence, the data sets in this chapter capture the entire reservoir of organizations actually and *potentially* participating in national political processes.

The main features of the British data are reported by Jordan and Greenan in Chapter 4. This chapter uses the recoding of the British material in line with the Policy Agendas Project to allow direct comparison with US trends. This allows us to go beyond single-country findings, as the directory instruments are so similar in their nature that the use of the same coding schema allows a cross-national comparison of subtypes of association.

The assumption of explosive growth in the interest group system

As noted above there is a broad consensus in the literature that there is a lack of authoritative data; nonetheless there is a commonplace assumption in political science that there has been an *explosion* in interest group numbers – at least in the UK and the US. Jordan and Maloney (2007, p. 3) quote Cigler and Loomis writing on the US: 'a participation revolution has occurred... large numbers of citizens have become active in an ever increasing number of protest groups, citizens' organizations, and special interest groups'. Jordan and Maloney use British data from the *Directory of British Associations* to show that 48 percent of recently recorded groups had startup dates after 1968. They say, 'Approximately at the same time as the explosion in the number and membership levels of groups, British political parties began to experience a hemorrhaging in the level of both membership and intra-organizational activity' (2007, p. 3).

So common is this theme in the US literature that Baumgartner and Leech include an entire section on 'The Recurring Discovery of an "Interest-Group Explosion"' (1998, pp. 100–102), tracing it back through the work of Croly (1915), Pollock (1927), Herring (1929), and Crawford

(1939) and onward through virtually every decade of the 20th century. They note that 'There can be no doubt that the American interest-group system has grown dramatically over the decades' (1998, p. 102). Nownes and Neeley similarly argue that 'Since 1960, the number of politically active public interest groups in the United States has skyrocketed. In fact, there are now more public interest groups active in Washington politics than at any other time in the nation's history' (1996).

In 'The Paradox of Interest Groups in Washington' Salisbury pulled together changes in the group system since 1960 under the heading 'The Explosion in Numbers' (1990, reprinted 1992, p. 340). He conceded, 'we have no reliable baseline of observation', but the following items he collated suggest the 'magnitude of expansion of the interest group universe' (p. 74):[3]

- The number of registered lobbyists increased from 3,400 in 1975 to 7,200 in 1985.
- The annual publication *Washington Representatives* managed to find and list more than 5,000 people in 1979; by 1988 it listed nearly 11,000 (Close *et al.* 1988).
- The proportion of US trade and professional associations headquartered in and around Washington grew from 19 percent in 1971 to 30 percent in 1982 (Colgate 1982).
- The number of lawyers belonging to the District of Columbia Bar Association (a requirement for practice in Washington) increased from 10,925 in 1973 to 34,087 in 1981.
- The number of business corporations operating offices in Washington increased from 50 in 1961 to 545 in 1982 (Yoffie 1985).
- Some 765 of the citizen groups and 795 of the welfare groups in Washington in 1981 had come into existence since 1960 (Schlozman and Tierney 1986, p. 76).

In sum, there is no doubting the existence of a scholarly and journalistic consensus identifying the 'interest group explosion' in both the US and the UK.

Several implicit propositions underpin the assumption of group proliferation. Berry (1999a, p. 17) pointed to the emergence of lower organization costs and the ability to more easily contact niche clienteles. He argued that newly formed groups are like cable TV channels that can make money by finding a small but faithful audience. Truman (1951) argued that the pattern of associations reflected the increasingly fragmented economic system. As the economy and the professions further fragment, new organizational niches are created, eventually to be filled by interest groups. Other commentators have more recently focused on such factors as increased education, income, and leisure time to explain the proliferation of groups, but since most groups have a professional or industrial link we suspect that Truman was once again mostly right as he put his emphasis on the professional nature of groups and their linkage to the economy.

The bottom line of the comparison between the UK and US is shown in Figure 7.1. It depicts US growth by plotting the number of associations listed in each of the 42 volumes of the *Encyclopedia* from 1956 to 2006. The UK data reflect three measurement points: 1970, 1992, and 2006.

The figure shows that in the US there was an increase from 12,000 recorded organizations in 1975 to 22,000 in 2005, or 79 percent growth over the 30-year period. It shows rapid growth in the early years (possibly due to increased accuracy of the directory through the first several editions, but certainly not due only to that in later years), rapid overall expansion throughout the 1960s, 1970s, and 1980s, and then stagnation and even some annual declines in the 1990s and since then. In the case of the UK the system is smaller (around 7,000) and very limited.

While there is sharp real overall growth in the US, perhaps a term such as 'surge' fits better than 'explosion'; in the UK the phenomenon is

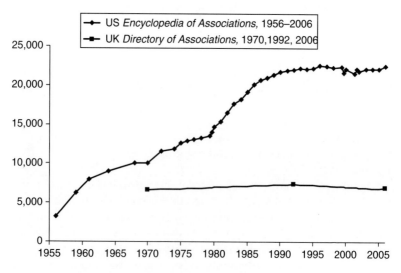

Figure 7.1   US and UK national association totals over time

even weaker. The understanding that there is a group explosion seems exaggerated. In part this may be an artifact of the asymmetry in visibility between growth and contraction. Press and other attention tends be on new examples, and groups tends to disappear by decline and eventual silent demise. In consequence perhaps there just *appears* to be more associational growth going on than death; this may be illusory.

While data from two systems are obviously desirable, when the results of separate exercises look inconsistent there is an initial tendency to query the accuracy of recording rather than accept unpredicted findings. The expectation was that similar pressures would be operating in both systems, leading to similar trend lines. In particular the UK line looks 'suspect' given the explosion expectation, but in fact these reservations were quite quickly set aside. The UK position is not that there was no growth; it is that the growth was offset by major declines in certain areas, notably employer and trades unions. These declines are confirmed by other work in these narrower research areas (see Chapter 4).

The assumption of differentiated sectoral change

The explosion seems to be rediscovered in the literature in most decades, but there is a second conventional wisdom that is not perfectly congruent with the first. This is an expectation that the overall growth in the field is the sum of a mixed pattern of group growth at different rates in different sectors. Alongside the explosion claims there is an extension that assumes a continual transformation or churning, with different sectors of the population growing and declining at differential rates. For example, Berry's *The New Liberalism* finds a 'staggering rise in the numbers of interest groups active in Washington' (1999a, p. 17), but Berry (1999b, p. 371) also draws attention to an explosion of liberal citizen groups from 1864 to 1980 and then a mobilization of conservative citizen lobbies in a later period. He does not assume uniform trends and stresses the rising power of citizen groups. While in part Berry subscribes to the explosion image, a strong subtheme for Berry and others is that growth was sectorally distinctive. He suggests that the three decades from 1968 to 1998 were a bull market for lobbying groups, but he raises the question as to whether all group sectors proliferated at equal rates. He says that newspaper reports on the formation of new associations implied that the number of groups was increasing, 'but...the number of citizen groups is growing more rapidly than all other types, creating a trend away from the predominantly occupational basis of the interest group system' (1999a).

Baumgartner and Leech (1998 p. 103), using the US *Encyclopedia of Associations*, show an increase from 5,843 associations to more than

23,000 in 1995.[4] But they too stress the variation across subpopulations. They note, for example, that trade associations in the *Encyclopedia* increased from 2,309 in 1959 to 3,973 in 1995, but that this represented a decrease in the percentage of all associations as the total population was growing even faster. Other important sources underpinning the assumption of group growth include Walker (1983) and King and Walker (1991). They assemble evidence to sustain an impression that 'there is no doubt that the number of citizen groups has grown rapidly during the past twenty years in several policy areas' (Walker 1983, p. 394). King and Walker conclude:

> Since about the time Martin Luther King, Jr. led 'a march on Washington' by thousands of citizens in the civil rights movement in 1963, there has been a march to Washington by interest groups as well. We have witnessed an explosive growth in the number of groups finding voice and redress in Washington. (1991, p. 72)

This leads to a qualification to the basic explosion image. Some sectors of the associational population have indeed exploded in numbers in recent years, whereas others have stagnated or even declined. The associational system can be said to be significantly more diverse, including many more citizen and social movement organizations, as well as showing overall increases. Walker says, 'all available evidence points in the same direction, namely that there are many more interest groups operating in Washington today than in the years before WWII and that citizen groups make up a much larger proportion of the total than before' (1983, p. 395). This chapter confirms these findings, but also points to the more complicated nature of the situation: it is not *only* citizen groups that have proliferated, and it is not *only* traditional economic groups that have stagnated.

The shaded areas in Figure 7.2 represent the numbers of associations listed in each volume of the *Encyclopedia*, simply using the publisher's categories. This makes clear that trade associations represent the largest single category of groups in the US system, but that this category is growing only very slowly in comparison with other types of groups. Other groups – including health and public affairs groups – have had overall growth rates in the period of up to 1,000 percent, as compared with the 79 percent growth rate across the entire system. Several association types have remained relatively stagnant, such as labor unions, chambers of commerce, and of course trade associations. This picture is also sustained to some extent by Schlozman's work (see Chapter 2).

The UK lines (Figure 7.3) show a less uniform pattern of expansion. In the US the picture is of less or more growth in different categories, whereas in the UK there is mainly limited growth offset by major decline in two categories: trade/business and chambers of commerce.

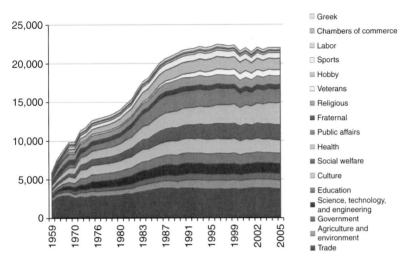

Figure 7.2   US trends in association numbers, by sector, 1959–2005

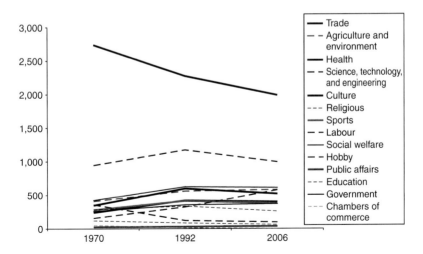

Figure 7.3   UK trends in association numbers, by sector

The broad pattern of the data

Both data sets were coded by associations' major focus of activity according to the topic classification system used in the US and UK Policy Agendas Project. The overall growth in the US system in the period was more than 79 percent, but growth ranged from 15 percent in local government to 210 percent in niches such as civil rights (Table 7.1).

In the US there is definitely some kind of general expansion, with all categories showing growth. However, the biggest category, business,

Table 7.1   US associations by sector, 1975–2005 (US coding)

Sector	1975	1985	1995	2005	Growth rate (%)
Civil rights	273	656	795	848	210.62
Family	139	274	371	401	188.49
Housing	69	160	183	192	178.26
Health	1,044	1,849	2,331	2,821	170.21
Law	192	380	468	507	164.06
Environment	226	362	513	564	149.56
Ideological	245	481	568	609	148.57
Other	69	116	128	143	107.25
Lands	74	122	161	151	104.05
Defense	329	553	689	655	99.09
Art	620	845	1,375	1,190	91.94
Social welfare	242	414	479	464	91.74
Economy	44	84	85	83	88.64
Energy	98	239	214	184	87.76
Science	623	940	1,139	1,149	84.43
Agriculture	539	822	914	988	83.30
Hobby	516	934	1,129	940	82.17
History	821	1,089	1,459	1,481	80.39
Average for all group types					79.35
Sports	450	778	874	792	76.00
Government	249	450	455	424	70.28
Transport	488	902	1,045	789	61.68
International	839	1,216	1,569	1,322	57.57
Religion	609	852	1,026	942	54.68
Business	2,213	2,747	2,808	2,879	30.09
Education	943	1,084	1,137	1,212	28.53
Labor	328	407	443	418	27.44
International trade	124	166	197	156	25.81
Local government	85	98	102	98	15.29
Total	12,491	19,020	22,657	22,402	79.35

shows comparatively modest growth and little overall growth since 1985. Labor shows modest growth, and even a reduction in the last decade.

In the UK (Table 7.2) the average growth rate was only 4 percent, but this minor growth was the net result of reasonably large expansion in areas such as hobbies (ignoring the very small 'Economy' category) and declines in a similar number of categories. While the decline is less in business groups than in some other categories, the group itself is so large that this decline represents the largest drop in raw numbers.

The least expected finding in the data may be the sizable reduction in associational totals in some sectors in the UK (and Ireland). However,

Table 7.2 UK associations by sector, 1970–2006 (US coding)

Sector	1970	2006	Growth rate (%)
Economy	1	4	300.00
Hobby	154	581	277.27
Law	46	89	93.48
Social welfare	213	388	82.16
Ideological	177	309	74.58
Art	273	464	69.96
Health	231	387	67.53
Agriculture	297	445	49.83
Government	8	11	37.50
Civil rights	22	30	36.36
Sports	279	379	35.84
Environment	117	141	20.51
Other	22	27	22.73
Family	41	45	9.76
Science	846	920	8.75
Average for all group types			4.16
Education	282	258	−8.51
International	86	76	−11.63
History	70	58	−17.14
Local government	42	34	−19.05
Transport	84	62	−26.19
Energy	15	11	−26.67
Business	2,742	2,002	−26.99
Defense	21	14	−33.33
Lands	3	2	−33.33
Religion	120	60	−50.00
Housing	36	17	−52.78
Labor	361	97	−73.13
International trade	50	4	−92.00
Total	6,639	6,915	4.16

reexamination suggests the data are robust. In fact this fits in with the British academic literature on trade union evolution that has documented a huge wave of mergers in the area in the face of related but not identical pressures of potential insolvency and membership losses. (This business concentration phenomenon is not unique to the UK.) Business in the UK has also of course seen the creation of new groups to respond to economic change, as Truman expected, but the larger wave has been toward associational simplification. This is due in part to economies of scale and/or the incentives operating for association executives, but also in part to the increasing importance of evidence-based policy making. Government departments have actively tried to reduce group proliferation in an attempt to simplify consultation and to secure better-researched responses. In other words, with hindsight, a pattern of a shrinking population of business and union groups fits in with our existing knowledge of the field, although this 'fact' is in conflict with the expansion expectation. Unrestricted growth is almost certainly the one outcome that will not be found over time.

Why is there a consensus about the group explosion?

Several reasons may have underpinned the clear tendency to characterize growth as an explosion:

1. *Some growth.* The first reason is that the data do show an overall net increase – particularly in the US. Some policy domains, especially those related to health care, civil rights, and so on, have seen truly dramatic increases, and the system as a whole has grown.
2. *Visible growth and invisible decline.* But probably the temptation to use the term 'explosion' stems from the visibility of births rather than net growth. Group observers see plentiful new startups, even in the UK. The offsetting group terminations are possibly less interesting to study and less easily picked up by looking at press reports, for example. So the explosion image may be caused by focusing on one side of the population ledger. This effect is so powerful that even observers in a regime of (overall) flat growth such as the UK become fixated by examples of startups.
3. *Generalizing from the atypical.* A further reason for acceptance of the explosion image is the slippage between accounts of growth in the associational universe and the narrower idea of citizen groups or campaigning groups. (The eye may be caught by a sharp rise in national lobbying groups.) The fact that there was undoubtedly growth in

that particular sector led to a spillover assumption that all groups were proliferating in like fashion. There are indeed many more public affairs, ideological, and overtly political organizations in the US and the UK, but there are also many policy areas where growth has been slow. Political scientists may tend to think the whole is like that part of the system that is of particular interest to them.

4. *Backward mapping.* The fourth suggested reason for the explosion characterization is the possible consequence of not using contemporaneously collected data of the type exploited in this chapter. Exercises that try to reconstitute past populations from one data collection date may well underestimate earlier examples, leading to an appearance of modern proliferation. Looking at how many groups existing today were created after some recent date gives a good idea of the actual number of births, but this strategy ignores the deaths. If a population is churning substantially, or a long retrospection is attempted, then a backward-mapping approach can be extremely misleading. The expectation that there was an exploding group universe was perhaps left uncriticized (or undercriticized) because it conveniently fitted in with antipluralist concerns about ungovernability and gridlock.

The phenomenon of varied growth rates in different sectors is well established; nonetheless the consequence seems often neglected. Walker said that the 'Evidence of the recent growth in the interest group structure also exists in the data from my survey' (1983, p. 394). He secured the startup date for the groups he surveyed in the 1980s. But as Walker immediately points out there is a flaw in this sort of retrospective exercise which draws conclusions from surviving groups. He notes:

It is possible, although unlikely, that citizen groups in areas ignored by historians were declining in numbers during the 1960s and 1970s, thus canceling out the reported gains. The analysis of founding dates of the groups in my survey is suggestive, but it may only be a statistical artifact because I have no data on the number of groups that were formed in earlier years but went out of existence before 1980, when the survey was conducted. (p. 394)

The data sets underlying this chapter allow some insight in this area. Because there are practically annual directories in each country, the estimates of group populations from a backward projection can be compared with the actual numbers of groups listed in earlier directories. A simple example is provided by analysis of our UK data (Figure 7.4).

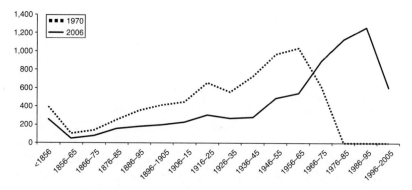

Figure 7.4   UK group creations as estimated from the 1970 and 2006 editions of the *Directory of British Associations*

The apparent rate of increase is different depending on when one takes a retrospective look at dates of birth. The line recording groups that survived until 1970 runs higher than the line of groups that survived to 2006. This is simply because the earlier line covers a population less contaminated by group death over time. The impression of the number of groups being born in decades further back from 2006 is artificially low, as groups have ceased to exist in the time between their startup and the data being recorded in 2006. What Walker considered to be a logical possibility is empirically captured in this simple graph: different time points yield different versions of group history, with more recent dates suggesting lower totals in earlier years. Some of these 'missing' groups were recovered by looking from a perspective (1970) closer to their birth decade. (This UK information ties in with Johnson and McCarthy's 2005 more systematic analysis of the difficulties of backward projection using a subset of organizations from the US *Encyclopedia of Associations*.)

The apparent decline in the rate of growth in the decade immediately before data collection shown for both 1970 and 2006 in the UK (Figure 7.4) reveals another predictable consequence of data collection practice – the problem of entry lag. When placed side by side, the curves for 1970 and 2006 showing reduction in new births almost exactly mirror each other. The similarity suggests that this is another artifact of data collection. It appears there is a fairly common lag between startup and inclusion in both the UK and US sources – the time taken for new groups to be absorbed into the data source. What might look like a decline in the rate of birth in the most recent phase may well be a consequence of recording delays.

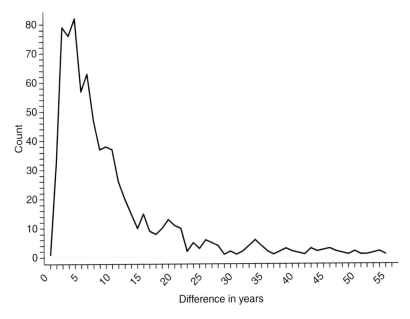

Figure 7.5   Differences between founding dates and first appearance in the US *Encyclopedia of Associations*

Note: The graph shows the count for each value of the number of years between the reported creation date and the year in which the organization was first listed in the *Encyclopedia of Associations*. The mean number of years is 10.5, median 6, mode 4, minimum 0, and maximum 129.

Source: Bevan (2008), data from the 'Public Affairs' section of the *Encyclopedia of Associations* only.

Shaun Bevan (2008) has performed a systematic analysis of the entry lag problem using the US *Encyclopedia* data (Figure 7.5). The figure depicts the frequency for each difference in number of years between a group's founding date and its first appearance in the *Encyclopedia of Associations* 'Public Affairs' section. As can be observed, the mean lag is more than 10 years, and the modal lag is 4 years since a very small number of organizations are listed decades or even a century after their actual founding.

The stability illusion

The argument in this chapter is that the contrast between the situations in the US and the UK is not between explosive growth and stability, as is perhaps suggested by Figure 7.1. First, a stable number is not the same as a stable population: the total can be the same while the cases have heavy turnover. This is easily illustrated with the specific example of chambers of commerce in the UK, and our example

Table 7.3   Illustration of turnover in UK chambers of commerce

1970	2005
Aldershot and District Chamber of Commerce	Arab-British Chamber of Commerce
Andover and District Chamber of Trade	Ashford (Kent) Chamber of Commerce, Industry and Enterprise
Anglo-Israel Chamber of Commerce	Australia and New Zealand Chamber of Commerce UK
Armagh Chamber of Commerce	Ayrshire Chamber of Commerce and Industry
Ashford (Kent) Chamber of Trade	Ballymena Chamber of Commerce and Industry
Ashford (Middlesex) Chamber of Trade and Commerce	Banbury and District Chamber of Commerce
Association of British Chambers of Commerce (ABCC)	Barking and Dagenham Chamber of Commerce
Association of Chambers of Commerce of Ireland	Belgian-Luxembourg Chamber of Commerce in Great Britain
Athlone Chamber of Commerce	Black Country Chamber
Aylesbury and District Chamber of Commerce	Brazilian Chamber of Commerce in Great Britain
Ayr Chamber of Commerce	Britain Nigeria Business Council
Ballymoney Chamber of Commerce	Britain-Nepal Chamber of Commerce
Barking and Dagenham Chamber of Trade and Industry	British and Colombian Chamber of Commerce
Barrow in Furness Chamber of Trade and Commerce	British American Chamber of Commerce Northern California
Batley and Birstall Chamber of Commerce	British Argentine Chamber of Commerce
Bechenham, Penge and Anerley Chamber of Trade	British Bulgarian Chamber of Commerce
Bedford Chamber of Trade	British Canadian Chamber of Trade and Commerce
Birkenhead Chamber of Commerce	British Chamber of Business in Southern Africa

highlights the usefulness of having more than one time point to study. In 1970, 238 chambers of commerce were listed; by 2005 this was down to 136 (a difference of 102). This makes sense in terms of other information about the reorganization of the chambers: this story indeed is part of the explanation of the decline of business groups in the UK reported above. But simply by looking at the first few chambers listed in each selected year it is immediately obvious that this example suggests something else: that there has been turnover as well as shrinkage (Table 7.3). The churning or replacement of defunct groups with new ones makes the overall shift in the population of groups much greater than a simple count would imply. Looking only at net growth or decline, not specific groups whose individual births and deaths can be identified, clearly overestimates stability. This is a picture of *both* decline and change.

This example demonstrates the difference between looking at individual groups over time, noting their creation and demise, and a simple focus on the net amount of growth or decline in a population over time. Net numbers systematically overstate the level of stability, but to a varying degree. That degree is determined by the individual death rate. The birth rate is equal to the growth minus deaths, but without knowing the latter we cannot know either the birth rate or the overall degree of change in the population. Hard work is required to collect the data needed to map these populations, in particular the degree of churning that may take place within them.

Conclusion

This chapter is a first cut at two data sets that offer some sense of the changing pattern of associational growth in the UK and the US over time. The advantages of linking these types of directory-based exercises are threefold:

1. The data sets are broad and yet allow subfields to be abstracted to match less all-embracing categories, for example campaigning groups or trade associations.
2. They offer the possibility of measurement over time to look for patterns.
3. The UK data set has been recoded to offer direct comparison with the US data.

One main theme of this chapter is to question the idea of an explosion in the associational population. Both the US and UK findings show growth, but the US position is much stronger. The national differences raise the question as to whether this is an artifact of data collection or an empirical gap. The rather gentle British slope of increase is actually the net result of strong birth rates with offsetting large-scale deaths. Some of the death rate is the result of economic change leading to redundant interests which cannot sustain representation; in part it is a shift to more national-level administration and effective lobbying; in part there may be finance-driven merger activity. In the US the pattern is also of growth, but the morbidity factors are less well developed, and *this* difference accounts for the different profiles. The picture is not one of growth versus stability but one of growth impacted by areas of decline versus growth less impacted by decline.

While the idea of explosion needs qualification even in the US, a picture of uneven growth is much more sustainable in both systems. In the US this unevenness varies from 210 percent down to 15.9 percent. In the UK (ignoring a very small example), the range is from 277 percent to *minus* 92 percent. However, the broad thrust of both data sets is that explosion might be an overdramatic image of the whole, and certainly within the subpopulations there is often apparent stability or even decline. But micro-level research in this area is needed. As seen in the UK chambers of commerce case, modest overall decline might actually be masking large-scale termination offset by a volume of startups.

The two national systems have some similarities but also differ in ways that may reflect both the different social and economic contexts on the one hand and the different public policy context on the other. It is striking and perhaps unexpected that the growth rates in the US for business and labor are 24th and 27th respectively in the list, and in the UK the same two categories are 24th and 26th. Of the 18 US association types with above-average growth, 13 also appear with above-average growth in the UK list (Tables 7.1 and 7.2). Moreover the noncongruent cases tend to be low volume.

This attempt to address the data gap identified in the early part of the chapter could only ever be partially successful. The exercise has brought to the fore some obvious and some less easily anticipated practical problems. There are practical difficulties in operationalizing the (apparently) simple ambition of looking at the pattern of association populations over time. But even more difficult than the (considerable) problems of capturing the data, there is the definitional issue over *what* is to be captured – particularly as the project is trying to offer material that is internationally equivalent. So in addition to the problem of recording national data, and the problem of deciding on a definitional focus, there is the added dimension of difficulty in seeking truly comparative findings with standard 'equivalent currency'.

These are not *the* maps over time of the UK and US interest group systems. Other chapters in this volume make as good cases for the sense of scale they reveal. But accepting that the processes involved in this comparison necessitate some compromise and tolerance of research shortcuts, the pictures reveal similarities and differences both over time and cross-nationally to give the data credibility. There are hints at the working out of big pressures both for group consolidation and for group differentiation in different fields. Above all there is endorsement of the idea of a complex, fragmented representation that makes this kind of research difficult, but, if it is anything like *the* pattern, makes it necessary.

Notes

1. The authors thank the publishers of the directories used for their cooperation and for their initiative in assembling these data.
2. Data for 2005 sometimes updated by 2006 supplementary information.
3. Salisbury was referring to the scale of group proliferation, and that group number focus is the key here. Gray and Lowery (1996, p. 7) point out that Olson himself in his 1982 study of institutional sclerosis uses data on members of groups rather than numbers of groups.
4. They also report Petracca's (1992) work on Washington representatives yielding an increase from 4,000 in 1977 to 14,500 in 1991.

References

Baumgartner, F. and B. Leech (1998) *Basic Interests* (Princeton, NJ: Princeton University Press).

Berry, J. (1999a) *The New Liberalism* (Washington, DC: Brookings Institution Press).

Berry, J. (1999b) 'The Rise of Citizen Groups', in T. Skocpol and M. Fiorina (eds.) *Civic Engagement and American Democracy* (Washington, DC: Brookings Institution Press).

Bevan, S. (2011) 'The Life Cycle of Voluntary Associations in the United States, 1972–2001' (doctoral dissertation).

Cigler, A. (1994) 'Research Gaps in the Study of Interest Representation', in M. Schwartz and J. Green (eds.) *Representing Interests and Interest Group Representation* (Lanham, MD: University Press of America).

Close, A., G. Bologna, and C. W. McCormick (1988) *Washington Representatives* (Washington, DC: Columbia).

Colgate, C. (1982) *National Trade and Professional Associations of the United States* (Washington, DC: Columbia).

Crawford, K. (1939) *The Pressure Boys* (New York: J. Messner).

160   *Grant Jordan* et al.

Croly, H. (1915) *Progressive Democracy* (New York: Macmillan).
Gray, V. and D. Lowery (1996) *The Population Ecology of Interest Representation: Lobbying Communities in the American States* (Ann Arbor: University of Michigan Press).
Herring, E. P. (1929) *Group Representation before Congress* (Baltimore, MD: Johns Hopkins University Press).
Johnson, E. and J. D. McCarthy (2005) 'The Sequencing of Transnational and National Social Movement Mobilization: The Organizational Mobilization of the Global and U.S. Environmental Movements', in D. Della Porta and S. Tarrow (eds.) *Transnational Protest and Global Activism* (Lanham, MD: Rowman & Littlefield).
Jordan, G. and W. Maloney (2007) *Democracy and Interest Groups* (Basingstoke, UK: Palgrave Macmillan).
King, J. C. and J. L. Walker (1991) 'An Ecology of Interest Groups in America', in J. L. Walker (ed.) *Mobilizing Interest Groups in America* (Ann Arbor: University of Michigan Press).
Nownes, A. and G. Neeley (1996) 'Toward an Explanation for Public Interest Group Formation and Proliferation: "Seed Money," Disturbances, Entrepreneurship, and Patronage', *Policy Studies Journal*, 24, 74–92.
Petracca, M. (1992) 'The Rediscovery of Interest Group Politics', in M. Petracca (ed.) *The Politics of Interests* (Boulder, CO: Westview).
Pollock, J. K. (1927) 'The Regulation of Lobbying', *American Political Science Review*, 21(2), 335–41.
Salisbury, R. (1992) *Interests and Institutions* (Pittsburgh, PA: University of Pittsburgh Press).
Salisbury, R. (1994) 'Interest Structures and Policy Domains', in M. Schwartz and J. Green (eds.) *Representing Interests and Interest Group Representation* (Lanham, MD: University Press of America).
Schlozman, K. and J. Tierney (1986) *Organized Interests and American Democracy* (New York: Harper & Row).
Truman, D. (1951) *The Governmental Process: Political Interests and Public Opinion* (New York: Alfred A. Knopf).
Walker, J. L. (1983) 'The Origins and Maintenance of Interest Groups in America', *American Political Science Review*, 77, 390–406.
Yoffie, D. B. (1985). 'Interest Groups vs. Individual Action: An Analysis of Corporate Political Strategies', Harvard Business School working paper no. 9-785-018.

8
The Usual Suspects: Interest Group Dynamics and Representation in Denmark

Peter Munk Christiansen

Some might think that being a researcher on interest groups in a corporatist country is an easy job. The accepted notion is that state–group relations are well organized and knowledge about the population of interest groups should be established and readily accessible – just push a button. Scandinavian-style corporatism, understood as the institutionalized and privileged integration of interest groups into policy making (Christiansen *et al.* 2010), may produce more knowledge about the population of groups than in many other systems, and consequently counting interest groups is easier than elsewhere – but probably not that much easier. Even in the Scandinavian 'corporatist' system knowledge about interest group populations is not that easy to collect. The reasons for the unexpected difficulties are various.

First, no country was ever fully corporatized. Even in the heyday of corporatism some policy sectors were more or less unaffected by corporatist structures (Damgaard and Eliassen 1978; Damgaard 1986), even in the few countries with stronger corporatist structures than Denmark. Second, there is much more pluralism in the landscape of interest groups than would be expected from Schmitter's original definition that the 'constituent units are organized into a limited number of singular, compulsory, non-competitive, hierarchically ordered and functionally differentiated categories' (1974, p. 93). The actual population is – even in countries and policy sectors conventionally characterized as having corporatist structures – much more multifarious than this suggests. Third, in a society with strong and dynamic civil society structures the population of interest groups and associations is a moving target and a target shaped by many different forces. In sum, the allegedly strong corporatist structures may not be that strong, and they may have less pervasive effects than initially believed.

This chapter focuses on the population of politically relevant interest groups in Denmark since the mid-1970s. It falls into three sections. The first section deals with classic and modern corporatist structures. Two large phenomena, the agricultural cooperative and the labor movement, have had a tremendous impact on modern Denmark and illustrate part of the dynamics of strong mobilization, collective action, corporatism, and public policy. Environmental interest groups, which emerged in the 1970s, illustrate how new groups in a new policy area develop their own type of relations with policy makers in a corporatist environment. Environmental interest groups were not active partners in the creation of corporatism, yet there are clear quasi-corporatist traits in the way environmental policy is formed and implemented. The second section deals with how public policies affect the formation of interest groups and thus how the state itself shapes the population of groups. This happens when the state establishes or sponsors interest groups, when public policy or welfare policy programs trigger the development of new groups of clients (Pierson 1996), or when government institutions form interest groups in order to provide services and take care of common interests. This dynamic is illustrated by the swift development in the number of patient groups. The third section looks at how the population of Danish interest groups has developed over time. It examines the population of Danish interest groups as they have been delineated in national surveys in 1976, 1981, 1993, 1999, and 2004.

The dynamics of interest group populations: classic and new examples

From civil society movements to corporatist partners

Danish society is in many respects affected by interest groups and associations, and vice versa. Two major movements in the late 19th and early 20th centuries – the agricultural cooperative movement and the workers' movement – had pervasive effects on Danish business structure, on labor market relations, on public policies, and on how political decisions were made for a large part of the 20th century.

The foundation of strong post–Second World War corporatism in Danish agriculture goes back to the late 19th century. In response to fierce international competition from overseas grain growers, from the 1860s Danish agriculture underwent a major change toward processing of animal products. A large number of cooperatives were established to handle collective functions in the agricultural export sector. Danish agriculture soon became internationally competitive, and the process was driven by rural civil organizations.

The Ministry of Agriculture was established at the turn of the century (1896) as a response to crises on the export markets. From then on the state's involvement in the agricultural sector increased, accelerated by the two world wars and the economic crisis in the 1930s. Group–government structures were created before the First World War and developed and strengthened through the late 1960s (Buksti 1974; Pedersen 1979; Gundelach 1988; Just 1992). Agricultural corporatism was characterized by self-governance, or what Streeck and Schmitter (1985) would call 'private interest government'. Implementation of certain public policies was delegated to interest groups. Relations between the ministry and agricultural groups were strong, and there was keen political interest in the structure of agricultural interest groups. Self-governance declined during the late 1960s because of Denmark's pending EEC (now EU) membership. The government was uneasy about having agricultural interest groups administer the many EEC schemes on behalf of Danish ministers. Informal hierarchy replaced corporatist governance, but most scholars agree that agricultural interest groups lost very little actual control over agricultural policy (Buksti 1974; Daugbjerg 1999). In recent years the landscape of agricultural interest groups has adapted further to the shrinking role of agriculture (Christiansen *et al.*, forthcoming).

In the late 1960s and early 1970s agriculture had a large and complex superstructure in terms of interest groups, yet insiders had no problems grasping it. It was captured in *Landbrugsårbog* (the Agricultural Yearbook), first published in 1899, which contained information on all agricultural interest groups.

At the high point of agricultural corporatism it was no simple job to draw the line between the state and agricultural interest groups. The latter were to a large extent formed by the former. In the years after Denmark joined the EEC the agricultural landscape became more diversified, among other reasons because of the growth of organic farming, which created its own interest groups, some of which are closely integrated with the ministry and some of which represent more *alternative* views (Daugbjerg and Møller 2010). Until recently it was still possible to draw the agricultural interest group population from the *Landbrugsårbog*, but the 105th edition in 2005 was the last.

In some important respects, the history of the Danish labor movement resembles that of the agricultural cooperatives. Strong collective mobilization in the late 19th and early 20th centuries created a labor movement with significant political impact on public policy; interest organizations were delegated public policy functions, and very close relations to the state blurred the lines between state and groups.

The mobilization of the urban labor class took place rather unevenly from the 1860s onward. After a long period of serious labor market conflicts, in 1899 the Landsorganisationen i Danmark (the Danish Confederation of Trade Unions) and the Dansk Arbejdsgiverforening (the Confederation of Danish Employers) entered into an agreement that became the foundation of the Danish labor market. The employees recognized the employers' right to manage their firms, and the employers recognized the employees' right to organize and ultimately strike if agreement could not be reached through negotiation. In 1907 an unemployment scheme based on the Ghent system was introduced, in which unemployment benefits are administered by funds associated with the unions even if unions are formally independent. The Ghent system tends to produce high rates of unionization (Scruggs 2002): Danish unionization has been more than 80 percent at times, but has declined in recent years to a still respectable level of around 70 percent.

Strong unions and their close cooperation with employers have endowed the Danish labor market with some special traits, most importantly that collective agreements in some respects are functional equivalents to legislation. A number of protective measures that in most countries are accomplished through legislation are in Denmark accomplished through collective agreements, which are even used by employers and employees who are not members of an employers' organization or a union (Due *et al.* 1994; Elvander 2002). The system raises some complex issues, especially concerning implementation of EU social chapter regulations, and it implies a close relationship between state actors and the main social partners.

State actors also have to be aware of developments in the population of labor market organizations because unions are entitled to negotiate collective agreements. The entitlement system implies privileging some groups at the cost of others: a union (or an employers' organization for that matter) has to be the biggest in the relevant area in order to negotiate on behalf of everyone in that area. Since public authorities are big employers they have to keep track of how different unions represent different parts of the labor market.

Very few countries have as regulated a labor market as Denmark. Moreover, few countries permit labor market organizations to play a bigger role in policy formation and implementation (although in

Denmark the role of labor market organizations in policy formation has been reduced over the last 15–20 years, and their role in policy implementation over the last 3–4 years; see Christiansen and Klitgaard 2008; Öberg *et al.*, 2011). Similar to *Landbrugsårbog* for the agriculture sector, *Arbejdsmarkedets håndbog* (the Labor Market Handbook) has been a valuable source of data on the labor market organizational population. Only unions that do not belong to the labor movement are not covered thoroughly.[1]

From anarchy to corporatism: environmental interest groups

Denmark's first Ministry of the Environment was established in 1971, and its first environmental protection act was passed in 1973. The bill was the result of close negotiations with the largest business and agricultural interest groups and the two interest organizations for counties and municipalities. Four environmental groups were invited to contribute to a written hearing, but the ministry did not meet with their representatives (Christiansen *et al.* 2004, pp. 192ff.). There are a number of reasons for this non-involvement of environmental groups. They were few in number at the time, and three of them were quite specialized: the Danish Society for Nature Conservation, the Danish Anglers Association, and the Danish Outdoor Council each had its own particular perspective on environmental issues. Only NOAH (the Danish member of Friends of the Earth) had a broader agenda, but the group was new and was not considered a relevant partner for the new ministry. The important thing was that industry and agriculture accepted the new legislative measures. Environmental groups thus did not play any significant role in this formative moment of Danish environmental policy.

This status drastically changed during the 1980s, when environmental groups came to play a much more prominent role (Andersen *et al.* 1992). The Nature Conservation Society in particular went through a metamorphosis and in the 1980s became a powerful environmental group that managed to set the agenda on several occasions. From some time in the late 1980s environmental groups were natural partners for the minister and the ministry in the formation and implementation of political decisions. There were more environmental groups, and the electorate's environmental awareness had grown; the foundation for a political exchange was established (Öberg *et al.*, 2011). A kind of very loose environmental corporatism had come into being. It is difficult for a ministry to engage with many differentiated and small groups at one time, and the environmental ministry welcomed the establishment of

Det Grønne Kontaktudvalg (the Green Contact Committee), which now consists of 14 environmental groups. The committee's only role is to represent environmental interests to ministries and parliamentarians. This has had the benign consequence that the ministry can ask the committee to send one or two representatives when a new administrative committee has to be established, and thereby reduces possible conflicts over the composition of a committee. Likewise the unified policies formulated by the committee make the activities of the ministry simpler, although from time to time also more troublesome to handle.

A few environmental groups, for example the Nature Conservation Society, have become institutionalized and privileged partners and may be compared to some of the major interest groups from the agricultural or labor market sectors. The Nature Conservation Society is by far the biggest environmental group; many groups are quite small, and groups come and go. There are various lists of 'Green organizations' or 'Environmental organizations' on the Internet, but they are not nearly as authoritative as the lists for the labor market sector and agricultural sector mentioned above. Nevertheless, it is not that difficult to compile such a list from different Internet sources. Very limited research in October 2010 generated a list of 54 nationwide, politically relevant environmental groups. A little more effort would undoubtedly reveal more groups, but not very many.

Policy-generated interest groups in a corporatist environment

State-sponsored interest groups: consumer groups

It is widely recognized that it is easier for some groups to organize and mobilize than for others to do so. Consequently, one might expect a bias in the stock of interest groups (Lowery and Gray 2004; cf. Olson 1965). It is, for instance, easier for producers (low numbers, high visibility of inaction) than for consumers (large numbers, *de facto* invisible free riding) to organize. Business groups are significantly stronger than consumer groups, and public sector unions are much stronger than groups that organize public sector consumers – at least in a country with a very high degree of unionization. The bias may be reduced in different ways. In the case of environmental groups the great popular support for a better natural environment has increased the number of entrepreneurs who offset the weak incentives for environmental groups to organize. In the case of consumer interests the patron/entrepreneur has been the state!

In recognition of the weak potential for consumers to organize, the Danish state subsidizes Forbrugerrådet (the Consumer Council), an umbrella organization for 32 organizations. Some have consumer issues as a main priority; for others these issues are only a minor part of their portfolio. Because of its approximately US$2.5 million subsidy, the Consumer Council probably feels obligated to report the stock of consumer groups in Denmark. The council lists around 140 groups on its Web site (www.forbrugerraadet.dk). Most are listed as something else because consumer tasks are only a small part of their job. Even if consumer groups are a difficult type of group to research because many consumer groups are small and have few resources, it is safe to assume that few consumer groups of political relevance would not be listed on the council's homepage.

The welfare state's client groups: patient groups

The dynamics of group formation is different for patient groups than for environmental groups and consumer groups, although they share some problems of mobilizing for collective action. In the case of these types of groups, public policies cause the establishment of client groups because policies create positive policy feedbacks (Pierson 1996, 2000). As the welfare state has increased in scope and intensity – and the Danish version implies a broad range of free or heavily subsidized services – this has resulted in the establishment of several groups who lobby for better or more services. Some of these groups would have existed in any case – that is, independent of the existence of welfare services – but the existence of welfare policies expands the groups' political roles.

Denmark – like most other countries, probably – has a few very large patient groups, such as the Danish Cancer Society (www.cancer.dk) and the Danish Heart Foundation (www.hjerteforeningen.dk). While large, these organizations are still ailment-specific in their focus rather than broad-gauge health organizations. Most patient groups are rather small, and many were established quite recently. The vast majority of the patient groups reported by Vrangbæk *et al.* (2010) were established after 1980, half of them after 1990, and one in four after 2000. Some are a consequence of new diagnostics or new treatments and are often subsidized by the medical or pharmaceutical industry. Medical treatment is free in Denmark, and groups with new and rare diagnoses push for more and better treatments. Of course, the producers benefit from patient groups having prescription success, for instance in the approval of medication by the National Board of Health. The state also contributes to the support of patient groups: more than half their income comes from public subsidies (Binderkrantz 2005b and data set). Despite the subsidies, patient groups typically have few resources. Consequently, they try to get their message across through the media, which makes them easier to find. Balslev (1999) reported the existence of almost 200 patient groups in Denmark. Ten years later Vrangbæk *et al.* (2010) reported finding 173 patient groups in different surveys. Some groups may not have been reported by these sources.

The public sector's producer groups

The public sector has two types of producer groups. One is unions that represent public sector employees; they generally work in the same way as unions on the private labor market, and they are included in the group of labor market organizations mentioned above. The other type is less obvious. Many groups represent public institutions (Salisbury 1984), among them employer groups with the capacity to negotiate collective agreements on behalf of their members. Local Government Denmark (www.kl.dk) and Danish Regions (www.danskeregioner.dk) are two powerful groups that handle the broad range of municipalities' and regions' interests. While the two groups are in a special class (Blom-Hansen 2002), a large number of other groups somehow represent public sector institutions. Danish Universities (www.dkuni.dk) represents the Danish universities in negotiations with the state on appropriations and regulation of the universities. The ministry has on various occasions encouraged the capacity of Danish Universities to act collectively because it is easier for the ministry to negotiate with one party instead of several universities. The same can be said about the Association of High School Principals (www.rektorforeningen.dk). Although there are several of these groups it is not difficult to count the population of public sector groups, because their activities are well covered in the media. The ministries' Web sites are also good sources for finding this type of group.

An estimate of the Danish interest group population

Compiling the population of interest groups requires a number of tools. As described above, it is more difficult to compile a nearly complete list of the population of some groups than others. It is easier to count in sectors with strong, formalized, and long-lasting relations between state actors and interest groups. These relations sharpen the focus on the stock of interest groups. After some years, different registers, handbooks, and so on show up, and even if they are not complete, they cover a significant part of the sector. It is more difficult in sectors with looser and briefer relations between groups and state actors. Few or none have incentives to get an overview of the stock of groups, and probably the stock itself is more volatile, because small groups come and go. It *is* easier to study interest group populations in corporatist-leaning societies than in noncorporatist countries, but only in sectors with corporatist traits.

There is no requirement in Denmark for interest groups that want to affect political and administrative processes and output to register. It is therefore left to researchers to make an estimate of the population. Over the last four decades (in 1976, 1981, 1993, 1999, and 2004), five surveys of all nationwide, politically relevant interest groups have been conducted.[2] Largely the surveys have utilized a standard textbook definition. Interest groups are a collective of actors in pursuit of a common cause, and they must meet the following criteria:

- *Formalization.* At a minimum the group must have written statutes and it must have members.
- *Political relevance.* The group must have as part of its purpose or strategy to affect political decisions regardless of how this endeavor is pursued. If it is not obvious whether the group is politically relevant, its statutes are examined and must state that it is part of the group's purpose to somehow affect political decisions.
- *Nationwide.* Local groups as well as local branches of national groups are excluded from the population. It would be an almost boundless task to include all groups in the country. Torpe and Kjeldgaard (2003) investigate the number of groups and associations in the municipality of Aalborg, the fourth largest city in Denmark, which has fewer than 125,000 inhabitants but no less than 2,031 groups and associations. Many of them were of course very small, and many would hardly play any political role. Transnational interest groups are only part of the population if they have a Danish division or at least a Danish office, and we count only the Danish division. Save the Children (www.savethechildren.org) is not registered as a Danish group, but its Danish division, Red Barnet (www.redbarnet.dk), is.

The criteria exclude several organizations: social movements without a formal organizational structure, religious sects, lodges, and pure hobby and leisure groups. Hobby or leisure groups such as sport associations that clearly may play a political role, for instance in the pursuit of public subsidies, are included. Most national sports associations are included in the population.

The political relevance criterion is not always easy to handle. What about professional societies? The Danish Society of Internal Medicine (www.dsim.dk) has as part of its purpose to advise the medical authorities about medical education in Denmark. Is this a sufficient 'political purpose' to be part of the population? It has been included because it was deemed politically relevant, among other reasons because it sometimes participates in the public debate on medical education. The judgment is not an exact science; some groups that should have been included are no doubt missed, and some groups are doubtless included that should not have been.

It is probably not coincidental that the only time a close-to-complete register of the Danish population of politically relevant interest groups has been published in a book was in 1977, at the time most observers see as the culminating years of corporatism (Christiansen *et al.* 2010, p. 31). Buksti and Johansen (1977, pp. 7–9; see also Buksti and Johansen 1979) made the first delimitation of the Danish interest group population, using the following procedure. From a large number of sources they compiled a list of 2,300 groups that might be relevant. These groups received a questionnaire. After further scrutiny the authors ended up with 1,890 interest groups that fell within the relevant population. The questionnaire was answered by 1,343. This procedure, and the following survey, were primarily intended to get information about the frequency and types of contact between interest groups and civil servants and politicians. The survey also worked as a check on the population, because it yielded more precise information about the groups.

The 1981 survey was shorter than the rather lengthy 1976 version, which perhaps explains the unusually high response rate of 94 percent, compared with 71 percent in 1976. As in the subsequent surveys the 1981 population was compiled on the basis of the previous list. New organizations were added – again from a large number of sources, including handbooks and directories, some of which are mentioned above – and organizations that had disappeared since the last survey were removed. The population that was first identified for the 1981 survey consisted of around 2,500 units; these were shaved down to 1,967. (It is not totally clear from the sources at http://ddd.dda.dk/ddakatalog/sdfiler/R00510. htm how the cut was made, but 1,967 appears to be a good estimate of the size of the population in 1981).

By the time of the 1993 survey the Internet had become a practical research tool. The gross population was estimated at 2,617 interest groups; it was reduced to 2,037 groups which received a questionnaire.

After a further screening the net population was set at 1,900 groups, with 1,316 returning the questionnaire (Christiansen and Sidenius 1995). The research team behind the 1993 and 1999 surveys were less interested in the population as such. For this reason only survey respondents, and not populations, are reported by group type in Table 8.1.[3]

The compilation of the 1999 population started with the 1993 population; new groups were added and dissolved groups deleted. The Internet made it much easier to determine whether a given interest group still existed and to search for new groups. The gross population was estimated at 2,469 groups; after scrutiny the net population was reduced to 2,008 (Christiansen and Nørgaard 2003, pp. 233ff. and data set).

The 2004 survey was conducted by Binderkrantz (2004, 2005b; see also 2005a). Her demarcation of the population was different. Her gross population consisted of 2,720 groups. After elimination of dissolved groups or groups whose addresses could not be found the net population was 2,465. In total, 1,722 groups responded to the survey (a combination of traditional mail survey and Web survey), but 493 groups reported that they had no politically relevant behavior. If we subtract these from the net population the total is somewhat below 2,000 (Binderkrantz 2005b, pp. 107ff.).[4] In the previous four studies the researchers rather than the interest groups had decided whether the groups were politically relevant, for instance by scrutinizing their statutes, but here groups self-defined.

Populations and responses from the surveys appear in Table 8.1, which also reports the distribution of the population for 1976 and 1981 and the survey respondents for the 1976, 1981, 1993, and 1999 surveys. The distribution of types of groups is not shown for Binderkrantz's survey (2005b) because, as noted above, she used a different classification than the other surveys.

The numbers for the years 1976 through 1999 in Table 8.1 suggest some interesting traits in the Danish interest group population. First, the traditional groups involved in corporatist exchange relations make up a shrinking part of the entire interest group population. Employees and business organizations made up no less that 56.3 percent of all groups in 1976. They still constitute a significant proportion, but in 1999 only slightly more than 40 percent (see Jordan and Greenan, Chapter 4, for a similar trend in the UK). This development was particularly strong in the 1970s and 1980s, whereas the drop in the 1990s was slower. In all years, business organizations were by far the largest group, with more than one out of four groups in the total population in the latest survey. The blue-collar unions have become a rather small group,

Table 8.1 Population and responding groups in surveys of national interest groups in Denmark, 1976, 1981, 1993, 1999, and 2004

	1976 questionnaire[a] (population)[b] %[c]	1981 questionnaire[a] (population)[b] %[c]	1993 questionnaire[a] %[c]	1999 questionnaire[a] %[c]	2004 questionnaire[a,d]
Employees, blue collar	51 (64) 3.4	48 (50) 2.5	34 2.6	35 2.9	n.a.
Employees, white collar	220 (302) 16.0	341 (357) 18.1	175 13.3	147 12.4	n.a.
Business organizations	465 (697) 36.9	583 (642) 32.6	356 27.1	310 26.1	n.a.
Organizations for education, science, and culture	266 (380) 20.1	413 (431) 21.9	307 23.3	249 20.9	n.a.
Charitable organizations	87 (118) 6.2	136 (139) 7.1	146 11.1	148 12.4	n.a.
National and international organizations	79 (109) 5.8	95 (102) 5.2	62 4.7	50 4.2	n.a.

Consumer and patient organizations	50	(61)	3.2	58	(59)	3.0	73 5.5	120 10.1	n.a.	
Organizations for youth and leisure	101	(128)	6.8	128	(132)	6.7	105 8.0	76 6.4	n.a.	
Environmental organizations	7	(8)	0.4	12	(12)	0.6	15 1.1	29 2.4	n.a.	
Other organizations[e]	17	(23)	1.2	39	(43)	2.2	43 3.3	26 2.2	n.a.	
Total number of respondents	1,343			1,853			1,316	1,190	1,722 (1,229)[f]	
Total number in final population	1,890			1,967			2,037	2,008	(~1,965)[f]	

[a] The questionnaire number is the number of interest groups that (1) answered the questionnaire and (2) fit the definition of interest groups.
[b] The 1976 and 1981 surveys distributed the nonresponsive groups by organizational type. That was not done in the 1993 and 1999 surveys.
[c] For 1976 and 1981 the percentage is calculated with the population number as the numerator, and the 1993 and 1999 surveys are calculated with the questionnaire number as the numerator. In both cases the final total population is the denominator.
[d] Binderkrantz (2005b) uses another classification. Only the population figures and figures on respondents are reported.
[e] Includes the associations of local governments and the regions.
[f] Binderkrantz (2005b) calculated the figures in a different way. Of the 2,465 groups in the final population she estimated that at least 500 did not consider themselves politically relevant. In the four preceding studies political relevance was calculated mainly on the basis of statutes.
n.a., not available.

primarily because of a strong trend toward amalgamation and concentration during the last couple of decades.[5] The Danish Confederation of Trade Unions currently has 18 unions as members, compared with more than 50 in the early 1970s. Blue-collar unions have become much bigger than they used to be, and thus fewer in number, at the same time as blue-collar jobs make up a shrinking proportion of the total number of jobs. Concentration also characterizes white-collar organizations and business organizations, even though both are more heterogeneous than the blue-collar groups.

A second development is an almost dramatic growth in the types of groups that were supposed by Olson (1965) to face almost insurmountable problems organizing. In 1976 consumer, patient, and environmental groups made up 3.6 percent of the total number of groups; in 1999 the figure was 12.5 percent. The theoretical obstacles to these kinds of groups forming are smaller in the real world. Finally, and in continuation of the second point, the proportion of charitable interest groups doubled, from 6.2 to 12.4 percent.

The landscape of interest groups is formed by many forces. Interest groups are established in response to needs in civil society when entrepreneurs successfully form groups; interest groups are shaped by public policies, and sometimes they are even established with the direct support of the actors they are supposed to affect. The organizational population thus mirrors the surrounding society. The first attempt to delimit the population was made in 1976. More than half of all groups were business organizations or unions, mirroring the heyday of Denmark's version of corporatism. By the turn of the century new groups had entered the population. Environmental groups, consumer groups, patient groups, and charitable groups reflect the fact that new political issues had entered the political agenda at the same time as these groups are shaped by the political agenda.

Conclusion

The point of departure for this chapter was whether group counting is easier in countries with a corporatist tradition. The simple answer is a little or somewhat, but not that much. It *is* easier to study interest group populations in corporatist-type societies than in countries without corporatist traits, but only in sectors with corporatist traits. Strong corporatist traditions somehow produce (1) a tendency for potential members to organize in groups with close relations to public authorities,

(2) a high awareness of the structure of interests and the structure of interest representation, and (3) a materialization of this awareness in the form of lists, registers, or directories of interest groups.

It is probably no coincidence that the best lists of interest groups were produced in the agricultural sector (*Landbrugsårbog*) and in the labor market sector (*Arbejdsmarkedets håndbog*). They included *almost* all politically relevant groups in the two sectors. Corporatism is, among other things, about privileging some at the cost of others: where *Landbrugsårbog* was almost complete in terms of traditional interest groups in agriculture, it was less complete in terms of organic agriculture. Organic agriculture was disliked for many years by traditional agriculture, and the organic groups were only slowly accepted by the traditional groups. Among the labor market groups, unions outside the traditional workers' movement (the Danish Confederation of Trade Unions) and unions that organize workers as well as employers are looked upon with great suspicion and condemnation. This was mirrored in *Arbejdsmarkedets håndbog*, which was silent on these so-called yellow unions (see note 1). Otherwise these two registers appear to have been close to comprehensive.

In terms of population counting, it is not yet clear what will happen as corporatism fades further from policy preparation activities in these traditional sectors (Öberg *et al.*, 2011; Blom-Hansen 2000, 2001). As mentioned, *Landbrugsårbog* has stopped publication, but this is more a consequence of the accessibility of addresses on the Internet than of the waning of corporatism. *Arbejdsmarkedets håndbog* is now published only as an Internet version. Since Danish corporatism is still strong in policy implementation (Christiansen *et al.* 2010) one would assume that data on interest groups in agriculture and the labor market will still be easily accessible for some years to come.

Corporatism is relatively strong in only a few policy sectors, such as labor market policy, agricultural policy, and industrial policy. In some sectors the corporatist legacy has had a visible effect on new policy areas: when the environment became a big political issue in the late 1960s a new administration and new policy had to be built from scratch. The corporatist legacy had some effects on how organized interests gain access to the administrative and political decision-making process (Christiansen 1999).

In other sectors the corporatist legacy may be there, but it is less clear. State policies have generated a large number of patient groups, and these groups are heavily subsidized. Yet corporatism is limited when it comes to characterizing the relations between patient groups and public authorities, and it would be difficult to establish such structures with most of the groups because many are ephemeral. For instance, half of the close to 200 patient groups in Denmark were established after 1990, and half of these after 2000.

Consumer groups also have some corporatist spillover: the state sponsors the Consumer Council to give consumers a voice and have one group to negotiate with when consumer issues are on the agenda. The Consumer Council is typically also the sole representative when the state establishes committees or commissions.

In summary, corporatism makes group counting easier because strong corporatist structures increase political and administrative awareness of the structure of interest representation. This somehow manifests in group registers and the like. However, corporatism is far from strong in all sectors, and even if there are spillover effects from a corporatist legacy to other policy sectors, group counting in most policy sectors is not that different in Denmark than in countries with a less strong corporatist tradition.

Another reason it appears a little easier to count groups in Denmark than in many other countries discussed in this book is size. Denmark has a population of 5.5 million, the UK about 10 times that, and the US 60 times that of Denmark. The 'markets' for interest groups in the UK and the US are much bigger, with the potential for much more differentiated formation of groups. The very high number of lobbyists reported to be active in Brussels – a figure of more than 15,000 has been mentioned – also reflects a much greater political complexity than in Copenhagen. In the case of Brussels not only size but also policy complexity matters.

The five estimates of the size of the Danish interest group population – from 1976, 1981, 1993, 1999, and 2004 – approximate to 2,000 nationwide, politically relevant interest groups. Binderkrantz's (2005b) estimate is somewhat lower, but it differs from the estimates in the previous studies. There may be more relevant groups than the 2,000, but hardly many of great importance. This implies that there has been no group explosion in Denmark like the one reported in the US. Denmark is much closer to Jordan and Greenan's UK (see also the Scottish data reported in Chapter 12). This is in part because unions and business groups have imploded rather than exploded. The only groups with a significant increase in numbers are charitable groups, consumer and patient groups, and environmental groups – but it is hardly meaningful to talk about an explosion.

Notes

1. For instance, so-called yellow unions, a term which in Denmark refers to unions that are part of an organization that also organizes employers, and in the international literature to unions established by employers (Müller-Jentsch 1985; see also www.billige-fagforeninger.dk).
2. All five surveys were conducted by researchers at the Department of Political Science, Aarhus University. Four of the surveys are available from the Danish Data Archives (DDA): 1976: DDA-0053, Interesseorganisationer i Danmark (Interest Groups in Denmark); 1981: DDA-0510, Interesseorganisationer i Danmark; 1993: DDA-6434: Interesseorganisationer i Danmark; 1999: DDA-6435: Interesseorganisationer i Danmark. See also Christiansen and Nørgaard (2003). The 2005 survey is documented in Binderkrantz (2004, 2005b). Researchers in the department are planning a 2011 survey.
3. In 1976 and 1981 the researchers were interested in the population of Danish interest groups, but in 1993 and 1999 the researchers registered only the type of groups that responded to the survey. Consequently, only the distribution of responding groups is shown in Table 8.1 for 1993 and 1999.
4. The total would have been even smaller had we known how many of the nonresponsive groups would have reported the absence of politically relevant behavior.
5. The general response rate was 59.3 percent in 1999. If we assume that this was also the response rate for the blue-collar groups, there were 58 unions and other interest groups in the true population in 1999.

References

Andersen, M. S., P. M. Christiansen, and S. Winter (1992) 'Denmark: Consensus Seeking and Decentralization', in K. Hanf and A.-I. Jansen (eds.) *Governance and Environment in Western Europe: Politics, Policy, and Administration* (Harlow, UK: Addison Wesley Longman).

Arbejdsmarkedets håndbog, annual (Copenhagen: AOF).

Balslev, J. (1999) *Patientforeningsbogen* (Frederiksberg, Denmark: Patientforum).

Binderkrantz, A. S. (2004) *Spørgeskemaundersøgelse blandt danske interesseorganisationer: Design og svarfordelinger* (Aarhus, Denmark: Department of Political Science, Aarhus University).

Binderkrantz, A. S. (2005a) 'Interest Group Strategies: Navigating between Privileged Access and Strategies of Pressure', *Political Studies*, 53, 694–715.

Binderkrantz, A. S. (2005b) *Magtens midler: Danske interesseorganisationer og deres indflydelsesstrategier* (Aarhus, Denmark: Politica).

Blom-Hansen, J. (2000) 'Still Corporatism in Scandinavia? A Survey of Recent Empirical Findings', *Scandinavian Political Studies*, 23, 157–81.

Blom-Hansen, J. (2001) 'Organized Interests and the State: A Disintegrating Relationship? Evidence from Denmark', *European Journal of Political Research*, 39, 391–416.

Blom-Hansen, J. (2002) *Den fjerde statsmagt? Kommunernes Landsforening i dansk politik* (Aarhus, Denmark: Aarhus University Press).

178   Peter Munk Christiansen

Buksti, J. (1974) *Et enigt landbrug? Konflikt og samarbejde mellem landbrugets organisationer* (Aarhus, Denmark: Erhvervsarkivet/Aarhus University Press).

Buksti, J. and L. N. Johansen (1977) *Danske organisationers hvem-hvad-hvor* (Copenhagen: Politikens Forlag).

Buksti, J. and L. N. Johansen (1979) 'Variations in Organizational Participation in Government: The Case of Denmark', *Scandinavian Political Studies*, 2, 197–220.

Christiansen, P. M. (1999) 'Miljøpolitik og interesseorganisationer: Mellem anarki og integration', in J. Blom-Hansen and C. Daugbjerg (eds.) *Magtens organisering: Stat og interesseorganisationer i Danmark* (Aarhus, Denmark: Systime).

Christiansen, P. M. and M. B. Klitgaard (2008) 'Institutionel kontrol med arbejdsmarkedsforvaltningen: jobcentrenes tilblivelse', *Tidsskrift for Arbejdsliv*, 10, 24–38.

Christiansen, P. M. and A. S. Nørgaard (2003) *Faste forhold, flygtige forbindelser: Stat og interesseorganisationer i det 20. århundrede* (Aarhus, Denmark: Aarhus University Press).

Christiansen, P. M. and N. C. Sidenius (1995) 'Korporatisme på retur?', *Politica*, 27, 436–49.

Christiansen, P. M., A. S. Nørgaard, and N. C. Sidenius (2004) *Hvem skriver lovene? Interesseorganisationer og politiske beslutninger* (Aarhus, Denmark: Aarhus University Press).

Christiansen, P. M., A. S. Nørgaard, H. Rommetvedt, T. Svensson, G. Thesen, and P. Öberg (2010) 'Varieties of Democracy: Interest Groups and Corporatist Committees in Scandinavian Policy Making', *Voluntas*, 21, 22–40.

Christiansen, P. M., A. S. Nørgaard, and N. C. Sidenius (forthcoming) 'Dänemark: Verbände und korporatismus auf Dänish', in W. Reutter (ed.) *Verbände und Interessengruppen in den Ländern der Europäischen Union* (Wiesbaden: VS Verlag für Sozialwissenschaften).

Damgaard, E. (1986) 'Causes, Forms, and Consequences of Sectoral Policy-Making: Some Danish Evidence', *European Journal of Political Research*, 14, 273–87.

Damgaard, E. and K. Eliassen (1978) 'Corporate Pluralism in Danish Law-Making', *Scandinavian Political Studies*, 1, 285–313.

Daugbjerg, C. (1999) 'Landbrugspolitik: Stabilitet eller forandring', in J. Blom-Hansen and C. Daugbjerg (eds.) *Magtens organisering: Stat og interesseorganisationer i Danmark* (Aarhus, Denmark: Systime).

Daugbjerg, C. and D. K. Møller (2010) 'Økologipolitikken og de økologiske interesseorganisationers kapaciteter i Danmark, Sverige og Tyskland', *Politica*, 42, 69–89.

Due, J., J. S. Madsen, C. S. Jensen, and L. K. Petersen (1994) *The Survival of the Danish Model: A Historical Sociological Analysis of the Danish System of Collective Bargaining* (Copenhagen: Danish Association of Lawyers and Economists Press).

Elvander, N. (2002) 'The Labour Market Regimes in the Nordic Countries: A Comparative Analysis', *Scandinavian Political Studies*, 25, 117–37.

Gundelach, P. (1988) *Sociale bevægelser og samfundsændringer* (Aarhus, Denmark: Politica).

Just, F. (1992) *Landbruget, staten og eksporten 1930–1950* (Esbjerg, Denmark: Sydjysk Universitetsforlag).

Landbrugsårbog, annual (Copenhagen: Royal Danish Agricultural Society).

Lowery, D. and V. Gray (2004) 'Bias in the Heavenly Chorus: Interests in Society and before Government', *Journal of Theoretical Politics*, 16, 5–30.

Müller-Jentsch, W. (1985) 'Trade Unions as Intermediary Organizations', *Economic and Industrial Democracy*, 6, 3–33.

Öberg, P., T. Svensson, P. M. Christiansen, A. S. Nørgaard, H. Rommetvedt, and G. Thesen (2011) 'Disrupted Exchange and Declining Corporatism: Government Authority and Interest Group Capability in Scandinavia', *Government and Opposition*, 46(3), 365–91.

Olson, M. (1965) *The Logic of Collective Action* (Cambridge, MA: Harvard University Press).

Pedersen, E. H. (1979) *Landbrugsrådet som erhvervspolitisk toporgan 1919–1933* (Copenhagen: Landbohistorisk Selskab).

Pierson, P. (1996) 'The New Politics of the Welfare State', *World Politics*, 48, 143–79.

Pierson, P. (2000) 'Increasing Returns, Path-Dependence, and the Study of Politics', *American Political Science Review*, 94, 251–67.

Salisbury, R. H. (1984) 'Interest Representation: The Dominance of Institutions', *American Political Science Review*, 78, 64–76.

Schmitter, P. (1974) 'Still the Century of Corporatism?', *Review of Politics*, 36, 85–131.

Scruggs, L. (2002) 'The Ghent System and Union Membership in Europe, 1970–1996', *Political Research Quarterly*, 55, 275–97.

Streeck, W. and P. Schmitter (1985) 'Community, Market, State – and Associations? The Prospective Contribution of Interest Governance to Social Order', *European Sociological Review*, 1, 119–38.

Torpe, L. and T. K. Kjeldgaard (2003) *Foreningssamfundets sociale kapital* (Aarhus, Denmark: Aarhus University Press).

Vrangbæk, K., H. Rommetvedt, and S. Opedal (2010) 'Patientorganisationer i Danmark og Norge: Karakteristika og strategier for interessevaretagelse', *Politica*, 42, 90–108.

9
Mapping the WTO Interest Group System: Exploring Density, Diversity, and Stability Over Time

Marcel Hanegraaff, Jan Beyers, and Caelesta Braun

The relationship between the World Trade Organization (WTO) and interest groups has been and still is a contentious topic in many political and scholarly debates.[1] One of the key issues in these debates is the access that the WTO offers to a variety of interest groups wanting to participate in trade policy making. Although access to the WTO's predecessor, the GATT (General Agreement on Tariffs and Trade), was always limited, since the establishment of the WTO in 1995 the number of access opportunities has slowly grown. Despite these new opportunities the level of openness of the WTO to societal interests is still among the lowest of all international organizations (Van den Bossche 2008). Many interest groups, in particular nongovernmental organizations (NGOs), have consequently contended that the WTO needs to become more responsive to their input (Steffek and Kissling 2006).[2] The call for more openness to interest groups on the part of the WTO has been much discussed in academic circles, attracting both proponents and opponents. Many students of international trade argue that in order to increase its expertise, accountability, and legitimacy, the WTO should allow a higher number of more diverse societal interests access to its decision-making process (Charnovitz 2000; Robertson 2000; Scholte 2000).[3] Opponents contend that the WTO should uphold its system of limited access for interest groups. Given the inherently biased nature of interest group systems, they argue, interest groups from developed countries would likely dominate the scene (Fried 1997; Spiro 2000).

The debate on the WTO and its interest group system revolves around a classic issue in the study of interest group politics, namely whether the involvement of interest organizations in policy making results in more legitimate and effective policies or whether it has a corrupting effect on public policy making. In the case of the EU it appears that expertise-based inside lobbying by business organizations dominates the grass-roots mobilization of social movement organizations (Berkhout and Lowery 2007; Beyers *et al.* 2008). While legal scholars working on the WTO mostly focus on normative implications, political science research can contribute considerably to our empirical and theoretical understanding of how interest groups organize to influence international venues such as the WTO. That is, without a systematic overview of the interest groups that effectively lobby the WTO, we do not know to what extent interest group representation is skewed toward one particular interest, nor can we make any meaningful comparison with national systems of interest intermediation.

The issues sketched above are typical of most research on transnational interest groups, because adequate efforts to map interest group populations at this level are quite rare and are mostly limited to one type of interest group, such as NGOs or transnational actors (Smith 2005, 2006; Smith and Weist 2005). This chapter aims to fill this gap in the literature by exploring the complete population of WTO interest representation over time. In addition, the application of a more general framework of interest representation allows comparison of interest group populations at different institutional levels, adding to the literature on interest populations more generally. The chapter is structured as follows. It begins with an overview of current research on transnational interest group communities, linking it to more general theories of interest representation. It then provides an operationalization to resolve the problem of establishing a population of interests active at the WTO. Next, on the basis of a novel dataset of 1,992 interest organizations that attended the seven Ministerial Conferences (MCs, the highest decision-making body of the WTO), the density, the diversity, and the volatility of the WTO interest group system are analyzed. The chapter concludes with an assessment of the main benefits of and obstacles to analyzing interest populations at the international level, including some specific recommendations for future research.

Global interest group systems

There are currently very few systematic mappings of internationally organized interest groups. However, the general assumption in the literature on transnational interest groups is that the number of interest organizations active at the global level has grown substantially during the last two decades. Moreover, NGOs have significantly increased their fundraising and campaigning activities, have adjusted their organizational structures to the international level, and have served as important advocates of new global rules, representatives of a global civil society, promoters of democracy, and actors who monitor compliance with international norms (Teegen *et al.* 2004; Werker and Ahmed 2008; Aldashev and Verdier 2009). A range of factors are used to explain the rise of these transnational nonstate actors, ranging from changes in the global political economy, to the growing number of democracies worldwide, to the revolutionary changes in communications technology. This chapter does not focus on these explanatory factors; rather, it takes one step back to deal with the issue of adequately mapping international interest group populations, because most research in this area has remained qualitative and descriptive, and few scholars have investigated the topic systematically. Moreover, most efforts have been limited to one particular type of actors, mostly global NGOs, and studies have seldom been longitudinal. In part this is a consequence of the fact that for most international venues no systematic data are available; where there are data, we face problems with regard to how well the data cover real populations. Moreover, the data available for one international venue are often not directly comparable to the data that may exist for other international venues.

Despite these obstacles some important research into the mapping of global advocacy has been done. One of the most notable examples is the work of the Global Governance Centre (GGC) of the London School of Economics,[4] which includes a wide variety of research on global governance. The mapping studies carried out by this center are mostly based on the Union of International Associations (UIA) database, which deals predominantly with transnational organizations, but does not explicitly include national organizations that lobby – occasionally or regularly – at the international level (see, e.g., the *Yearbooks* of the GGC since 2001). Yet, as this chapter shows, national organizations constitute a substantial proportion of the civil society participation at international venues, as many national interest groups enter the global domain alongside transnational interest groups. Even starker, when it comes to interest groups that have attended WTO MCs, national organizations vastly outnumber transnational organizations. Thus, relying on GGC data only when aiming to explain general patterns of global advocacy would be to ignore a substantial portion of the population that mobilizes at the international level.

Keck and Sikkink (1998) provided another overview of what they call 'social change organizations' at the global level in which they observe growth in all issue areas since 1953. Their analysis is also based on the

UIA dataset, which means that national interest groups were not explicitly included in this mapping effort, although Keck and Sikkink do include national interest groups among their case studies. In line with Keck and Sikkink, Smith's study of the mobilization of transnational interest groups is an even more systematic effort to map the global population of social movements (Smith 2005, 2006; Smith and Weist 2005). This work is largely cross-sectional and focuses on international social movement organizations, yet it does not cover business associations or, due to its reliance on the UIA as its main data source, national groups which lobby at international venues. Interestingly, Smith's research shows that the growth of the international interest group population is not infinite (2006, p. 420). Growth was particularly marked in the late 1980s and the 1990s, which coincides with the growth in the number of conferences organized by the UN and other international organizations (Keane 2009, pp. 716–21). Since the turn of this century, however, there has been a decline in the number of organizations, which seems to correspond with the constraints interest organizations face in realizing policy change at the international level. Especially because decision making at this level is extremely time-consuming, due to the many veto players and the requirement for unanimity among the member states of international organizations, and because international negotiations are conducted primarily by states, many interest groups stop their lobbying efforts at the international level prematurely. Moreover, given that, compared with state governments, international organizations do not provide extensive selective benefits to interest groups, international venues seem less crucial for the organizational maintenance of interest organizations. Other important observations reported in the studies cited above are that national-level factors are, in addition to international factors, of crucial importance in explaining the international-level presence or exit of international interest groups, and that a large number of international NGOs are based in the Northern hemisphere, most notably Europe and North America.

Despite these important findings, studies that map interest representation at the international level currently focus primarily on transnational interest groups, thereby excluding a large proportion of the interest groups that lobby in the international domain, most prominently national interest groups. Thus we do not know whether these findings hold true for the broader population of interest groups mobilizing at the international level. In order to fill this knowledge gap, our approach aims to trace the development of multiple types of interest groups at one specific global venue, namely the population of interest groups that attended the MCs of the WTO between 1996 and 2009. Starting from an international venue has the benefit of allowing us to determine how many interest groups in total, including national interest groups, aim to make their way globally.

Analyzing the WTO interest group system

In order to characterize the interest system of the WTO MCs, in this chapter the density, diversity, and volatility of this population are analyzed. Although the concepts used in this chapter originate from studies of domestic interest group systems, we believe that they travel across systems of interest representation at various levels of government (Messer *et al.* 2010). Together these three characteristics help us offer insights into how the overall WTO interest group system has developed over time.

Density is a relational concept referring to the number of interest groups (or organized interests) active within a certain area, either in geographical terms (Gray and Lowery 1996; Halpin and Thomas, forthcoming) or in terms of substantive policy area (Browne 1990). Gray and Lowery (1996) provide the most rigorous exploration of interest group population densities (see also Nownes, Chapter 5). They posit that the number of interest groups registered to lobby at any one time is shaped by a density-dependence mechanism, implying that maintaining a lobbying function depends on the existing number of interest groups in a given population relative to the amount of available resources (Gray and Lowery 1996, pp. 54–55). It follows that relatively young interest representation systems tend to display linear growth in the number of interest groups, but that growth will eventually slow down when such systems mature and become more densely populated. It is important to stress that this density-dependence mechanism will probably be less marked for our transnational interest group population, because most of the interest groups in the WTO population do not depend on the WTO for their survival, and thus the WTO interest system is less homogeneous than are most interest populations elsewhere. Nonetheless, we did expect a rather stable presence of interest organizations at the MCs because these meetings show consistency in terms of issues on the agenda. First, the structure of MCs is characterized by ongoing rather than separate negotiations, that is, by so-called negotiation rounds (Hoekman and Kostecki 2001). Before the Doha MC more or less the same issues were dealt with (during Singapore, Geneva 1998, and Seattle). Since the Doha MC again mostly the same issues have been on the agenda at each meeting. For instance, currently, 10 years after the start of the Doha Development Round in 2001, the negotiation round is still not concluded (Doha, Cancún, Hong Kong, and Geneva 2009). Moreover, as some issues were not concluded during the first set of MCs, they reappeared during the later negotiation rounds. Because MCs show substantial consistency and stability in terms of agenda issues, the WTO population of interest groups is expected to show a relatively steady pattern of attendance over time.

The diversity of interest group systems is a recurring topic in the literature (Baumgartner and Leech 1998; Beyers *et al.* 2008). Limited diversity – or, put differently, a biased pattern of interest representation as opposed to a balanced or more normally distributed pattern – is often considered problematic because of the potentially unequal distribution of influence that results. While early interest group scholars differed markedly in their normative assessments of the potentially limited diversity of a given interest community (Truman 1951; Schattschneider 1960; Olson 1965), recent empirical studies have repeatedly shown a substantial bias in the pattern of interest representation, in particular a dominance of business interests in both national systems and supranational systems (Baumgartner and Leech 2001; Berkhout and Lowery 2007). In that sense, the preponderance of business interests in the WTO interest group system is not *sui generis* to the WTO, but more a generic feature of how interest group systems develop (Esty 2001).

Volatility, finally, points to the extent to which interest groups are able to enter a specific area and maintain their lobbying efforts over a period of time (Schlozman and Tierney 1986). Volatility is important for three reasons (Berkhout and Lowery 2010). First, it tells us something about how easy it is for new organizations to enter a policy venue. If a system is biased toward a single interest or biased in favor of a small number of players, it may be much more difficult for new organizations to enter. Second, stability and volatility are important for the role interest organizations play. The more stable the pattern of representation is, the more interest organizations are capable of building experience in lobbying and constructing lasting networks with key policy makers. Organizations that maintain only a temporary presence are much less likely to create these vital resources. Third, decreasing exit rates over time suggest a stable and overall more mature interest group system, while strongly fluctuating entry and exit rates suggest a more volatile interest group system (Gray and Lowery 1996). Due to the stable nature of the issues on the MC agenda we expect to observe stability, or low volatility, in the WTO interest system because interest groups that have an interest in one particular MC will also be interested in other MCs.

Mapping the WTO interest group system

Our map of the WTO interest population was created by looking at all organizations that were registered by the WTO Secretariat as eligible to attend and/or did attend one of the seven MCs organized between 1996 and 2009. The database consists of organizations which sought (and were accredited for) access to an MC by applying to the WTO Secretariat. Our approach can best be characterized as an example of top-down measurement, whereby the mapping is strongly driven by the interest organizations that seek to influence policy-making processes at a given government venue, in our case WTO Ministerial Conferences. This strategy is different from a bottom-up approach in which organizations are sampled because they engage in some form of collective action which is potentially, but not necessarily, related to public policies. Top-down approaches may run the risk of biased results because it is difficult to assess whether the organizations present at a given government venue are representative of the interest community at large (Berkhout and Poppelaars 2009; Poppelaars 2009a, 2009b). But bottom-up approaches require a reliable census of interest organizations, which is something that is not readily available either for international venues or for most domestic policy-making systems. Therefore, we applied a top-down method of counting interest organizations that lobby the WTO MCs.

In total we identified 1,992 different organizations that were eligible to attend and/or did attend at least one of the seven MCs between 1996 and 2009. All of these organizations were coded on the basis of a number of variables which were identified by systematically reviewing all available Web sites. For 1,593 organizations a Web site could be identified which offered relatively elaborate data on the organization; for 370 organizations we were not able to find a Web site, but information on other Web sites enabled us to code at least some basic features of these organizations. Only 29 organizations could not be traced. In the few cases of organizations changing their name, we coded the organizations on the basis of their last name. Mergers happened more frequently, but not during the period covered by our research; most mergers happened before that period and therefore do not affect the results presented in this chapter. The complete dataset with Web-based information gives us a comprehensive insight into, for example, the types of organizations interested in WTO policies, the region or country they come from, their respective areas of interest, and how they are organized. Moreover, because all MCs from 1996 (Singapore) to 2009 (Geneva) are included, the changes in density, diversity, and volatility over time can be calculated. Table 9.1 provides an overview of the participation of interest groups at the different MCs. In addition, during the fall of 2009, we conducted a series of semistructured interviews with 3 WTO officials in Geneva, 4 representatives of the Dutch and the Belgian governments, and 14 representatives of global, national, and European interest groups who attended one or more of the MCs. These interviews help us to contextualize the quantitative data.

When we were constructing the database several obstacles came up. The records kept by the WTO Secretariat lack some accuracy (see Table 9.1). For some MCs (Singapore, Geneva 1998, Doha, Hong Kong) there are only lists of the organizations that effectively attended. In the case of three conferences (Singapore, Doha, Hong Kong) these lists differ by more than 20 percent from the number of organizations which were accredited by the WTO Secretariat. There are no data available on which organizations were accredited but did not attend and why these eligible organizations did not travel to the MC. For three conferences (Seattle, Cancún, and Geneva 2009) the number of organizations on the WTO list is substantially larger than the number of organizations that, according to the official WTO sources, attended the MC. In these cases the numbers are very close to the number of eligible organizations, which leads us to presume that the data here correspond to the eligible organizations. As the Secretariat of the WTO did not store any other lists than the ones they provided (third column of Table 9.1), we cannot systematically trace the organizations that asked for accreditation but did not show up at the conference.

Next, not all interest groups who want to attend MCs of the WTO are allowed to do so. There is gate keeping to the venue. Before each MC interest groups have to submit an official request stating the reasons they want to attend and how their interests are related to WTO issues. A small number of officials at the WTO Secretariat then decide on the basis of Article V, para. 2 of the WTO Agreement[5] whether interest groups are eligible to attend. One important criterion for the WTO Secretariat is that accredited actors should be interest organizations – business associations, labor unions, NGOs, think thanks, local governments – and not individual firms. The WTO does not keep a full record of all groups that seek attendance at MCs, so it is not possible to check the implications of the way the WTO Secretariat accredits organizations. However, given the fact that most interest groups are organized at the level of

Table 9.1 Number of eligible and attending organizations and number of organizations in the WTO dataset, 1996–2009

Ministerial Conference	Eligible organizations	Attending organizations	Organizations in WTO dataset	Difference between eligibility count and dataset records (%)	Number of individuals who attended
Singapore (1996)	159	108	108 (= attended)	32	235
Geneva (1998)	153	128	128 (= attended)	16	362
Seattle (1999)	776	686	738 (< eligible)	5	~1,500
Doha (2001)	651	370	370 (= attended)	43	370
Cancún (2003)	961	795	948 (< eligible)	1	1,578
Hong Kong (2005)	1,065	812	812 (= attended)	24	1,596
Geneva (2009)	435	395	430 (< eligible)	1	490

the WTO member states and that the WTO is a membership-driven organization in which different member states pursue different, often opposing, policy views, there is no reason to suspect that the Secretariat would systematically bias its decision in favor of a particular interest. Moreover, WTO officials who are responsible for the selection process assured us that only a small number, about 1 percent, of groups are denied access.[6] Usually the organizations that are deemed ineligible are those that seek access for reasons not related to WTO policy issues (for instance, seeking visas for entry to developed countries). Not including these organizations in the dataset will, therefore, probably have only very limited influence on the outcomes of the analysis.

It is not only the WTO Secretariat, however, that determines who gets accredited. Much also depends on the host member state. It may limit access, for instance, by applying strict visa requirements. Moreover, WTO member states may have very different domestic legal rules with regard to interest group involvement. To illustrate, the sharp decrease in the number of organizations participating during the 2001 MC in Doha is the result of fewer interest organizations asking for access to the MC and a combination of limited hotel accommodation, strict visa requirements, and the aftermath of 9/11 leading to a much smaller number of eligible organizations being able to attend the conference. This does present a problem because in the case of Doha almost half of the organizations that were accredited to attend the meeting did not show up. As we do not have data on these organizations we cannot trace them or explain their absence systematically. Moreover, during WTO MCs many interest organizations, in particular NGOs, assemble outside the conference venue and organize a visible public presence in order to put pressure on what takes place within the conference venue. Systematic longitudinal data on these outside events is currently lacking. On the basis of information in NGO archives it would be possible to assemble such a list,[7] but, as many of the organizations that protest outside the conference venue also formally attend the MCs, the impact of excluding these actors on the total population would be limited.[8]

Another important issue is to what extent our dataset is representative of the interest groups which potentially could lobby the WTO. For instance, access to MCs is not valued equally by all interest organizations who have a stake in trade policies; how such access is valued differs according to the domestic contexts from which groups originate (Browne 1985; Berkman 2001). The lists could, therefore, be biased toward those groups that are likely to value access to the MCs more highly than other organizations (Poppelaars 2009a, 2009b). This variation potentially affects the shape of our population as groups from some countries or interest organizations with radical political views might be less likely to ask for accreditation. Related to this, the dataset we constructed deals only with access to one specific venue of the WTO. Interest groups also use other venues to seek influence, such as their domestic governments, foreign delegates, or other WTO fora. Yet the MC is the highest decision-making body of the WTO and all of the interest groups that we interviewed indicated that attending these meetings was an essential, although not the only, ingredient in lobbying on WTO policy. This makes it plausible to expect that most of the interest groups that have an interest in influencing WTO decision making will aim to attend these meetings as part of their lobbying strategy.

To summarize, compared with other data that map policy activity – such as data from the US and Scotland (Lowery, Chapter 3; Halpin *et al.*, Chapter 6) – our data include organizations that managed to overcome a higher access threshold and more gate keeping than domestically mobilized interest organizations. This could have a substantial effect on the composition and development of an interest community as it takes more effort to maintain lobbying at the WTO than in many domestic political venues.

The density, diversity, and volatility of the WTO interest group system

We now turn our attention to the empirical part of our analysis, which focuses on the density, diversity, and volatility of the WTO interest group system. With regard to density, our expectation is that the number of mobilized interest groups will initially grow due to the increasing openness of the WTO and the fact that over time interest organizations themselves professionalize, become more effective, and learn how to cope with the constraints they face when mobilizing at the international level. However, due to the limited possibilities for interest groups to influence the policy process at MCs and the slow pace of the decision-making process, at some point some groups are likely to encounter more and more constraints in realizing their policy goals, and in response they may exit and/or seek access to other international organizations (Smith 2005, 2006, p. 420; Smith and Weist 2005; Alter and Meunier 2009; Murphy and Kellow 2009).

The density measure in Figure 9.1 seems to confirm this trend, which Smith also identified for international NGOs, namely that WTO lobbying is not an infinite-growth business (Smith 2005, 2006). Although there are clear differences between the number effectively attending and the number eligible to attend for several MCs (see Table 9.1), overall the numbers follow the same trend. The data indicate a process that starts with slow growth (from 1996), enters a stage where the population grows rapidly (1999–2003), and finally reaches a stage where the number of active organizations starts to decline (2005 onward). Figure 9.1 also clearly shows a 'Doha effect', a sharp decrease in the number of organizations eligible for/attending that particular MC as a result of constrained access, less explicit demand for access, limited hotel accommodation, and stricter visa requirements. Although we cannot pinpoint any direct causes for the observations in this chapter, for which we need additional data such as the exact issues on each of the MC agendas, we do observe a rather similar trend to that found in other international political systems (Smith 2005, 2006).

In terms of diversity we analyze two indicators that are repeatedly discussed with regard to international venues such as the WTO, namely diversity in terms of organizational type and diversity in terms of the country or region from which they originate. For both diversity measures the density rates across different categories are outlined. For organizational type, we differentiated between business associations, labor unions, NGOs, and institutions (Table 9.2).[9] The difference between business associations and NGOs as a percentage of all organizations lobbying at the MCs is not large, and their proportions do not fluctuate

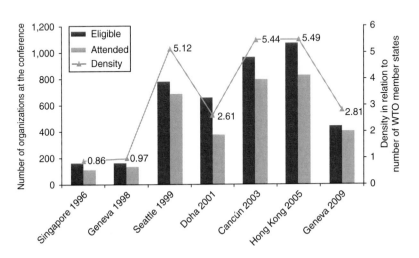

Figure 9.1   Density of the WTO interest group population, 1996–2009

Table 9.2   Type and origin of organizations lobbying during WTO MCs, 1996–2009 (%)

	Singapore (1996)	Geneva (1998)	Seattle (1999)	Doha (2001)	Cancún (2003)	Hong Kong (2005)	Geneva (2009)
Organization type							
Institutions	19	15	18	17	12	13	15
Labor unions	11	17	7	10	9	9	13
NGOs	36	37	35	35	37	34	39
Business associations	35	31	40	38	42	44	33
Primary level of political mobilization							
National (including subnational)	43	42	60	53	59	58	60
Regional	21	21	17	23	20	19	19
Global	36	37	23	24	22	23	20
Type of country of origin							
Least developed countries	5	7	3	6	6	6	17
Undeveloped countries	36	19	16	23	29	29	30
Developed countries	59	74	81	71	65	65	53
Region of origin							
Africa	5	9	4	9	10	8	16
South America	2	3	5	2	5	3	6
Oceania	2	0	2	3	2	5	1
Asia	36	15	11	21	18	25	24
Europe	33	24	23	38	28	25	30
Northern America	22	48	54	27	32	32	20

substantially over time: they remain between 33 and 44 percent. The proportion of labor unions remains rather low (between 9 and 17 percent), a finding which is consistent with other observations on this type of interest organization and the WTO (Beyers and Kerremans 2007). These results suggest, first, that there is no systematic underrepresentation of nonbusiness interests compared with business interests. It appears that noneconomic interests are quite well represented at the WTO (Piewitt 2010). Second, there is no strong growth of one type of organization, such as NGOs or business organizations, at the cost of other types. True, there are some fluctuations, but we do not observe substantial growth or decline in one particular direction.

The second diversity indicator we analyzed was the territorial origin of the interest groups. Table 9.2 shows that domestically based groups constitute by far the largest set of lobbying organizations, and their share has grown considerably over the years. The proportion of such groups[10] has increased by 17 percent, from 43 percent in 1996 to 60 percent during the 2009 MC in Geneva. Regionally based organizations (of which 44 percent are EU-level business organizations and NGOs) constitute a relatively stable share – between 17 and 23 percent – of the overall population. Although, we cannot take for granted that domestically based groups will represent national interests, the strong and growing presence of such groups leads us to refine the general assumption of a growth in importance of transnational interests groups and global social movements. Our data suggest that MCs are increasingly used by domestic groups for all sorts of purposes, which could include the continuation of their domestic lobbying and the monitoring of national governments at international venues. This general picture fits with the notion that domestic groups play a key role in potential policy changes when it comes to protectionism, and might also be a result of the fact that most regulatory policies are still originated at the national level (Goldstein and Martin 2000). In addition, these numbers clearly indicate that if we were to rely only on data dealing with transnational interest groups, such the *Yearbook of International Organizations* or the GGC database, we would exclude a large portion of the interest groups that become active at the international level. In the case of the WTO this could exclude up to 60 percent (Geneva 2009) of all organizations active at the MCs.

The remainder of Table 9.2 concerns the country or region of origin of organizations and confirms on first glance the strong representation of countries of the Northern hemisphere (Piewitt 2010). When we scrutinize the data, however, the picture becomes more nuanced. In addition to the overrepresentation of Northern hemisphere countries, we observe a potential geographical effect, namely a strong presence of organizations from countries or regions close to the conference venue, which is most obvious when we compare the Seattle MC with the Doha MC. Organizations from North America far outnumbered other organizations at the Seattle MC (54 percent), whereas at Doha the proportion of North American organizations sunk to 27 percent of the overall population. At Doha we also see an increase in the number of Asian and African organizations. This is most likely the result of the proximity of Doha to these regions. In general, however, organizations from developed countries still constitute the bulk of the organizations that attend WTO MCs.

Finally, we deal with volatility. As our mapping is largely a top-down exercise and not driven by a bottom-up census, our data do not measure group formation, deaths, and births.[11] Hence, we cannot refer to organizational mortality, but conceive volatility as the (dis)continuous participation of interest groups at the MCs, or political hibernation at MCs (see Schlozman, Chapter 2). The way we constructed the dataset allows us to analyze when groups enter MCs and when they exit. Because of the rather stable policy agenda, interest groups can be expected to maintain a durable interest in several MCs. Entry and exit rates are, therefore, robust indicators of the volatility of the WTO interest group system, because the stability in terms of policy agenda could generate considerable stability in terms of attendance.

Our database codes exit and entry rates for MC attendance for all interest groups that attended at least one MC. In this chapter we restrict the analysis to exploring the variation in exit and entry over time. Entry levels differentiate between organizations that are newcomers to the WTO and those that regularly participate at MCs. Exit rates indicate organizations that drop out from lobbying at a particular MC. We differentiate between those that had never been present at a previous conference but were at the one in question (new entrants), those that were present at all previous MCs (repeat players), those that were present at one or more but not all of the earlier MCs (partial repeat players), those that were present at all of the previous MCs but not at the one in question (exiters), those that were present at one or more but not all of the earlier MCs but not at the one in question (early exiters), and those that were not present at the MC in question or any of the earlier MCs (not [yet] lobbying) (see Table 9.3).

Table 9.3   Categories of entry and exit

New entrants	Never been at a previous conference but present at the conference in question
Repeat players	Present at each of the previous conferences and at the one in question
Partial repeat players	Present at one or more but not all of the previous conferences and at the conference in question
Exiters	Present at each of the previous conferences but not at the one in question
Early exit	Present at one or more but not all of the previous conferences but not at the conference in question
Not (yet) lobbying	Not present at this conference or at any of the earlier conferences

From Figure 9.2, one obvious observation is that each MC attracts new organizations, but that since the conference in Cancún the number of new entrants has started to decrease. Second, repeat players (organizations present at all previous conferences) are an extremely rare species. More substantial is the category of partial repeat players, a category that grows until the Cancún conference, but starts to decline after Cancún. The number of organizations that were present at one or more but not all of the previous conferences grows until 2003, but many of these organizations did not return after 2003. This suggests that the population is characterized by strong fluctuations and a decreasing level of stability.

High volatility is confirmed by looking at exit rates. The rate of early exits is substantial and grows over time, indicating that many organizations had attended a particular MC in the past but dropped out from later MCs. Compared with new entrants, the category of early exit is relatively large, which confirms the high volatility of the total population. Partial repeat rates also increase, while, as mentioned, the number of new entrants declines. Where a steadily declining number of new entrants could suggest competition effects – that is, that the dense nature of the population does not leave much space for additional organizations – the growing number of partial survivors suggests additional mechanisms, such as policy-area concentration effects whereby

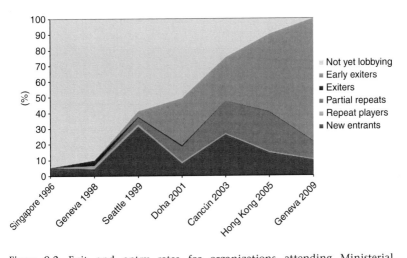

Figure 9.2 Exit and entry rates for organizations attending Ministerial Conferences, 1996–2009

flocks of organizations active in a particular sector keep on lobbying while others exit. In addition, for Doha, the visa restrictions did not have much impact on the group of exiters, which is after all a small group, but affected the groups characterized by early exit substantially. These trends potentially indicate the importance of contextual variables, such as the selection criteria of the WTO, but they could also point to the strategic behavior of interest groups as they adapt to the success or failure of their individual lobbying efforts. It could also be that the absence of any prospect of policy changes stimulates interest groups to hibernate. Further and more elaborate research is needed to draw more accurate conclusions on this matter.

Table 9.4 looks at how many newcomers at each MC returned to a subsequent MC, allowing us to say something about the effect of different MCs. The left-hand column lists the number of new organizations at each conference. For instance, at Doha 233 new organizations entered that had not attended Singapore, Geneva 1998, or Seattle. The subsequent columns show what proportion of these new organizations attended one of the later summits. When these percentages are compared substantial differences can be observed between the MCs. For instance, the Seattle conference was very successful in attracting new entrants, but less than half of these new entrants showed up at later conferences. Similarly for Cancún and Hong Kong, two MCs with large numbers of new entrants, a rather low proportion of organizations returned to later conferences. This is especially significant when compared with Singapore and Geneva 1998, two early MCs at which only a small number of new groups attended. The proportion of returning organizations is much higher for these conferences than for later MCs

Table 9.4 Returning newcomers at WTO Ministerial Conferences, 1998–2009 (%)

Number of newcomers at each Ministerial Conference	Percentage of newcomers returning to subsequent Ministerial Conferences					
	Geneva (1998)	Seattle (1999)	Doha (2001)	Cancún (2003)	Hong Kong (2005)	Geneva (2009)
Singapore, $n = 108$	38	56	33	51	40	22
Geneva, $n = 120$		68	45	64	54	34
Seattle, $n = 714$			29	45	36	16
Doha, $n = 233$				79	65	36
Cancún, $n = 763$					57	29
Hong Kong, $n = 448$						43

such as Seattle, Cancún, and Hong Kong. Interesting is Doha, a conference where the number of new groups (as well as the overall number of participants) was low compared with the other MCs but after which a majority of these new groups showed up at later conferences. Possibly, more selective conferences such as Doha, Geneva 1998, and Singapore attract more active and resourceful interest organizations. In sum, it is evident that most MCs create an almost entirely new set of attending interest groups, which points to a high level of volatility. Yet, in order to explain these observations, more research is needed that explicitly links exit, entry, and survival rates to key organizational characteristics and contextual factors to examine the precise mechanisms behind the development of the WTO population.

Conclusions and lessons learned

Mapping international interest group populations is still a rare phenomenon. Until now, most empirical work on the mobilization of interest groups at the international level has focused on a limited set of organizations, in terms of both numbers and types of groups. The few studies that do deal with international interest populations focus on just one type of interest group – most prominently social movement organizations and/or transnational interest organizations – and seldom take into consideration population dynamics. In this chapter we made a first attempt to more systematically analyze a specific global interest group system: all interest groups that participated at WTO MCs during 1996–2009. More specifically we analyzed the density, diversity, and volatility rates during these meetings.

What are the most striking trends? In terms of density, we found that more openness in terms of allowing interest groups to participate at MCs is no guarantee of linear or indefinite growth. When it comes to diversity we observed that the composition of the WTO interest group system does not favor business interests over other interests, at least not in terms of the number of organizations that attend MCs. The data also demonstrate that the largest set of interest groups lobbying at the MCs are national interest groups, and that the share of these organizations is growing in both relative and absolute terms. Finally, as far as volatility is concerned, the WTO system of interest representation seems rather unstable. Repeat players – organizations that attend MCs more than once – remain a minority, and the number of organizations exiting after attending one MC has grown over time. This means that despite the aggregate stability we observe, the individual interest organizations that defend trade interests are almost never the same. The WTO interest group system therefore might not be as stable as it seems at first glance, and is potentially prone to sudden and radical disturbances. However, the data used in this chapter cannot explain these trends in detail. For this we need additional studies and data.

Despite our systematic effort to analyze the WTO interest population, comparisons with other interest group populations remain challenging. First, the available data are much more limited and less systematic than data for some domestic arenas, such as the US. Second, we know that many interest groups lobby at multiple venues, most prominently of course at the national level. The mapping procedure we used cannot account for this potentially very large number of trade-interested lobbying organizations. Third, gaining access to MCs clearly does not imply that all the organizations in our dataset were equally influential. In fact, we have only limited knowledge of the activities of interest groups at MCs. It could very well be that groups attend MCs not only to seek direct influence but also to monitor the activities of government delegations or to use these venues to exchange information with allies. Fourth, there is an issue of labeling. For instance, do we include organizations that only occasionally 'visit' an MC as a genuine part of the WTO population? This issue is quite similar to what we are confronted with when studying domestic interest group systems – namely, how to delineate the boundaries of an interest group system. In an era when the distinction between domestic and international politics is becoming more blurred, this seems even more difficult.

Our general findings provide a unique perspective into the development of an interest group system at the global level. The results show that it is possible, if difficult, to map interest representation at this level in more or less the same fashion as is done for other political arenas. Some of the observed trends require further examination and can therefore been seen as an avenue for future research on global interest representation.

Notes

1. In this chapter we use the terms 'interest group', 'organized interest', 'nonstate actor', and 'civil society actor' interchangeably. These terms all point to the set of (1) organizations that (2) seek political influence yet (3) have no interest in gaining executive or legislative power themselves (Beyers *et al.* 2008).
2. We use the term 'nongovernmental organization' to refer to organizations that work on issues that are beneficial to the common good, such as development aid, the environment, or human rights.

3. It is interesting to add that most of these scholars use the concept 'civil society organization' as a way to emphasize the presumed positive contribution nonstate actors make to the functioning of international organizations such as the WTO.
4. The GCC is dedicated to research, analysis, and dissemination of information on the topic of global governance. It aims to increase understanding and knowledge of global issues, to encourage interaction between academics, policy makers, journalists, and activists, and to propose solutions. This includes the mapping of (parts) of global civil society.
5. This article, which dates from 1995 (the Marrakesh Agreement that established the WTO) is vague on the criteria that are used in practice ('The General Council may make appropriate arrangements for consultation and cooperation with non-governmental organizations concerned with matters related to those of the WTO').
6. Only for the 2009 MC in Geneva was the percentage higher (around 10 percent).
7. See, e.g., www.ourworldisnotforsale.org.
8. Some of the interest group representatives interviewed in Geneva attended such outside meetings or knew people who attended such meetings. They indicated that many of these organizations also register for the formal meetings.
9. Institutions include a variety of organizations without members (companies, individuals, or direct supporters) and encompass organizations such as think tanks, local governments and authorities, and universities.
10. We include subnational interest groups, such as the province of Quebec or the city of Los Angeles, as domestically based groups.
11. Our dataset consists of existing organizations which gained formal accreditation by the WTO. As a result, our data say nothing about the formation and disbanding of trade interest groups and how the political opportunity structure of international organizations such as the WTO affects the creation of transnational interest organizations. Moreover, many organizations in our dataset are national groups whose organizational survival does not depend primarily on international venues such as the WTO. The fact that we could find Web sites for most organizations suggests that many organizations in our dataset still exist. This indicates that organizations that attended early MCs but did not show up during later MCs did not necessarily disband or disappear.

References

Aldashev, G. and T. Verdier (2009) 'When NGOs Go Global: Competition on International Markets for Development Donations', *Journal of International Economics*, 79, 198–210.
Alter, K. J. and S. Meunier (2009) 'The Politics of International Regime Complexity', *Perspectives on Politics*, 7(1), 13–24.
Baumgartner, F. R. and B. L. Leech (1998) *Basic Interests: The Importance of Groups in Politics and Political Science* (Princeton, NJ: Princeton University Press).

Baumgartner, F. R. and B. L. Leech (2001) 'Interest Niches and Policy Bandwagons: Patterns of Interest Group Involvement in National Politics', *Journal of Politics*, 63(4), 1191–1213.

Berkhout, J. and D. Lowery (2007) 'Counting Organized Interests in the EU: A Comparison of Data Sources', *Journal of European Public Policy*, 15(4), 489–513.

Berkhout, J. and D. Lowery (2010) 'The Changing Demography of the EU Interest System since 1990', *European Union Politics*, 11(3), 447–61.

Berkhout, J. and C. Poppelaars (2009) 'Going to Brussels: A Population Perspective on Interest Representation in the EU', paper presented at the EUSA conference, Los Angeles, April 23–25.

Berkman, M. B. (2001) 'Legislative Professionalism and the Demand for Groups: The Institutional Context of Interest Population Density', *Legislative Studies Quarterly*, 26(4), 661–79.

Beyers, J. and B. Kerremans (2007) 'The Press Coverage of Trade Issues: A Comparative Analysis of Public Agenda-Setting and Trade Politics', *Journal of European Public Policy*, 14(3), 269–92.

Beyers, J., R. Eising, and W. Maloney (2008) 'Researching Interest Group Politics in Europe and Elsewhere: Much We Study, Little We Know?', *West European Politics*, 31(6), 1103–28.

Browne, W. P. (1985) 'Variations in the Behavior and Style of State Lobbyists and Interest Groups', *Journal of Politics*, 47(2), 450–68.

Browne, W. P. (1990) 'Organized Interests and Their Issue Niches: A Search for Pluralism in a Policy Domain', *Journal of Politics*, 52(2), 477–509.

Charnovitz, S. (2000) 'Opening the WTO to Non-governmental Interests', *Fordham International Law Journal*, 24, 171–216.

Esty, D. C. (2001) 'The World Trade Organization Legitimacy Crisis', *World Trade Review*, 1(1), 7–22.

Fried, J. (1997) 'Globalization and International Law: Some Thoughts for States and Citizens', *Queen's Law Journal*, 23, 259–74.

Goldstein, J. and L. L. Martin (2000) 'Legalization, Trade Liberalization, and Domestic Politics: A Cautionary Note', *International Organization*, 54(3), 603–32.

Gray, V. and D. Lowery (1996) 'A Niche Theory of Interest Representation', *Journal of Politics*, 58(1), 91–111.

Halpin, D. R. and H. Thomas (forthcoming) 'Evaluating the Breadth of Policy Engagement by Organized Interests', *Public Administration*.

Hoekman, B. M. and M. M. Kostecki (2001) *The Political Economy of the World Trading System: The WTO and Beyond* (Oxford: Oxford University Press).

Keane, J. (2009) *The Life and Death of Democracy* (London: Simon & Schuster).

Keck, M. E. and K. Sikkink (1998) *Activists beyond Borders: Advocacy Networks in International Politics* (Ithaca, NY: Cornell University Press).

Messer, A., J. Berkhout, and D. Lowery (2010) 'The Density of the EU Interest System: A Test of the ESA Model', *British Journal of Political Science*, 40(5), 161–90.

Murphy, H. and A. Kellow (2009) 'Shopping Around: States, Business Groups and NGOs in Multiple Arenas', paper presented at the 21st IPSA World Congress of Political Science, Santiago, Chile, July 12–16.

Olson, M. (1965) *The Logic of Collective Action: Public Goods and the Theory of Groups* (Cambridge, MA: Harvard University Press).

Piewitt, M. (2010) 'Participatory Governance in the WTO: How Inclusive Is Global Civil Society', *Journal of World Trade*, 44(2), 467–88.

Poppelaars, C. (2009a) *Steering a Course between Friends or Foes: Why Bureaucrats Interact with Interest Groups* (Delft, Netherlands: Eburon).

Poppelaars, C. (2009b) 'Corporatism or Lobbyism behind Dutch Dikes? Interest Representation in the Netherlands', in C. McGrath (ed.) *Interest Groups and Lobbying, Volume II: Europe* (Lewistone, NY: Edwin Mellen).

Robertson, D. (2000) 'Civil Society and the WTO', *World Economy*, 23, 1119–34.

Schattschneider, E. E. (1960) *The Semi-Sovereign People: A Realist's View of Democracy in America* (Hinsdale, IL: Dryden).

Schlozman, K. L. and J. T. Tierney (1986) *Organized Interests and American Democracy* (New York: Harper & Row).

Scholte, J. A. (2000) 'Civil Society and Democratically Accountable Global Governance', *Government and Opposition*, 39(2), 211–33.

Smith, J. (2005) 'Globalization and Transnational Social Movement Organizations', in G. F. Davis, D. McAdam, R. W. Scott, and M. N. Zald (eds.) *Social Movements and Organization Theory* (Cambridge: Cambridge University Press).

Smith, J. (2006) 'Social Movements and Multilateralism' in E. Neuman, R. Thakur, and J. Tirman (eds.) *Multilateralism under Challenge? Power, International Order, and Structural Change* (Tokyo: United Nations University Press).

Smith, J. and D. Weist (2005) 'The Uneven Geography of Global Civil Society: National and Global Influences on Transnational Association', *Social Forces*, 84(2), 621–52.

Spiro, P. J. (2000) 'The New Sovereigntists: American Exceptionalism and Its False Prophets', *Foreign Affairs*, 79(9), 9–12.

Steffek, J. and C. Kissling (2006) 'Civil Society Participation in International Governance: The UN and the WTO Compared', TranState working papers (Bremen, Germany: University of Bremen).

Teegen, H., J. P. Doh, and S. Vachani (2004). 'The Importance of Nongovernmental Organizations (NGOs) in Global Governance and Value Creation: An International Business Research Agenda', *Journal of International Business Studies*, 35, 463–83.

Truman, D. B. (1951) *The Governmental Process: Political Interests and Public Opinion* (New York: Alfred A. Knopf).

Van den Bossche, P. (2008) 'NGO Involvement in the WTO: A Comparative Perspective', *Journal of International Economic Law*, 11(4), 717–49.

Werker, E. and F. Z. Ahmed (2008) 'What Do Nongovernmental Organizations Do?', *Journal of Economic Perspectives*, 22(2), 73–92.

10
Above and Below the Radar: Mapping the Distribution of Civil Society Associations in England

John Mohan

As is reported regularly in this volume attempts to map the contours of associational life must resolve questions about how best to draw boundaries around eligible populations of organizations. A widely used point of departure for such investigations in the civil society area is the *Almanac of Civil Society*, which uses a definition developed by a team from Johns Hopkins (Salamon and Anheier 1996). Organizations are considered part of civil society if they are

- *organized* (that is, there is a degree of formality in the way they conduct their business, evident in governing documents and reporting structures of some kind);
- *private* (that is, they are formally separate from government, self-governing, and do not distribute profits to external stakeholders, but instead reinvest any surpluses in the organization); and
- *voluntary* (that is, there is at least an element of voluntary labor in the day-to-day running of the organization, or of voluntarism in its governance).

One way to map associational populations would therefore be to draw upon the records of regulatory bodies, such as the Charity Commission or Companies House in the UK, with which such organizations must register if they meet certain criteria (e.g., eligibility for charitable status or a financial threshold). As shown in the next section of this chapter, there is reliable information on the numbers and distribution of these 'registerable' organizations. The majority are charities, but there is a larger population of organizations which take a nonprofit legal form.

The collective noun for such entities widely used under the Labour government (1997–2010) was the 'third sector', and although that term is clearly no longer current, it is used here because it circumscribes the population of interest in important ways. In particular, not all non-profits are necessarily seen as providing public benefits, whereas the third sector was said to be characterized by its distinctive values and orientations.

Of course, many organizations do not appear on such 'radars'. David Horton Smith (1997) has argued that unless attention is paid to the organizations which do not show up – which he terms the 'dark matter' of the voluntary sector – there is a risk of producing 'flat earth maps'. Research would thereby neglect organizations which (for various reasons) are not subject to formal regulatory requirements, and which therefore do not appear on lists compiled by governments or regulators. These may be relatively ephemeral groups, formed around a particular threat (e.g., to resist a new road project), or they may have a long-term existence sustained by exchange of services and limited amounts of money (e.g., playgroups or groups organized to maintain a small area of public space). They may be very small and operate at the scale of a few streets, or they may draw on a broad base of support, bringing together diverse groups of people to campaign around shared interests and operating almost as a social movement. They may range from organizations with an agenda no wider than the delivery of a needed service (self-help groups) to organizations that have much grander campaigning ambitions.

As argued in Chapter 1 there are good reasons to be interested in such (easily undercounted) groups. (But clearly this is a much wider focus than in some other counting exercises.) They may play a vital role in civil society and social cohesion, as well as providing much-needed social, cultural, or educational services. They may also provide an environment in which political issues can be debated and campaigning skills developed. Furthermore, at the present time, the UK's coalition government has differentiated itself from its predecessor by its focus on the so-called 'big society'. The prime minister has expressed his desire that every adult should be part of a neighborhood group, and is talking about recruiting 5,000 community organizers to stimulate such activity. It is also envisaged that charities and social enterprises will take over many functions previously carried out by public sector agencies. But what capacities are available through the 'big society'?

Given what is known about patterns of participation, substantial differences between communities in numbers and types of organizations can be expected. These can be mapped for regulated third sector organizations, but without an understanding of the distribution of the less formalized small-scale community groups our picture of the capacities of communities will remain partial.

Some previous studies serve to illustrate the potential and challenges of researching the distribution of organizations. Fyfe and Milligan (2003) mapped the distribution of voluntary organizations in Glasgow, drawing on listings provided by local agencies such as the Glasgow Council for the Voluntary Sector, the City Library, and the Healthy City Partnership. They were particularly interested in a contrast between apparent concentrations of voluntary organizations in particular locations and gaps in the distribution in others, especially peripheral housing estates. Maloney *et al.* (2000; see also Chapter 11) accessed similar listings for Birmingham. Their sources included directories provided by Birmingham Voluntary Services Council, a trade union resource center, a yearbook compiled by the main Birmingham newspaper, the city council's lists of residents and tenants associations, and the 1997 version of the 'index of Birmingham charities'. They found a minimum of 5,700 organizations in Birmingham, which compares with some 2,000 registered charities plus several hundred other nonprofit entities, although they do not appear to have cross-referenced their sources against the records of regulators to establish the extent to which they were discovering organizations below the regulatory radar. They also attempted a classification of these entities. One notable feature was that the number and proportion of sports clubs appeared to have declined dramatically compared with an earlier study from the 1970s. This illustrates the importance of considering the source material on which such studies rely.

In later work (Smith *et al.* 2004) they looked at contrasts between Birmingham and Glasgow in the numbers and types of organizations. They were interested in organizations which had some kind of relationship with governance structures in their respective cities rather than in producing a comprehensive mapping of voluntary organizations. Again this in an interesting question for students of how societies cohere, but it is a different ambition from a comprehensive register. However, neither of these studies cross-referenced their work against the records of regulators, so it was not possible to determine how typical their data were compared with other studies. The survey reported in 2004 found a more substantial proportion of larger organizations than would be the case if one examined the Register of Charities. As shown below, the organizations that appear on local listings tend to be larger than the charity population as a whole, so their findings on the distribution of organizations are unsurprising, if unrepresentative. In the case of Smith *et al.* (2004), which was a comparative study of two cities, it is also possible that differences between the cities in organizational populations simply reflected the priorities and capacities of those who compiled their source material. It is a general problem in this area that even exercises that are broadly similar in aim may be operationalized differently.

There are numerous other, nonacademic local studies of the voluntary and community sector which have attempted to estimate numbers and characteristics of organizations, and their findings are rarely if ever comparable, because of variations in the methods used. In its 2001 study 'Low Flying Heroes', the New Economics Foundation compared findings from a number of such studies and found great variability in the results produced, from 3 groups per 1,000 people to more than 20 per 1,000 (McGillivray *et al.* 2001). The figure for Birmingham, at around 6 organizations per 1,000 population, would be toward the lower end of this range. Extrapolation of the figure of 20 organizations per 1,000 people generated a national estimate of between 600,000 and 900,000 community organizations, but it should also be pointed out that if the lower estimate were representative, the extrapolated figure would be around 135,000, which is rather less than the total number of registered charities. If the upper limit were correct it would suggest around 1 group per 50 people – which seems somewhat unlikely unless a very broad definition were used that encompassed many small and *ad hoc* groups with only a few members and limited characteristics of a formal organization. This estimate nevertheless seems to have become something of a conventional wisdom: a figure of 600,000 community organizations was added, uncritically and without qualification, to other estimates of the size of civil society in the National Council for Voluntary Organisations (NCVO) *Almanac*.

In this chapter the focus is on how one might understand variations among communities in the numbers and characteristics of associations. A distinction is made between two types of organizations: regulated third sector organizations are differentiated from what are sometimes known as 'below-radar' organizations, entities which are not legally required to register with the Charity Commission or other regulatory agency. As with other chapters in this volume the aim is both to report findings and to reflect on research method.

On the first type of organization (regulated), attention is drawn to the range of entities which make up the associational population and to initial work on the composition and distribution of these organizations. For the second type of organization (below-radar), extensive studies of the voluntary and community sector in northern England are drawn upon (the North East and the Yorkshire and Humberside government office regions, plus the county of Cumbria). The sources used cover a range of organizations, many of which are small and possibly ephemeral, while, at the other end of the spectrum, others are very large regional or even national entities. Many are not associations directly concerned with influencing the policy process ('policy-active' in the language of other chapters); they nevertheless make a contribution to civil society in their locality – from providing opportunities for sport and recreation to campaigning for specific causes and delivering welfare services.

The next section begins with a discussion of what might be found out by analyzing lists, from national regulatory bodies, of the broad population of third sector organizations. The focus is on variations among local communities in terms of the numbers and types of such organizations, and how such variations might be interpreted. The chapter then describes the methods and general findings of a study of the below-radar organizations appearing on lists of voluntary sector infrastructure bodies in parts of northern England. This gives insight into Horton Smith's 'dark matter' dimension, but it also raises questions about whether the distinction between the below-radar organizations and those which are on the radar is as watertight as might appear at first sight. It also suggests that much of the apparent variation is likely to reflect the priorities of those capturing the information.

Mapping the regulated third sector: organizational densities and social capital

The starting point for this work was involvement in research programs designed to delineate, and assess the impact of, third sector organizations in the UK. The immediate stimulus was the growing interest in the sector's contribution to economic and social life, exemplified by the Labour government's strongly pro third sector policies and by the coalition government's belief in the virtues of the big society. Before the 2010 UK general election, Conservative spokespeople such as Iain Duncan Smith referred to the idea of 'charity deserts' – measured as the ratio of registered charities to population – as an index of the capacity of the local voluntary and community sector. Elsewhere, analysts have used measures of the distribution of nonprofit organizations as an index of social capital (Rupasingha *et al.* 2006; Scheffler *et al.* 2008), while policymakers in the UK have incorporated measurement of the formation of third sector organizations into a basket of indices of the success of community regeneration efforts. A strong civil society can no doubt have beneficial social outcomes, but whether maps of organizational densities should be taken at face value is surely questionable. The population of third sector organizations, which in the UK numbers more than 250,000 legally regulated entities in various forms, is extremely heterogeneous. Below are presented some initial findings from work on the gamut of nonprofit organizations, including not just registered charities but various other legal forms, and encompassing work on the composition and distribution of this population.

The core of the third sector is registered charities. Since these organizations are established for a public purpose, are independent of government, have formal governance structures, have a substantial degree of voluntary input, and do not distribute profits or services, it might seem uncontroversial to regard all of them as part of the third sector and civil society, but some classification is in order at the margins. There are arguments about which organizations should be included: private schools are now having to pass more stringent scrutiny of their public benefits; a number of charitable organizations are controlled directly by public sector bodies (e.g., charitable trusts which exist for the benefit of particular National Health Service hospitals), raising questions about their independence from government; some nondepartmental public bodies are registered charities so that they can take a legal form entirely independent of government, as well as receive charitable donations; and there are many small grant-making trusts which, while no doubt providing help to those in need, nevertheless operate on a small scale, often being administered out of the offices of local government or legal firms, with no clear opportunities for volunteer involvement. Because of these and other definitional and conceptual questions, the NCVO has worked over a number of years to develop its 'general charities' definition, which is more restrictive. There are some 190,000 active charities in England and Wales, but the population of those identified as general charities is smaller, at around 145,000 after the exclusion of subsidiary charities and various categories of charity described above. Many charities are of interest as contributors to associational life and participation which involves face-to-face interaction; the great majority (96 percent) report that they have volunteers.[1] However, these by no means represent an exhaustive list of associations.

The potential population in the UK also includes entities taking nonprofit legal forms such as industrial and provident societies (IPSs) and companies limited by guarantee (CLGs). These forms are used by organizations formed to represent the collective interests of their members and/or providing benefits only to their members and/or engaging substantially in trading activity; for these reasons they are not eligible for charitable status. There are very large numbers of such organizations. In the case of IPSs, there are some 14,000, comprising a range of entities: some 3,000 are concerned with housing, 650 are credit unions, and there are 1,500 cooperatives; a further 3,000 or so are sports and social clubs. Smaller categories include allotment societies (self-sufficiency horticulture) and various organizations concerned with community development or tenants' representation. Many of the remainder are associations of various kinds designed to advance the interests of a collective group (e.g., producer organizations such as grain growers associations) or to provide collective services for a group of people or a community (e.g., village shop associations). IPSs may conduct any business other than trading for a profit, and their share capital is purely nominal and held in common for the benefit of the members. Some may trade purely for the benefit of their members and others may do so to advance a wider public purpose.

There are more than 100,000 registered CLGs, which include clubs, membership organizations, residential property management companies, and sports associations; they may also include workers cooperatives and social enterprises, NGOs advancing causes which mean that they cannot have charitable status (e.g., Greenpeace, Amnesty), and charities engaging in substantial trading activities (many of the latter hold dual registration as charitable companies). Whether an entity incorporates as a CLG or an IPS depends on its purpose and stakeholders – company law permits multiple voting constituencies, for example, which may predispose an organization toward selection of the CLG legal form. Numerically, the largest single category is probably residential property management companies (it is estimated that there are approximately 12,000 of these), which are established, as the name implies, to provide collective services for leasehold properties such as apartment blocks. It is difficult to see how these might be regarded as part of civil society.

This is clearly a very diverse population, and the extent to which all of these organizations are of interest depends on the purpose of study. Measuring the density of nonprofit organizations in localities has been the subject of some studies of social capital, and the implication is that organizations contribute, in some way, to its formation. However, the extent to which associations and organizations do this, and the ways in which they do so, vary considerably. In the case of sports and social clubs it may not be clear what differentiates them from their more commercial rivals, and this may also be true for the working men's clubs of the industrial parts of the UK: squeezed by competition in the licensing trade, they no longer have the extensive links into the local community that they formerly did. If the interest is in social capital formation, Putnam's paradigmatic example – choral societies (many of which exist as registered charities) – obviously have barriers to entry and membership in the form of auditions and subscriptions; thus they are by no means examples of nonhierarchical associational life which cuts across social boundaries in the harmonious manner envisaged by Putnam. Property management companies are unlikely to involve much more than paying an annual subscription to the company to cover a leaseholder's share of repairs and maintenance. Conversely there are large third sector organizations delivering welfare services which have relatively little voluntary involvement.

Nevertheless, one of the notable features of the map of associations is the extent to which the distribution varies throughout the country. Overall there are approximately 3 per 1,000 population, but upward of 25 percent of the population – approximately 16 million people – live in areas where there are fewer than 1.5 charities per 1,000. In some disadvantaged regions nearly half the population live in areas with under 1.5 charities per 1,000. One might argue that the distribution of charities is not a good reflection of where they operate; there are large numbers of charities in some parts of the country which have very limited resources and these might arguably represent historical anachronisms. With the per capita incidence of registered charities varying two- or threefold among local authorities, opportunities to participate in voluntary action also vary considerably. Elsewhere, different ways of apportioning charitable expenditures across local authorities are explored (Mohan 2011); this gives a slightly more nuanced picture of where charitable expenditures are concentrated.

When more detailed information about where organizations operate is analyzed, and one focuses down on the neighborhood scale, very substantial variations are found. In the 2008 National Survey of Third Sector Organizations (NSTSO) some 20,000 responses were from charities saying they operated only at the neighborhood scale. Typically there were more than twice as many such organizations per head in the most prosperous parts of the country than in the most disadvantaged areas (Clifford and Mohan, forthcoming).

To what extent does the map of noncharitable third sector organizations exhibit a similar pattern? There is a strong suggestion that this pattern does not simply mirror the distribution of charities. Figures suggest that in many southern and rural parts of the country, the nonprofit population is dominated by registered charities, which may account for over 85 percent of the total number of organizations in an area. This is based on analysis of survey data which used as a sampling frame a narrow definition of the third sector in an attempt to ensure sampling from a population which shared a distinctive value orientation. In contrast, although charities remain numerically the largest category, in many large industrial and urban areas they account for below 70 percent of the nonprofit population. If the pattern is related to levels of deprivation, many of the noncharitable entities tend to be located in more disadvantaged local authorities. To a degree this could be related to the historic heartlands of working-class organizational activity in the UK – especially when we look at particular types of organizations in such areas, which include working men's clubs. However, it might also reflect more recent rounds of intervention and investment – for instance, the creation of housing associations and credit unions, often backed by the public sector, which *ceteris paribus* would be expected to be found in the less prosperous areas.

All this raises the question of how these variations might be interpreted. Clearly, historical legacies are very important. It is likely that the distribution of charities will reflect the economic history of particular localities. In the case of noncharitable entities the distribution will have something to do with local social and political traditions, particularly in the case of cooperative and mutual entities. There is also evidence from the recent past that the distribution of third sector organizations reflects state intervention: it seems that a higher proportion of charities were founded in the more deprived parts of England during the term of office of the Labour government (1997–2010), and this likely reflects the availability of public funding for needy groups and areas.[2] Therefore further work is necessary before accepting that a strong third sector presence in an area can be taken as an unproblematic index of social capital (as is the case with the use of a county-level measure of the distribution of nonprofits in the US by Rupasingha *et al.* 2006, or the use of the percentage of employment in nonprofits as an index, also in the US, by Scheffler *et al.* 2008). The concentration of the third sector in a particular area may have little to do with contemporary socioeconomic conditions, though a strong third sector presence may well improve quality of life in a community and potentially help generate social capital by providing opportunities for people to volunteer.

Mapping below-radar organizations

The discussion above shows that it is possible to generate maps of the distribution of regulated third sector organizations. But to what extent is it possible to produce reliable estimates of the numbers of below-radar organizations? The first question is how one would define such entities. One could simply classify an organization as 'below-radar' if it was not regulated (in other words, if it was not on the listings of bodies such as the Charity Commission or Companies House). Thereafter one finds a degree of subjectivity. For example, working definitions produced by the Third Sector Research Centre (McCabe and Phillimore 2009) refer to incomes below various thresholds (surprisingly, up to £50,000 or even more in some studies), the absence of assets, and expectations about an organization's role in campaigning and representation. Attempting to differentiate among organizations in this way is problematic. For organizations which are not registered, there is no background information on whether they meet those criteria. In fact there is very little information about how many such entities there are at all. There are in essence two methods by which estimates of the below-radar population might be derived.

One approach is that used by the LOVAS (Local Voluntary Action Studies) implemented by the UK Home Office in the 1990s. Intensive local, on-the-ground methods were used to record and survey volunteer-using groups and voluntary organizations. The LOVAS methodology used 'local mappers', researchers who lived in or close to the area mapped, to produce lists of a wide range of local organizations. The methodology concentrated on likely sites of voluntary activity, such as schools, public houses, and churches, and also drew upon pre-existing lists, such as those held by councils for voluntary service (CVSs, infrastructure bodies charged with providing support to local voluntary and community organizations). The method was essentially one of snowballing: contacts were made with CVSs and other umbrella bodies to obtain lists of organizations from them; from these listings the researchers then made personal contact with other useful organizations or people. The methodology contained a defined set of expected organizations, including Neighbourhood Watch, parent and toddler groups, and youth groups; the researcher concentrated on each of these in turn. Emphasis was placed on the importance of personally visiting sites of activity to find new organizations.

The bottom-up approach meant that the information was reasonably up-to-date and based on local knowledge; the methodology found organizations and activity that a more top-down approach would not have done. However, the reliance on the initiative of individual researchers and possible variations in how the methodology was applied means that it is not necessarily possible to directly compare results from different areas. Furthermore the methodology was resource-intensive and extension across the UK would be unrealistically costly. Indeed the LOVAS studies (mentioned above) mostly covered only parts of their respective local authorities.[3]

An alternative is to follow the 'local area profiles toolkits' initially developed by the Audit Commission (NAVCA and Audit Commission 2006); this approach is less intensive in terms of resources and can be applied consistently across locations. Listings of organizations are gathered from relevant local sources (see below), collated, de-duplicated, and cross-referenced to registers of regulated third sector organizations. This is not straightforward. Names are recorded in different ways; very rarely will a name on a local listing correspond perfectly with the name of the organization appearing on the Register of Charities. The potential for false positives – identifying an organization as a unique entity, and identifying an organization as a below-radar entity when it is not – is significant. A rigorous and consistent methodology for identification and removal of duplicates, and for matching against master lists of regulated third sector organizations, is essential. The methods used by the author are described in more detail elsewhere (Mohan *et al.* 2011). They include various measures to clean up name and address information and to apply consistency to currently used terms or abbreviations (e.g., 'Ltd' or 'Limited', in the case of companies). Even so, names of organizations may be recorded inconsistently, with the component parts of a name appearing in different ways in different sources: one listing had the 'League of Friends of the Wigton Hospital', for example, while another had 'Wigton Hospital League of Friends'. If names were simply sorted alphabetically and compared these might be treated as different entities. The research team of which the author was a part therefore developed a routine for splitting text strings and resorting them in alphabetical order. This entity became 'Friends Hospital League Wigton' in both sources, and was recognized as a duplicate. As was pointed out to us, an example from the film *The Life of Brian* illustrates the limitations of this approach. Had they appeared in our source data, the Judaea People's Front and the People's Front of Judaea would both have been rendered as 'Front Judaea People', but devotees of the film will recall that they are splinter groups with quite different political views![4]

However, the cases where accuracy is improved seem to heavily out-number any new problems generated. Additional methods included comparisons of nested names (often the only difference between two names is the addition of a place name) and comparisons of postcode data (for example, similar postcodes within the same local authority may indicate a duplicate). Finally, every organization in the listings was compared with every other organization in the listings. In pro-gramming terms this is not a trivial task.

There are, then, technical challenges with this work, and there is a tradeoff which has to be accepted: electronic de-duplication will get most of the way (the research team assessed that this method found about five-sixths of all duplicates in the database), but manual checking is the only way of being certain. Nevertheless, the methods achieved substantial removal of duplicates: the process began with a combined total of some 58,000 entities, which was reduced to approximately 45,000 unique entities using these routines.

How valid is this method as a means of estimating the below-radar population? As is a strong theme in other contributions to this volume, Grønbjerg and Clerkin (2005) suggest that, in the context of the non-profit sector, what you find will depend on where you look: listings will undoubtedly reflect the capacities and priorities of those compiling them and the willingness of those organizations on the list to supply data. In most local authority areas there were several potential sources of such listings and there were also lists from regional and national umbrella bodies (often sector-specific), as well as from community foundations, upon which we could draw. The research team obtained more than 80 listings from third sector infrastructure bodies and foun-dations and from local authorities, covering most of northeast England, Cumbria, and Yorkshire and Humberside. The principal infrastructure bodies in this area are councils for voluntary service, and listings from 30 such agencies covering nearly all local authorities in our region were obtained. CVSs can generally be regarded as the first port of call for information about the local third sector, although the extent and cover-age of their listings are variable. Listings were also gathered from some community foundations – philanthropic intermediaries which pool resources for a defined area.

What were the findings? If one looks at the organizations which fea-ture on local listings of third sector organizations such as those pro-duced by CVSs, there seem to be around three or four community groups for every regulated third sector organization. But to then mul-tiply the numbers of registered charities by a factor of three or four to arrive at an estimate of the below-radar population is methodologically questionable. These listings are not representative samples of the regulated third sector population. Only a minority of regulated third sector organizations appear on local listings. The analysis shows that many infrastructure bodies have on their lists between 10 and 30 percent of the registered charities in their respective local authorities; this would imply that, *relative to the numbers of charities on those listings*, there are between three and six organizations which are not registered third sector organizations. But because many charities do not appear on local listings at all, the true ratio may be more like 1:1.

Furthermore the upper-bound estimates of the below-radar population may rest on a misunderstanding of the nature of the third sector population. There is potentially considerable overlap between what might be perceived as below-radar organizations and registered charities. Large numbers of organizations which might be thought of as small community organizations do in fact appear on the registers of regulatory bodies, particularly the Charity Commission; many Scout groups, civic societies, playgroups, parent–teacher associations, and playing field associations are on the register, even though their economic weight is very small (a few hundred pounds or less). Nearly half of the 20,000-plus registered charities in these regions have an income of below £10,000; just under 30 percent have an income of £5,000 or less. This is well below the thresholds in the studies reviewed by McCabe and Phillimore (2009). What may differentiate these regulated third sector organizations from other community groups is that they have legal obligations with which they must comply (e.g., in relation to the management of assets or property) for which charitable status is required or advantageous. It was therefore possible to capture considerable detail about small community organizations from the Charity Commission database where these are registered charities. As examples, consider the following, which collectively account for more than 10 percent of registered charities in these regions:

- *Scout groups.* There are more than 800 such organizations in the areas for which we have local listings, of which just over 500 are registered charities.
- *Women's Institutes.* In our region there are some 750 of these, but as far as we can tell the vast majority (676) are registered charities.
- *Playgroups.* We can identify more than 400 organizations with 'playgroup' in their title which appear on the register of the Charity Commission, and a further 160 which do not.

In view of this, perhaps the distinction between the below-radar population and the population of other third sector organizations is more apparent than real.

Nevertheless, what can be concluded from the data collected? Having made the process of cross-referencing as complete as was feasible, we considered that on average – for the 42 local authorities for which data were available – the number of below-radar organizations and groups is around 4 per 1,000 population. This is some 10 percent higher than the number of regulated third sector organizations, but it is by no means as large as the estimates from the New Economics Foundation. In a small number of local authorities the estimates arrived at were more than 6 organizations per 1,000 population, and the ratio in one area reached 9 per 1,000, but it is clear that in these areas very substantial efforts had been made to enumerate organizations by collating lists which included some very informal and small community groups, as well as very large numbers of sports clubs: one small rural local authority, with a population of under 100,000, appeared to have more sports clubs than some of the major cities of our study region. Because of the multiplicity of lists supplied for this area in particular, there were heightened possibilities for false positives in the identification of unique entities. It was found that in areas where many listings were supplied, more than a quarter of all entries proved to be duplicates.

So one answer to the question of how many such entities there are is that it depends on how hard, and where, you look. Nevertheless, in no local authority area did the research team's findings suggest that there were anything like the numbers of organizations suggested by the New Economics Foundation. Consideration of the effects of drawing on different types of listing, and the potential overlaps between them, led us to suggest that there may be between 1.25 and 1.5 times the number of registered charities appearing on listings compiled by local infrastructure bodies – possibly adding up to between 200,000 and 300,000 community organizations. This is a substantial number but is not as large as previous estimates. The team also suspect that this may still be an overestimate; the matching process eliminates many possibilities for duplication but is by no means exhaustive, so we may still be incorrectly identifying entities as below-radar when in fact they are not.

What do these organizations do, and can we conclude that we are capturing a different population from that of the regulated third sector? There seem to be some fairly clear findings here. All the organizations in the combined listings were classified against standard schema such as the International Classification of Non-Profit Organizations

(ICNPO) (United Nations 2003), using keywords from organizational titles. Compared with the population of registered charities, the largest single element of the registered third sector population, the below-radar organizations are more likely to be involved in the ICNPO categories of sport and recreation and of arts and culture; these categories account for some 27 percent of those organizations that could be classified (Table 10.1). In contrast, in the regulated third sector population – particularly registered charities – the modal class seems to be in the area of social care. It is possible that these variations reflect what the compilers of the lists (the councils for voluntary service, principally) regarded as important: on some listings, the proportion of below-radar organizations we assessed as being part of the ICNPO classification of social care was as high as 35 percent; combined with the number of organizations concerned with community development, this figure exceeded 50 percent for several listings. However, organizations on the mailing lists of community foundations, which give many small grants to community groups, seemed much more likely to be concerned with culture and recreation. Clearly the only way around this particular challenge is to assemble every conceivable list relevant to each local authority, but such efforts are likely to encounter difficulties; despite repeated requests the research team was simply unable to gain access to all the listings which had been requested. Note also that some of these differences will reflect regulatory practice: sport *per se* is not a charitable purpose, so sports clubs must generally take either a noncharitable legal form or no legal form at all. This is why, in our study regions, some 70 percent of the 'culture and recreation' organizations on the listings were classed as below-radar.

There are also relatively clear findings in relation to the location of these below-radar organizations. These entities seem to be more concentrated in the disadvantaged parts of communities. If one links organizations to socioeconomic data using their postcode and categorizes areas by deciles of the distribution of the Index of Material Deprivation (a social index encompassing dimensions of poverty and exclusion such as worklessness, proxies for income, and housing tenure and quality), one finds that there is a fairly clear gradient, with greater numbers of below-radar organizations in the more deprived parts of the region (Figure 10.1). If these organizations were distributed equally across these areas, one would expect approximately 10 percent in each area, but it is plain that the proportion of below-radar groups is much higher in the most disadvantaged areas. That conclusion is reinforced when we compare the distribution with that of registered charities,

Table 10.1 Classification of below-radar organizations and registered charities

	Legal form											
	BTR			Charities			Charitable companies			Total		
	No.	Row %	Col. %	No.	Row %	Col. %	No.	Row %	Col. %	No.	Col. %	Cum. %
Culture/recreation	5,417	70.9	29.6	1,785	23.4	12.5	440	5.8	15.6	7,642	21.6	21.6
Education	1,919	36.4	10.5	3,021	57.3	21.2	335	6.4	11.9	5,275	14.9	36.5
Health	600	50.5	3.3	421	35.5	3	166	14.0	5.9	1,187	3.4	39.8
Social services	4,127	51.0	22.5	3,340	41.2	23.4	631	7.8	22.3	8,098	22.9	62.7
Environment	715	59.0	3.9	349	28.8	2.4	148	12.2	5.2	1,212	3.4	66.1
Development	3,170	52.0	17.3	2,347	38.5	16.5	584	9.6	20.7	6,101	17.2	83.4
Law, advocacy, politics	518	60.4	2.8	223	26.0	1.6	117	13.6	4.1	858	2.4	85.8
Promotion of voluntarism	251	20.9	1.4	840	70.1	5.9	108	9.0	3.8	1,199	3.4	89.2
International	137	34.3	0.7	239	59.8	1.7	24	6.0	0.8	400	1.1	90.3
Religion	1,419	42.6	7.7	1,653	49.6	11.6	258	7.7	9.1	3,330	9.4	99.7
Other	48	48.5	0.3	37	37.4	0.3	14	14.1	0.5	99	0.3	100
Total	18,321	51.8	100	14,255	40.3	100	2,825	8.0	100	35,401	100	100

BTR, below-radar organization.

Note: Row % provides a breakdown of charities operating in a specific area; column % provides a breakdown by area of operation within a single legal form.

which are clearly more likely to be found in the prosperous areas of these regions. In some senses, then, the below-radar groups complement the distribution of regulated organizations, though it is clear that the organizational population is somewhat different.

A further finding may be of note. This is that while considerable efforts were made to ensure that below-radar organizations were correctly identified, in practice, when we administered a small-scale survey to them, many respondents believed that they were a regulated third sector organization (they were asked a filter question to eliminate those organizations which were registered charities, CLGs, IPSs, or community interest companies). Of 1,000 organizations approached, some 500 responded to the filter question by stating they were a registered charity. When their names were checked individually, it was discovered that they were not. Whether this is because they were operating out of premises owned or leased by larger organizations, or because they had

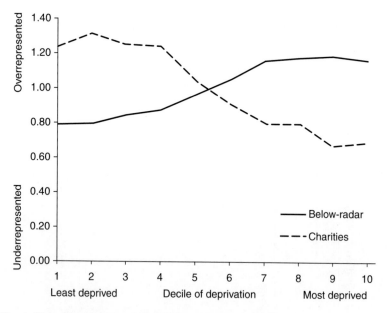

Figure 10.1 Distribution of charities and below-radar organizations, by decile of deprivation

Note: A figure greater than 1.0 on the *y*-axis indicates there are more organizations in each area of these regions (when ranked by level of deprivation) than their share of population would indicate. A score below 1.0 indicates that there are fewer.

close working relationships with such organizations, was not something probed, but again it does call into question any neat division between below-radar and on-radar organizations.

The results of that survey were also interesting for other reasons. It was difficult to draw any hard-and-fast distinctions between below-radar and other organizations on the basis of resources. Although in most cases the former operated on small budgets, these still often ran into four figures and in some cases exceeded £10,000. In terms of sources of income, they were likely to draw primarily upon membership subscriptions, donations, and fundraising activities, and in this regard their profile is very similar to that of charities whose incomes are below £10,000. Nor was it easy to determine, without further survey research, whether organizations were interest groups, protest organizations, or campaigning organizations as opposed to simply delivering a service or providing a social focus.

In summary, then, this work has established what is by some distance the largest database compiled from local listings of third sector organizations in the UK, and it seems to point to some areas of complementarity – for example, that there appear to be more regulated third sector organizations in more prosperous localities than there are in more disadvantaged ones, and that they appear to be operating in somewhat different areas of activity. It is a matter for further investigation whether this reflects real differences among areas or whether there are differences in the likelihood of organizations choosing to go through the process of registration, for instance, with the Charity Commission.

Conclusions

What can mapping exercises of this kind tell us? One initial finding would be that there are rather fewer below-radar entities than claimed by previous studies. Unless one adopts a very catholic interpretation of community groups that encompasses almost any small and informal grouping, the upper limit of our estimates is some way below those of the New Economics Foundation and others. A second finding would be that the distribution and composition of third sector organizations varies between different types of communities, but we are a long way off a comprehensive understanding of the underlying processes. That is true *a fortiori* in the case of so-called below-radar organizations, where we are still at an early stage of mapping and measuring their distribution and impact. Other research, probably of a very intensive kind involving local case studies, will be needed here.[5] One possibility would be to follow up the study of local listings of third sector organizations with case studies in places which appear to have more (or fewer) such entities.

How might we understand variations in these distributions? A well-known metaphor in geographical research is that of 'rounds of investment'; in other words, the fortunes of regions and localities wax and wane depending on whether a particular location is attractive given the spatial division of labor at any point in time. That is likely to be very true of charitable organizations and associational activity of various kinds – whether this be philanthropic in intent, associated with political mobilization in defense of particular interests, or collectivist in orientation. Long-term studies of the dynamics of organizational growth and decline are needed here.

There are grounds for skepticism about whether simply mapping the distribution of associations and organizations tells us a great deal about social capital, as some commentators seem to suggest. The presence of an organization is no guarantee that it has public benefits. Multipurpose indicators of social capital, such as those developed by Rupasingha *et al.* (2006), have the failing that they aggregate large numbers of disparate kinds of organizations. In the work of Rupasingha *et al.*, a range of public and private clubs and facilities are combined with a global total of the number of nonprofit entities in a jurisdiction. But if the largest single type of nonprofit entity is residential property management companies, of which there are some 12,000 in England and Wales, it is difficult to see how social capital is generated through such entities or, if it is, what the mechanisms are and how they vary among different types of organizations. On the other hand, the presence of a range of small community organizations is more likely to generate the kind of face-to-face interaction beloved of social capital theorists. We need to specify the grounds on which we choose particular organizational types in relation to the purposes of a particular study.

Likewise, from the perspective of political scientists concerned with interest groups and public policy, the mere presence of an organization, as Halpin and Jordan note in Chapter 1, is not enough for all purposes: many researchers also want to look at the question of action in pursuit of public policy. Many small community organizations would fail this test. On the other hand, the Wolfenden Committee pointed out more than three decades ago that 'the soil for voluntary action is more fertile in some areas than others' (1978, p. 58), and if that is the case we should note the possibility that the future great oaks of civil society are currently lurking as seedlings below regulatory radars. Studies of the kind reported here might at least lay the foundations for understanding the dynamics of change in this underresearched area.

Notes

The material on which this chapter draws comes from research projects funded by the Northern Rock Foundation; the Economic and Social Research Council (ESRC), the Office of the Third Sector, and the Barrow Cadbury Trust (Third Sector Research Centre, www.tsrc.ac.uk); and the ESRC, the Office of the Third Sector, and the Scottish Office (Centre for Charitable Giving and Philanthropy, www.cgap.org.uk). I am grateful in particular to many local infrastructure bodies who supplied listings of voluntary organizations in the northern regions of England. I would like to acknowledge the support and advice of Rob Williamson and Penny Wilkinson of the Northern Rock Foundation, and of Mark Crowe of the Yorkshire and Humberside Regional Forum. The research was a collaborative venture with the National Council for Voluntary Organisations (NCVO), and I am grateful to Karl Wilding, David Kane, and Jenny Clark of the NCVO for their contribution to the work and constructive advice; to Ruth Beattie, who collated many of the local listings for us; and finally to Julia Branson (Geodata, Southampton) and Steve Barnard for their sterling efforts to devise solutions for de-duplicating complex lists of organizations.

1. In a way this is a surprising finding: the figure should arguably be 100 percent, since one of their distinguishing features is that governance is voluntary and unpaid, but for those who wish to check it, the survey data on which this claim is based are available from www.nstso.com.
2. The source for this is unpublished work with Peter Backus on long-term trends in the foundation of new charities. Contact the author for further details.
3. Note that the recently established Third Sector Research Centre is conducting a program of work on below-radar organizations that includes a detailed 'micro-mapping' exercise which focuses on areas even smaller than those covered in the LOVAS studies; see www.tsrc.ac.uk/Research/BelowtheRadarBtR/tabid/450/Default.aspx.
4. I am grateful to Steve McKay of the Third Sector Research Centre for this observation.
5. See some of the early work of the Third Sector Research Centre on this theme at www.tsrc.ac.uk/Research/BelowtheRadarBtR/tabid/450/Default.aspx.

References

Clifford, D. and J. Mohan (forthcoming) 'Neighbourhood Organizations: Evidence from the National Survey of Third Sector Organizations about Their Distribution, Characteristics and Resources', TSRC working paper, in preparation.

Fyfe, N. and C. Milligan (2003) 'Space, Citizenship and the 'Shadow State': Exploring the Voluntary Welfare Sector in Glasgow', *Environment and Planning C: Government and Policy*, 35, 2069–86.

Grønbjerg, K. and R. Clerkin (2005) 'Examining the Landscape of Indiana's Nonprofit Sector: Does What You See Depend on Where You Look?', *Nonprofit and Voluntary Sector Quarterly*, 34, 232–59.

Horton Smith, D. (1997) 'The Rest of the Non-Profit Sector: Grassroots Associations as the Dark Matter Ignored in Prevailing "Flat Earth" Maps of the Sector', *Nonprofit and Voluntary Sector Quarterly*, 26, 114–31.

Maloney, W., G. Smith, and G. Stoker (2000) 'Social Capital and Urban Governance: Adding a More Contextualised "Top-Down" Perspective', *Political Studies*, 48, 802–20.

McCabe, A. and J. Phillimore (2009) 'Exploring below the Radar: Issues of Theme and Focus', TSRC working paper no. 8; available from www.tsrc.ac.uk.

McGillivray, A., C. Wadhams, and P. Conaty (2001) *Low-Flying Heroes: Micro-social Enterprise below the Radar Screen* (London: New Economics Foundation).

Mohan, J. (2011) 'The Idea of a "Charity Desert": Effects of Methods of Assessing the Distribution of Charitable Resources across Communities in England and Wales', CGSP/TSRC working paper.

Mohan, J., D. Kane, J. Branson, and S. Barnard (2011) *Entering the Lists: What Can Be Learned from Local Listings of Third Sector Organizations*, report to the Northern Rock Foundation; available from www.nr-foundation.org.uk.

NAVCA and Audit Commission (2006) 'Getting to Know Your Local Voluntary and Community Sector: Developing Voluntary and Community Sector Profiles', available at www.navca.org.uk/NR/rdonlyres/9D87AB09-07E4-4959-89E2-25A2E0285E54/0/VCSProfiles.pdf.

Rupasingha, A., S. Goetz, and D. Freshwater (2006) 'The Production of Social Capital in US Counties', *Journal of Socioeconomics*, 35, 83–101.

Salamon, L. M. and H. K. Anheier (1996) *The Emerging Nonprofit Sector: An Overview* (Manchester: Manchester University Press).

Scheffler, R., T. Brown, L. Syme, I. Kawachi, I. Tolstykh, and C. Ibarren (2008) 'Community-Level Social Capital and Recurrence of Acute Coronary Syndrome', *Social Science and Medicine*, 66, 1603–13.

Smith, G., G. Stoker, and W. A. Maloney (2004) 'Building Social Capital in City Politics: Scope and Limitations at the Inter-organizational Level', *Political Studies*, 52, 508–30.

United Nations Department of Economic Affairs (2003) *Handbook on Nonprofit Institutions in the System of National Accounts*; available at http://unstats.un.org/unsd/publication/SeriesF/SeriesF_91E.pdf.

Wolfenden Committee (1978) *The Future of Voluntary Organizations: Report of the Wolfenden Committee* (London: Croom Helm).

11
Counting at the Local Level

Jan W. van Deth and William A. Maloney

As argued by Schlozman in Chapter 2 (see also Mohan, Chapter 10), one reason for trying to get a sense of scale of local organizations is that the democratic learning that is assumed to take place in groups is central to many arguments in the literature – most notably, the neo-Tocquevillean 'schools of democracy' thesis. The democratic lessons that take place within groups are most likely to occur in local organizations that offer opportunities for face-to-face interaction, rather than through 'pocket book participation' in national 'mail-order' bodies. This chapter reports the experience of conducting research on civic and political organizations active at the local level. It discusses the intellectual and logistical problems involved in researching the local and informal end of the organizational spectrum. The chapter describes an international collaborative project – Citizen, Involvement, Democracy (CID)[1] – to investigate local organizations and citizens' involvement in these associations using a top-down research approach.

Empirical research on the consequences and meaning of associational engagement usually focuses on individual features of participants or on the perceptions of activists. The most common strategy for this kind of research is bottom-up – that is, to interview citizens and decide on the basis of the information provided how to proceed with the research endeavor. If a respondent indicates that he or she is active in voluntary associations or works as a volunteer, additional questions are presented about the goals and circumstances of, and time devoted to, organizational activities. Bottom-up approaches obtain information about the respondent as well as the organization's activities from a single source, the respondent questioned. While such techniques are intuitive and useful, there are many pitfalls and limitations. An alternative approach is to gather information directly from the organizations themselves instead of relying on specific cases or subjective assessments and opinions. This strategy provides much more reliable and systematic contextual information. Moreover, it can be used to gather data from citizens affiliated to these groups about their attitudes and behavior and their direct organizational experiences. Accordingly, the CID project proceeded by analyzing the combined impact of (1) objective features of the specific associations concerned, (2) the type and scope of citizen engagement within these associations, and (3) the individual characteristics of participants. Integrating these various sources enables us to study the impact of organizational characteristics on individual voluntary orientations and behavior.

Comparative empirical research linking aspects of civil society and organizational features, on the one hand, to attitudes of people engaged in these associations, on the other, is very rare. To date comparative data of this kind have been collected only by the CID project. This project has three main parts: (1) a study of voluntary associations (the CID Organization Study), (2) a study of activists in selected voluntary associations (the CID Activists Study[2]), and (3) a study of citizens (the CID Population Study). This chapter begins by presenting the main characteristics of the CID Organization Study, which focused on the associational landscape of six European communities: Aalborg (Denmark), Aberdeen (UK), Bern (Switzerland), Enschede (The Netherlands), Mannheim (Germany), and Sabadell (Spain).[3] It then describes in detail the methodology used to map the associational universes in these six locales, providing empirical examples from the Aberdeen and Mannheim studies. In addition, the post-mapping process of collecting demographic data for each of the organizations found is explained. Finally, the integration of the CID Organization Study and the CID Activists Study with the CID Population Study is discussed and some of the main findings from the integrated data are presented.

Exploring local organizational landscapes

Finding communities and associations

The major innovative aspect of the CID research design is the generation of data that directly link the organizational context and the relevant activist, volunteer, member, or supporter; that is, the data locate individual citizens within their specific associational environment. The research design allows us to evaluate the impact of the organizational context (membership or staff size, participatory opportunities, budgets, etc.) on individual activity profiles (patterns of volunteering, group-based activities) and political and civic attitudes. In this respect the CID project represents an advance on previous studies that have focused on single organizations or samples of activists, volunteers, members, or supporters. It is also worth noting that our investigation of these local organizational landscapes is set in two contextual layers: first, the city/country where the associations and their members are located;[4] second, the associational universe. In the CID project the primary research context is the associational universe (discussed in detail below).

The research design combines elements of previous studies of organizational life at the local level. It builds upon primarily two different approaches. The first of these is citizen surveys that examine the attitudes and behavior of individuals with (local) organizational affiliations. This prior research has made a significant intellectual contribution to the academic literature. However, its value as a standalone approach is limited in two main ways: (1) the focus tends to be on formal organizations, and much important informal activity crucial for the generation of social capital is potentially missed or underrecorded (see Mohan, Chapter 10); (2) one key aim of our research is to connect the individual to the organizational context. Therefore, individual surveys need to be supplemented with surveys of organizations (formal and informal) – the second approach on which we build.

Several organizational surveys have been conducted over the last 50 years (e.g., Newton 1976; Hansen and Newton 1985; van Deth and Leijenaar 1994; Lelieveldt 1999; Maloney *et al.* 2000). These studies begin by mapping associational activity, but the focus tends to be on larger formal organizations. Accordingly, there is again a failure to capture much informal activity. Much added value can be gained from a research design that seeks to capture all associational activity – or to get pretty close to that goal – because it allows for greater confidence in drawing generalizations about the possible impacts of associational features on citizens' orientations and activities. In addition, capturing more informal associational activity allows for the measurement and assessment of the social capital generated within these 'looser' organizational structures. But, of course, the less formal the activity, the more challenging the task of recording it (see Font *et al.* 2007, pp. 20–22, for a more detailed discussion).

In the CID project organizations were selected as the unit of analysis because they play a crucial role as generators and/or facilitators and/or mediators of social and political participation. Associations are seen as making an important, multifaceted contribution to the functioning of democracies as vehicles for citizens' participation. In the post-social capital era, a vibrant and diverse associational life is increasingly perceived as a basic democratic necessity.

We chose six medium-sized municipalities[5] because they had associational universes that were large and diverse enough to provide the maximum variation of organizational types within the same (and varying) institutional structure(s). The areas included in the study had populations in excess of 100,000, a wide range of economic activities, a fully fledged educational system (with at least one university and, where applicable, a vocational school), a developed welfare system, a major hospital, and a cosmopolitan city centre. There were also pragmatic and logistical reasons for the choice of cities. The location of the researchers (all based in, or very close to, these cities) and their local information and contacts provided an efficient means to conduct this research. Indeed, such local embeddedness or connectedness means that the research teams have a good appreciation of several key characteristics, which allows more authoritative interpretation (Font *et al.* 2007, p. 20). The research design is predicated upon the assumption that these cities are appropriate venues for a comparative analysis of extensive associational universes. To illustrate the procedure a detailed account of the methodology as implemented in Aberdeen and Mannheim is presented here. This approach was also followed in the other four cities (see Font *et al.* 2007).

Aberdeen and Mannheim[6]

The UK and German parts of the CID project sought to assess the shape and structure of associational life in two medium-sized cities: Aberdeen (UK) and Mannheim (Germany). The research design covered three distinct steps: organizational mapping, organizational surveys, and an activist survey. First, exhaustive mapping of the organizational universes in Aberdeen and Mannheim was completed.[7] The mapping methodology took pains to get as close as possible to identifying all social and political organizations active in Aberdeen and Mannheim. Mapping went beyond a restricted focus on large or institutionalized groups. We aimed to capture as large as possible a proportion of formal and crucially active informal groups to provide a comprehensive map of the density, shape, and structure of these associational universes. Groups were identified through a wide variety of sources, and mapping was implemented in four discrete phases.[8] First, we contacted local authorities, journalists, other local bodies, and voluntary sector umbrella organizations to obtain basic information about the community organizations. Second, we conducted a documentary analysis by examining local authorities' and voluntary organizations' newsletters, citywide and local newspapers, and neighborhood leaflets and magazines. Third, we carried out detailed searches of local archives and registers, local directories of organizations and large institutions, telephone directories and Yellow Pages, local Web sites, and national Web addresses looking for national-level organizations with local branches or chapters. Fourth, there was a final consolidation and validation phase. We telephoned schools, churches, community centers, community education centers, and hospitals. During the validation and mapping processes we eliminated double-counting that resulted from organizations being listed in several directories. What made the process particularly challenging was that a specific group might appear under its acronym as well as its full name, or have 'The' prefixed to its name, or have its name misspelled. We also decided that we would not stop mapping until it became clear that we were repeatedly finding the same organizations. When we reached an unacceptable scale of diminishing returns, mapping was officially ended. However, we remained open to finding more associations even at that stage. The robustness and rigor of our mapping is evidenced by the fact that we generated the same organizational names several times from different sources. We also identified some *ad hoc* and ephemeral organizations. For example, in Aberdeen there was a local NIMBY (not in my back yard) group called STOP (Stop Tesco Opening Premises) opposing the opening of a supermarket in their neighborhood (see Maloney *et al.* 2001). We invested heavily in a comprehensive mapping exercise in both Aberdeen and Mannheim because it was critical for the methodological and theoretical robustness of the project that we identify as many associations as possible. We needed to maximize the variety of organizational types in terms not only of their goals but also of their organizational characteristics.

Once mapping was completed a postal survey of all organizations identified was conducted. The theoretical assumption was that different organizations would have a differential impact on their activists, volunteers, members, or supporters. In order to test this hypothesis we needed detailed information about institutional designs in terms of constitution, staffing levels, financial resources, membership size, activities, contacts and networks, income sources, main and subsidiary objectives, structure, and outputs.

The organization survey enabled us to identify organizations for the third stage of the project. Not all associations had to be involved in this step. A selection could be made from the groups of very similar organizations (e.g., sports clubs), but the inclusion of much smaller groups or unique organizations had to be guaranteed. A nonrepresentative sample was drawn on the basis of an empirical typology along seven variables or dimensions (Maloney *et al.* 2008, p. 266):

1. vertical integration (part of peak organization),
2. horizontal integration (summary measure of 'part of networks' and 'contact with other organizations'),
3. size (summary measure of membership levels, number of volunteers, number of clients, etc.),
4. degree of institutionalization,
5. political contacts,
6. financial strength, and
7. source of finance.

To select activists in each city a sample of organizations was drawn from the associational universe mapped by the CID Organization Study on the basis of an empirical typology of voluntary associations. The objective was to collect a subsample that contained all possible associational variations. Up to 20 organizations (if possible) were selected per issue area in each city on the basis of a carefully drawn sample. Extensive data analysis was carried out on both the original total and the sample taking into account the organizational features mentioned above. In cases where the sample did not include all types and organizational variations it was corrected. In this way, the selection procedure focused on representation of variations and not on representation of the population of voluntary associations or activists (see Maloney *et al.* 2008, p. 266, for a fuller discussion).

Choosing to locate individuals within their organizational contexts had logistical implications. It meant that we included the name of the organization in each question about the individual's organizational involvement. Accordingly, we produced 272 separate questionnaires in Aberdeen and 257 in Mannheim (one per organization in each sample). We wanted to ensure that respondents were continually reminded that they were being asked about their experience in a specific organization. A very small number of individuals had affiliations to several organizations and received a questionnaire for more than one organizational membership. In these cases we instructed them to select the group which they considered to be the most important to them and to complete only one questionnaire. It was crucial to ensure that respondents were clear when they were completing the survey that all of the questions related directly to a specific organization, because our aim was to assess the impact of organizational traits on various features of activism.

The questionnaires distributed among activists in many associations were mailed back to us directly without further involvement of the associations. In this way we surveyed their members' or supporters'

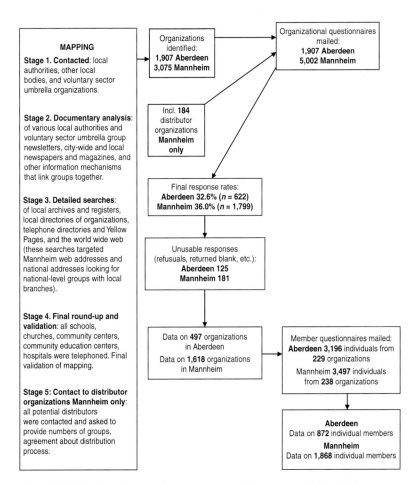

Figure 11.1 Methodology and response rates, Aberdeen and Mannheim

Note: See note 8 for an explanation of the fifth stage of mapping in Mannheim.

Source: Adapted from Maloney *et al.* (2001, pp. 78–79).

political and social trust and confidence, civic skills and attitudes, civic and political participation, social integration, and socioeconomic demographics. In addition to its more general aspects, the membership survey asked a series of questions relating to the specific organization in which the individual respondent was active. These included questions about activities within the organization, skills acquired, satisfaction with the organization, perceived impact of the respondent on several organizational traits and the management structure and procedures, time spent with the organization, attempts to change or improve the organization, importance of this organization in comparison to other areas of life, frequency and type of contact with other organizational members, and frequency of political discussions within the organization. For each respondent, then, we have extensive information about her or his social and political orientations and associational engagement based on the activists' questionnaire. Furthermore, we know in which organization the activities are carried out (see Maloney *et al.* 2008; Maloney and van Deth 2010). The main steps and the results obtained for the studies in Aberdeen and Mannheim are summarized in Figure 11.1.

Specifying the research object: defining a voluntary organization[9]

Definitional debates are not always the most fruitful academic activity. Nevertheless, it is important to specify the research object as clearly as possible. Given the expansive nature of the mapping exercise conducted in the CID project, providing a clear definition of voluntarism was crucial. We developed a structural operating definition of a voluntary association that shared several criteria with the definition used in the Johns Hopkins study on the voluntary sector (also see Mohan, Chapter 10). However, there were some important differences. (The definitional criteria set out here are based on and adapted from Kendall and Knapp 1996, p. 18.) To be included in our study an organization had to meet the following criteria. First, it could have a *formal or informal structure.* We did not require organizations to have a constitution or a formal set of rules. If we had insisted on such formal structures we would have excluded many neighborhood-based organizations, which are an integral part of European civic life. It was also theoretically important to map all political and social involvement in these cities. One of our key research questions was to assess the extent to which the level of 'civic vibrancy' in a locale is an important variable in accounting for the number and diversity of political and civic organizations. We deliberately targeted loosely structured and informal organizations because we saw no *a priori* reason why more informal groups would be less efficient in generating social capital. Second, organizations should be unequivocally *independent of government and self-governing*. Third, groups should be *not-profit-distributing and primarily nonbusiness*. However, we included voluntary associations of businesses (e.g., Chamber of Commerce, Federation of Small Businesses); these organizations may well undertake philanthropic civic activities in addition to the political advancement of business interest. Fourth, groups should be sustained by the *voluntary* activity of citizen involvement and *voluntary* philanthropic contributions. We adopted a wide definition of 'voluntary citizen involvement' to capture as much of the associational activity as possible. Kendall and Knapp (1996) excluded parent–teacher associations, leagues of hospital friends, and trust funds operating in support of National Health Service facilities because even though these bodies were constitutionally independent and many enjoyed charitable status, they funded public sector activities and facilities. However, we included these bodies because they were voluntary and independent and they supported the welfare state through contributions of time and money (see Kendall and Knapp 1996 for a fuller discussion; see also Maloney *et al.* 2001).

Some main characteristics of the associational universe in the six cities are summarized in Table 11.1. As can be seen, the number of voluntary associations found varies considerably among the cities. Since the CID project relied on implementing very similar research strategies

Table 11.1   The relative density of civil society in six cities

	Number of groups mapped	Number of inhabitants	Ratio of organizations to inhabitants	Relative density[a]
Aalborg[b]	2,031	161,661	1 per 80	12.6
Aberdeen	1,907	212,650	1 per 112	8.9
Bern	1,198	122,537	1 per 102	9.7
Enschede	1,658	150,499	1 per 91	11.0
Mannheim	5,002	319,944	1 per 64	15.6
Sabadell	1,129	185,270	1 per 164	6.1

[a]Number of organizations per 1,000 inhabitants.
[b]As mentioned in note 3, Aalborg (Denmark) was part of the CID Organization Study, but no data were collected at the activist level.
Source: Maloney and Roßteutscher (2007b, p. 41).

in each city the differences illustrated in Table 11.1 provide a reliable estimate of the distinct universes of voluntary associations.

Linking organizations, activists, and citizens[10]

Three major studies

As mentioned the CID project has three main parts: (1) a study of voluntary associations (the CID Organization Study), (2) a study of activists in selected voluntary associations (the CID Activists Study), and (3) a study of citizens (the CID Population Study). It should be noted that the last part of the activists' questionnaire, which dealt with orientations and behavior, was similar to the survey instrument used for the CID Population Study (see below).

The CID Population Study was developed in parallel to, but mainly independent of, the Organization and Activists Studies. The samples for the Population Study are all representative of the adult population of a number of European countries: 18 years old (and over), the minimum voting age in of all the countries in the study. Data were collected in 12 European countries (Denmark, Switzerland, [East and West] Germany, Russia, Portugal, Norway, Spain, The Netherlands, Slovenia, Moldova, Romania, and Sweden). An extensive survey instrument was designed that included a series of questions on several main topics, including political participation at different levels and in several areas, social participation and voluntary associations, engagement in 'small democracy' (workplace, health, education), social trust and confidence, political equality, and networks and social contacts.[11] Comparative analyses of citizens' orientations based on the full set of 13 societies were published in van Deth *et al.* (2007).

Integrating the three studies

The country-specific conditions for associational engagement can be seen as the first contextual layer for our analyses. Cross-national differences in this area have been documented in a number of empirical studies, and these findings are most likely to be corroborated by the six countries selected here. The second contextual layer consists of the particular cities and communities which provide the direct environment for the associations selected. The varying historical, institutional, and cultural settings of these six localities result in different associational universes but do not necessarily have consequences for the orientations or behavior of active members. The primary context here, however, is established by the specific associations and their impact on individual orientations and activities. The key research aim is to assess the impact of organizations on active members. Thus the challenge is to obtain an empirical assessment of the link between specific organizational characteristics and demographics, on the one hand, and the social and political orientations of active members, on the other. To this end, the first key task is to link the information from the Activists Study with that from the Organization Study. Second, in order to assess the similarities between active members of associations and average citizens, a link between the Activists Study and the Population Study is required.

Since the first two contextual layers (country and city/community) are only indirectly relevant for the primary context (voluntary associations), the empirical analyses are carried out for each country/city separately. In this way, the analyses are replicated six times and both the interrelationships between various factors and the levels or distributions of specific factors can be studied. For each country/city the three parts of the CID project are merged and extended. The Activists Study contains the most relevant information and is used as a starting point for the construction of the six integrated data sets:

1. The rectangular data set of activist information (see matrix A in Figure 11.2) consists of activists' responses to the questionnaire (one case for each activist). For a particular voluntary association V, let the number of activists be p.
2. For each volunteer or activist the specific organization, V, in which he or she is socially active is known. This information can be used to establish a link to the Organization Study.
3. The rectangular data set of organizations, however, consists of cases for organizations. In order to provide the organization information for each activist p within organization V the organizational information has to be replicated for each activist; that is, the information for organization V is provided p times in the expanded organizational data set (matrix B).
4. After the replication of the organizational information for organization V, each activist p obtains the same organizational information by simply merging the two matrices. In this way, the associational features of organization V are transformed into individual features of each active member p of organization V separately.
5. The merged data set (matrix A+B) can be used for the analysis of various features of individual activists (e.g., a comparison of the average age of activists in small and large associations or a comparison of associational resources available for men and women).

6. Since the new organizational data set (matrix B) is now weighted by the number of activists interviewed within each organization, the organizational features in the new data set should be handled very carefully.

The addition of the population information is the next step. The questionnaires for the activists and the citizens are similar, and so the

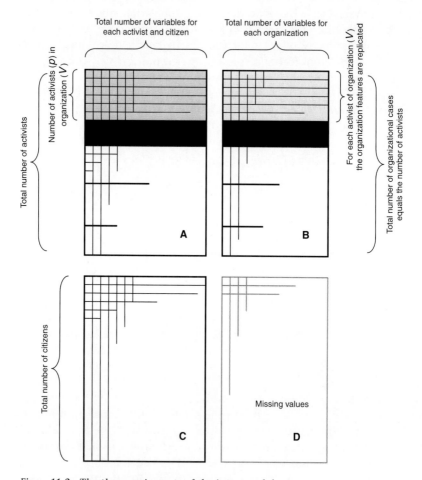

Figure 11.2   The three main parts of the integrated data set

Matrix A: Activists Study; Matrix B: expanded Organization Study; Matrix C: Population Study.

Source: van Deth and Maloney (2010, p. 11).

respective variables can be easily identified and matched. The rectangular data set for the Population Study (matrix C) can be used to expand the number of cases of the Activists Study (matrix A). In this way, the features of activists can be directly compared with corresponding features of average citizens (e.g., the difference in the level of education between activists and citizens or possible over- or underrepresentation of specific orientations among active members of voluntary associations as compared with other citizens). Although a number of the citizens interviewed indicated they were engaged in voluntary associations, none was active in one of the organizations in the Organization Study. For that reason the lower right-hand part of the resulting data set consists of missing values only (matrix D).

The resulting data set (matrix A+B+C+D) offers a large number of opportunities to relate features of activists to organizational characteristics and to compare them with the total population. By constructing similar data sets for each of the six countries/cities separately the contextual impacts on voluntary engagement can be compared among various areas systematically.

Activists, socially actives, and non-actives

By definition, the Activists Study contains information about citizens active in a voluntary association. Yet a substantial number of the citizens involved in the Population Study also indicated that they were actively involved in some association. For these respondents, however, the information about their activities is restricted to reported behavior and perceptions of organizational opportunities only. Therefore, the resulting integrated data set enables us to distinguish three types of citizens:

1. *Activists.* For these respondents of the Activists Study we have objective information about their activities and the specific organizational context. The fact that they are active in a voluntary association is not based on self-reporting, and their inclusion in our study is not based on self-selection.
2. *Socially actives.* These are respondents in the Population Study who explicitly indicate that they 'participate in activities' and/or 'do voluntary work' in at least one of the 27 types of associations presented. By excluding respondents who are members only or donate money for this group, the socially actives selected are, in principle, similar to the activists interviewed in the Activists Study. Yet being identified as a socially active depends on self-reporting only.

Table 11.2 Main characteristics of activists, socially actives, and non-actives in six cities and countries

	East Germany			West Germany			The Netherlands		
	Activists	Socially actives	Non-actives	Activists	Socially actives	Non-actives	Activists	Socially actives	Non-actives
Gender (% male)	53.95	51.29	43.88	53.21	47.45	39.30	62.04	45.73	48.23
Age (years, mean)	48.18	48.65	49.11	52.54	48.49	51.88	51.19	48.14	46.20
Education (% tertiary)	40.22	19.62	11.36	33.24	15.36	8.34	48.02	33.50	22.22
Political interest (1–4, mean)	2.90	2.82	2.21	2.99	2.61	2.18	2.74	2.66	2.42
Left–right placement (0–10, mean)	4.06	4.41	4.61	4.82	4.92	5.12	4.93	5.17	4.99
General trust (0–10, mean)	5.97	4.44	3.95	6.10	5.55	4.16	7.01	6.40	6.00
Satisfaction with democracy (1–4, mean)	2.25	2.49	2.31	2.72	2.97	2.85	2.98	3.00	2.91
Satisfaction with life (0–10, mean)	7.63	7.62	6.68	7.75	8.11	7.54	8.04	8.10	7.93
N (min)	1,196	390	483	1,773	1,043	699	423	938	601

	Spain[a]			Switzerland			United Kingdom		
	Activists	Socially actives	Non-actives	Activists	Socially actives	Non-active	Activists	Socially actives	Non-actives
Gender (% male)	49.72	52.66	46.17	55.50	47.86	41.40	37.88	37.82	41.82
Age (years, mean)	41.67	43.22	45.62	47.67	47.06	49.72	55.08	48.36	51.66
Education (% tertiary)	47.80	25.37	11.25	31.97	27.69	18.47	37.95	26.63	23.42
Political interest (1–4, mean)	2.53	2.16	1.71	2.75	2.76	2.48	2.71	n.a.	n.a.
Left-right placement (0–10, mean)	3.57	4.50	4.62	4.44	5.01	5.16	5.05	5.12	5.18
General trust (0–10, mean)	6.01	4.97	4.29	6.62	6.34	5.37	6.22	6.82	6.57
Satisfaction with democracy (1–4, mean)[b]	2.17	2.65	2.66	2.80	2.73	2.68	2.65	2.95	2.99
Satisfaction with life (0–10, mean)[b]	n.a.	7.67	7.40	8.08	8.31	8.10	8.03	3.90	3.84
N (min)	1,191	1,202	2,152	893	895	1,022	789	730	1,571

[a] Spanish data weighted.
[b] Satisfaction with democracy/Satisfaction with life in the UK population file scaled 1–5.

Source: van Deth and Maloney (2010: 14).

3. *Non-actives.* These are the respondents in the Population Study who neither volunteer nor participate in activities of voluntary associations. They can, however, be engaged in these organizations in less active ways. Being identified as non-active depends on self-reporting only.

Some main characteristics of activists, socially actives, and non-actives are summarized in Table 11.2 for each of the six countries/cities considered here. As can be seen, the three categories show repetitive differences when we go from the evidently active respondents to the self-reported activists and then to those who are not clearly involved. Compared with other groups, activists tend to be relatively highly educated, relatively interested in politics, more supportive of left-wing positions, and relatively satisfied with democracy and their life as a whole. However, even a cursory glance at these findings shows that the differences between the various countries/cities are considerable.

Main findings from the integrated analysis of activists, socially actives, and non-actives[12]

In this section we outline the main research questions and some of the key research findings from the fully integrated CID project – that is, the analysis of the data from activists, socially actives, and non-actives. Some findings from the research of our colleagues are presented here as examples of the substantive results obtained from the integrated CID data.

Bernhagen and Maloney (2010) examined the extent to which associations with internally democratic features can be portrayed as better schools of democracy than organizations lacking these characteristics. Their evidence presented a significant challenge to the 'school of democracy' perspective by showing that the democratic characteristics of associations were *at best* marginally related to individual political participation. The political participation levels of activists were comparable irrespective of whether they were members of formally or behaviorally democratic associations or nondemocratic groups. Accordingly, if voluntary associations act as schools of democracy, inculcating and enhancing participatory habits and civic attitudes, then nondemocratic organizations are as efficient (or inefficient) as their democratic counterparts. Van Deth (2010) drew a similar conclusion, suggesting that it would be more accurate to speak of 'schoolyards of democracy' than of schools of democracy. Discriminating between democratic and nondemocratic associations is irrelevant for the development of democratic attitudes among active members of these organizations. Membership of any organizational type will do.

Lelieveldt (2010) and Dayican *et al.* (2010) examined the impact of various associational characteristics on intra-organizational efficacy (Lelieveldt) and sense of political efficacy – or 'subjective political empowerment' (Dayican *et al.*). Lelieveldt speculated that members who feel they are able to affect decisions are also more likely to exhibit higher participation levels in decision-making processes. His results demonstrated that there is a substantial amount of participation in organizational management and decision making among the activists and socially actives; hence, unsurprisingly, efficacy and participation are strongly related. However, individual-level background variables and organizational factors appear to have very little impact on participation rates. Individuals heavily involved in running organizations are also most likely to possess the highest levels of intra-organizational efficacy, and those on the organizational margins the lowest. In their complementary analysis Dayican *et al.* (2010) identified a strong relationship between membership and activism and empowerment, and found that citizens involved in different types of political organizations feel more politically empowered. They also discovered (somewhat unsurprisingly) that membership of various types of political organizations is related to political efficacy. This led them to consider the direction of causality: that is, does such membership increase political efficacy (the social capital model) or are politically efficacious citizens more likely to join political organizations (the self-selection thesis)? They concluded that self-selection was most likely for political organizations. However, Dayican *et al.* advocated caution here, arguing that there is likely to be a process of reciprocal causation. While it may be the case that relatively self-confident individuals are more likely to join political organizations, there remains the distinct possibility that through membership they may enhance their political self-confidence. Self-selection, then, is clearly a significant factor in explaining why self-confident people are likely to be active in voluntary associations, but the associational impact cannot be fully discounted.

Van Deth (2010) and Caiani and Ferrer-Fons (2010) addressed the issue of political interest in the European Union. Van Deth (2010) analyzed whether active participation has a differential effect on interest in European politics (compared with interest in local, national, and international politics) and whether organizational characteristics (size, formal structure, resources) are relevant for the development of political interest and willingness to engage in political discussions. Caiani and Ferrer-Fons assessed whether associational participation *per se*, higher participation levels, or different associational characteristics (size, resources, formal structure) and concerns (welfare, politics, environment) affect the levels of interest and trust in European politics among activists. Van Deth (2010) discovered that while large cross-national differences in political interest were prevalent, there remained a consistent pattern of interest among the three groups of respondents (activists, socially actives, and non-actives). The level of political interest is highest among activists, a bit lower in the socially active category, and lowest among the non-active group. Caiani and Ferrer-Fons (2010) found some evidence that while associational activity contributed to a more engaged European citizen, it did not generate only fully supportive Euro-enthusiasts, but also more critical Europeanists. However, when they assessed the relative impact of associational characteristics, engagement levels, and individual features of activists on different types of support for Europe, they discovered that engagement levels and organizational features were unimportant. The crucial aspect that explained support for Europe was at the individual level. Accordingly, their key finding lends some support to the self-selection hypothesis; that is, 'associations attract people with specific individual features and that explains the associational impact on attitudes towards Europe' (Caiani and Ferrer-Fons 2010, p. 153). In this way, their conclusion evidently is in line with the findings presented by Dayican *et al.* (2010) that self-selection can be an important explanation for the reciprocal relationship between voluntary associations and their active members.

A final general conclusion can be based on Iglič's (2010) analysis of the strength of social integration and quality of social relations within associations. Do associations characterized by high levels of social integration facilitate identification with bodies such as Europe? Alternatively, do these types of organizations bolster more locally based identities and possibly even thwart more distant identifications? Iglič found that associational involvement did strengthen European identity: organizations that had frequent political communication and high levels of social integration built European identity. She also found that organizations that were smaller in scope, such as neighborhood or locally based groups, generated strong pro-European attachment – more so that bigger groups engaged in wider networks. Iglič's analysis demonstrated an inverse relationship between locally or regionally based identities and those based on geographically larger identities such as the nation-state or Europe. Citizens who are not strongly embedded in any type of organized social network, but who are younger and more highly educated and have high levels of confidence in European institutions also exhibit high levels of attachment to Europe.

Conclusion

Counting associations at the local level and interviewing activists is a time-consuming task. Expanding this task to cover the associational universe in several large cities across Europe implies the active engagement of many researchers and assistants over a long period. The question that should be addressed is whether the use of these resources is justifiable. In short, does collecting information about organizations, activists, and citizens contribute to our understanding of the impact of voluntary associations in democratic societies?

Each of the three parts of the CID project provided information about a specific aspect of the role of voluntary activities. Whereas the Population Study enabled us to explore the individual antecedents of social and political orientations and behavior, the Organizational Study provided detailed information about the associational universe across Europe. However, the advantages of the complex design of the CID project become especially apparent when the Activists Study is considered and the three parts of the project are integrated. First, it is clear that conventional data-collection methods that rely on interviewing randomly selected people about their associational activities underestimate the relevance of these activities for their social and political orientations and behavior. Reliable information in this area, then, can be obtained only if a top-down approach is selected that starts with organizations and interviewing people active within a specific organization. Survey research among randomly selected people provides no more – but also no less – than reports about situations and conditions known to the respondent only. Survey research, however, should not be seen as a second-order surrogate for studying associational context. If we want to study that context, mapping the associational universe is the point to start with.

Second, analyzing integrated information about organizations, activists, and populations in a cross-national setting shows that the still fashionable neo-Tocquevillean approaches are clearly underspecified. As the results of the CID project show, individual features of people are usually much more relevant for their social and political orientations and behavior than opportunities for engagement provided by various voluntary associations. Only a carefully planned and extensive project

242   *Jan W. van Deth and William A. Maloney*

is able to provide appropriate empirical information required to test expectations and speculations. But who said that counting at the local level would be an easy task?

Notes

1. The Citizenship, Involvement, Democracy (CID) network was funded by the European Science Foundation; see www.mzes.uni-mannheim.de/projekte/cid or the edited volumes by van Deth *et al.* (2007) and Maloney and Roßteutscher (2007a) for further information and acknowledgments. Some sections of this chapter draw on previously published research with CID colleagues, and we acknowledge these outputs at the relevant points.
2. We use the 'activist' label for this survey, but we are fully aware that the respondents cover several categories, including active and passive members, volunteers, donors, and supporters.
3. Aalborg (Denmark) was part of the CID Organization project, but since data were collected only at the organizational level and not at the activist level we have excluded it from our discussion here.
4. With regard to the first layer it is, of course, crucial to recognize that associational universes are located in specific cultural, economic, social, and political contexts that impact its shape, structure and *modus operandi*.
5. In three of the six countries (Germany, Spain, and Switzerland) more than one municipality has been researched. The choice of the municipalities was based on factors such as size and cultural, linguistic, and regional cleavages. The additional locales are not considered here.
6. This section draws extensively on Font *et al.* (2007) and Maloney *et al.* (2001); see also Maloney *et al.* (2008).
7. One potential criticism of our decision to map associational universes in medium-sized cities is that we should have selected even larger metropolitan areas because there will be more organizations in a city of 1 or 2 million people than in one with 100,000 inhabitants. However, mapping such areas would be extremely labor-intensive, and the payoff would probably not justify the cost. It is highly likely that one can uncover close to the same organizational diversity in medium-sized cities as in metropolitan centers. There will, of course, be many more organizations in metropolitan centers, but not necessarily greater diversity. There is also a greater possibility of overlooking some crucial associational features in such large areas.
8. In Manheim, a fifth mapping stage proved to be necessary because some umbrella organizations (e.g., self-help and religious organizations) were reluctant to provide the contact details for local branches and chapters. The Mannheim team solved this problem by recruiting a trusted volunteer to coordinate the distribution of questionnaires to the local branch in these areas without providing the research team with contact names and addresses. The Mannheim team faced a simple choice. Either make use of the trusted coordinator to distribute the survey or fail to reach a large number of self-help groups and religiously affiliated organizations active in Mannheim. The Mannheim team knew this solution was not risk-free, but they believed the payoff of reaching a larger and more diverse range of groups was justified.

9. This section draws extensively on Maloney *et al.* (2001).
10. This section draws extensively on van Deth and Maloney (2010).
11. An integrated data set is available. Data from the CID Population Study can be obtained from the Zentral Archiv in Cologne, study number 4492 (http://info1.za.gesis.org/DBKSearch12/SDesc2.asp?no=4492&search=CID&search 2=&db=E). For the UK the situation is more complicated, since country representatives from Britain dropped out of the CID project at an early stage. However, they subsequently developed the Citizen Audit of Great Britain (www.data-archive.ac.uk/findingData/snDescriptionasp?sn=5099), and these data can be used as a surrogate data set for the UK population (see Pattie *et al.* 2004).
12. This section draws extensively on Maloney and van Deth (2010).

References

Bernhagen, P. and W. A. Maloney (2010) 'Civil Society Organizations as "Little" Democracies?', in W. A. Maloney and J. W. van Deth (eds.) *Civil Society and Activism in Europe: Contextualizing Engagement and Political Orientations* (London: Routledge).
Caiani, M. and M. Ferrer-Fons (2010) 'Voluntary Associations and Support for Europe', in W. A. Maloney and J. W. van Deth (eds.) *Civil Society and Activism in Europe: Contextualizing Engagement and Political Orientations* (London: Routledge).
Dayican, B., B. Denters, and H. van der Kolk (2010) 'Associations and Political Empowerment', in W. A. Maloney and J. W. van Deth (eds.) *Civil Society and Activism in Europe: Contextualizing Engagement and Political Orientations* (London: Routledge).
Font, J., P. Geurts, W. A. Maloney, and M. Berton (2007) 'Organizations in Context: Politics and Culture Shaping Associational Life', in W. A. Maloney and S. Roßteutscher (eds.) *Social Capital and Associations in Europe: A Comparative Analysis* (London: Routledge).
Hansen, T. and K. Newton (1985) 'Voluntary Organizations and Community Politics: Norwegian and British Comparisons', *Scandinavian Political Studies*, 8, 1–21.
Iglič, H. (2010) 'The Relational Basis of Attachment to Europe', in W. A. Maloney and J. W. van Deth (eds.) *Civil Society and Activism in Europe: Contextualizing Engagement and Political Orientations* (London: Routledge).
Kendall, J. and M. Knapp (1996) *The Voluntary Sector in the UK* (Manchester: Manchester University Press).
Lelieveldt, H. (1999) *Wegen naar macht: Politieke participatie en toegang van het maatschappelijk middenveld op lokaal niveau* (Amsterdam: Thela Thesis).
Lelieveldt, H. (2010) 'Governing Associations: Member Involvement and Efficacy towards Associational Decision-Making', in W. A. Maloney and J. W. van Deth (eds.) *Civil Society and Activism in Europe: Contextualizing Engagement and Political Orientations* (London: Routledge).
Maloney, W. A. and S. Roßteutscher (eds.) (2007a) *Social Capital and Associations in Europe: A Comparative Analysis* (London: Routledge).
Maloney, W. A. and S. Roßteutscher (2007b) 'The Associational Universe in Europe: Size and Participation', in W. A. Maloney and S. Roßteutscher (eds.)

Social Capital and Associations in Europe: A Comparative Analysis (London: Routledge).

Maloney, W. A. and J. W. van Deth (eds.) (2010) *Civil Society and Activism in Europe: Contextualizing Engagement and Political Orientations* (London: Routledge).

Maloney, W. A., G. Smith, and G. Stoker (2000) 'Social Capital and Urban Governance: Adding a More Contextualized "Top-Down" Perspective', *Political Studies*, 48, 802–20.

Maloney, W. A., L. Stevenson, M. Berton, S. Roßteutscher, and J. W. van Deth (2001) 'Welfare through Organizations: A Comparative Analysis of British and German Associational Life', Anglo-German Foundation end of award report.

Maloney, W. A., J. W. van Deth, and S. Roßteutscher (2008) 'Civic Orientations: Does Associational Type Matter?', *Political Studies*, 56(2), 261–87.

Newton, K. (1976) *Second City Politics: Democratic Processes and Decision-Making in Birmingham* (Oxford: Clarendon Press).

Pattie, C., P. Seyd, and P. Whiteley (2004) *Citizenship in Britain: Values, Participation and Democracy* (Cambridge: Cambridge University Press).

van Deth, J. W. (2010) 'Schools and Schoolyards: The Associational Impact on Political Engagement', in W. A. Maloney and J. W. van Deth (eds.) *Civil Society and Activism in Europe: Contextualizing Engagement and Political Orientations* (London: Routledge).

van Deth, J. W. and M. H. Leijenaar (1994) *Maatschappelijke participatie in een middelgrote stad. Een exploratief onderzoek naar activiteiten, netwerken, loopbanen en achtergronden van vrijwilligers in maatschappelijke organisaties* (Rijswijk, Netherlands: SCP).

van Deth, J. W. and W. A. Maloney (2010) 'Introduction: Contextualizing Civil Societies in European Communities', in W. A. Maloney and J. W. van Deth (eds.) *Civil Society and Activism in Europe: Contextualizing Engagement and Political Orientations* (London: Routledge).

van Deth, J. W., J. R. Montero, and A. Westholm (eds.) (2007) *Citizenship and Involvement in European Democracies: A Comparative Analysis* (London: Routledge).

12
Politics Is Not Basketball: Numbers Are Not Results

Grant Jordan and Darren Halpin

The original intention underpinning this book was to address both the 'what' and the 'how' of researching numbers and groups: to set out conclusions from recent research but, just as importantly, to provide something of a manual anticipating practical issues that will need to be faced in future research. In scholarly enterprises, one can easily start off with hopes of seamless synthesis, but this volume is as much about celebrating diversity as looking for coherence. So great is the diversity captured that in reflecting on the messages of the contributions, one cannot escape asking whether there is a common scholarly enterprise stretching from Mohan's search for community activity 'below the radar' in England to Schlozman's tracking of organizational activity in Washington. However, on balance, the conclusions are positive. While the volume of course leaves us short of a full understanding of the pattern of groups, organized interests, and associations in different countries over time, we can now much more clearly see the issues that set that up as an unrealistic aim. The chapters focus on activity at different levels – supranational, national, subnational, and local. They span different institutional arenas – legislative, media, administrative, and legal. And they focus on counting efforts guided by different (defensibly so) approaches. A single overarching research approach is unlikely to meaningfully capture this scope.

The process of counting leads to conclusions that might have emerged without empirical work – but did not. The empirical processes prompt all kinds of reconsiderations of definitions and boundaries and throw up theoretical issues beyond the value of the quantification itself. In that sense, the material in the volume transcends best guesses and moves us closer to firmer empirical rules of thumb. As noted by Jordan *et al.* in Chapter 7, ' "wrong" numbers which develop the debate can be more useful than no numbers'; it is this ethos that permeates the contributions to this volume. Getting numbers 'right' will not happen in one research project; if 'right' emerges, it will be at the end of competing approaches and repeated efforts. This is a start. But the modesty about results can be overdone. It is important to note the emergence through the chapters of a broad sense of the differences among certain countries in terms of expanding or stable populations. Furthermore, we have sufficient pointers to sense that there are major general shifts afoot in terms of, say, the representation of business or the expansion of 'cause' organizations. As discussed below, numerous chapters – regardless of level of analysis – seem to point to a less dominating place for business (in terms of numbers of participants). Instead (Halpin *et al.*, Chapter 6), we find a rise of public institutions, as foreshadowed in the work of Salisbury (1984), and more generally there is evidence of increased citizen group activity, as noted by Berry (1999).

Similarly, we can start to discuss changing patterns of group diversity and how similar or different they are cross-nationally. The literature has perhaps broadly split into camps of pluralist and (neo) corporatist expectations. The former camp anticipates fluid populations with no obvious core, and where key players are not always easy to find. In contrast, the latter expects small, well-organized, and settled populations of interest groups.[1] The contributions suggest the former rather than the latter as a contemporary style. All regimes studied appear complicated and densely populated. Where, now, the corporatist simplicity?

This 'story' is not simply a byproduct of methods or of history. For, as the Danish contribution notes (Christiansen, Chapter 8), even in a fairly strong corporatist system, these corporatist interactions with the state were always limited to a small number of policy sectors, and thus other sectors were always more diverse and volatile (pluralist?). The finding for Denmark is that counting is easier than for pluralist situations, but then still not that easy, which underlines the need to rethink the expectations that inform comparative work. Paradoxically, counting groups may be more difficult in open democracies than in some other situations. A case with a relatively precise and countable group population and perhaps fewer rather than more groups (two dimensions) might be an authoritarian and regimented regime.

Having secured various numbers in different chapters, the volume effectively emphasizes that politics is not a basketball game where the running totals tell you who is ahead and where who has more is declared the winner. Instead, social scientists securing group numbers are (at best) more like doctors using temperatures in diagnosis. Increases or falls could mean many things, and there is no direct line between metric and prescription. But the doctor would prefer to have the statistic in the overall analysis. Nevertheless, the assumption that numbers are sufficient and make other criteria redundant is hard to break. In particular, the data undermine the idea that business power can be 'read' from business group numbers: numbers give us some sense of magnitude, but not a scale of power and influence. Numbers do of course give us some sense of magnitude, but of what? Our sense is that they are best deployed to challenge conventional wisdom and articles of faith long held but not often tested. For instance, Salisbury's reminder that interest groups may not be the most common participants in policy processes and in interest representation was given some force by his illustration with (some crude) mapping data. Arguably, his point was obvious enough, but then again, generations had concluded otherwise, content to see interest groups as the only interests in the game. Taking Schlozman's approach, a more realistic assessment of organizational headcounts is that of 'voice'. When one is assessing policy data, a headcount of an organization is literally a count of presence in a policy arena, and thus one might reasonably argue that this indicates the range of opinion in the debate. But, of course, *whose* voice counts cannot be resolved by maps alone.

Groups as the canaries of democracy?

One major justification for counting populations is a keen sense that organized interests and interest groups constitute an important avenue for linking society to policy makers. In a democratic society, a vibrant and fluid system might be viewed, from a normative perspective, as a positive finding. Accordingly, a fall in the number of groups would raise questions, perhaps, about some clamp-down by the state against possible opposition. The reduction in itself would not resolve the questions, but it would flag a situation that needed investigation. A fall in group totals might be an *indicato*r of a (possible) democratic problem, as a canary in a mine indicates air quality deterioration, but it would not be conclusive on its own and would require supporting evidence. The volume shows that some reductions are about increasing the influence of interests by reducing the organizational 'noise' and maximizing the increasingly limited organizational resources. A reduction could mean reorganization to produce more effective group representation. Nonetheless, there is no sense in the various chapters that an associational world with low entry costs and limited restrictions is other than a democratic 'good'.

The primary rationale for work in this area is to try to get a sense of what is happening in terms of associational or group numbers. Interpretation is the next stage. Mapping might identify the absence of organizational representation where it would be expected. For instance, as the salience of the issue of migration rises in Western Europe, groups could be expected to emerge to voice the views of these migrant constituencies (and, of course, of those who oppose them). This might be especially acute where migrants and asylum seekers are electorally marginalized or even without franchise. Numbers can tell us whether such groups are present; even better, numbers over time can tell us whether and when these groups emerge. But as Mohan observes in Chapter 10, not only is it difficult to draw conclusions about influence from population headcounts, but there are also problems with interpreting densities in relation to social benefits such as social outcomes. He says, 'A strong civil society can no doubt have beneficial social outcomes, but whether maps of organizational densities should be taken at face value is surely questionable.' Numbers are an element in an assessment, not a straight-line indicator.

A rapid expansion of groups in an area may signal, or perhaps even cause, a new policy agenda that leads to changes in public policy, but the explosion in numbers may be the result of changed public policy: policy causes politics. *A priori* argument does not clarify the sequence. Either way the link between group numbers and policy activity (or even change) is not likely to be clear. Certainly, classic mobilizations such as the anti-slavery or anti-Prohibition movements *preceded* change, but other mobilizations have been less effective (and thus mostly less studied). Mobilizations to oppose nuclear weapons proliferation are perhaps a case in point of policy begetting politics.

All of this draws attention to explanatory approaches to emergence and subsequent patterns of policy mobilization by organized interests. Population ecology (PE) has had a strong influence on the field, arguing that environmental changes shape within-population dynamics and thus the contours (or density) of populations (see Lowery, Chapter 3; Nownes, Chapter 5). As argued by Halpin and Jordan (2009), the basic animal population material of biologically based PE is not a perfect analogy for groups, as group leaders are able to reposition their organizations more nimbly than animal populations.[2] The natural sciences ecological model tracking species dynamics emphasizes competition over finite resources and partitioning of such resources; populations need to be of the same species to be usefully analyzed in this approach. Thus, groups need to be 'ecologically equivalent' in order for ecological models to be persuasively applied. Group research perhaps closest to this ideal is that conducted on organizational formation and disbandment which utilizes specific *organizational* theories of density dependence (see Nownes, Chapter 5).[3]

In his chapter, Nownes suggests that the term 'community' be used to denote a set of organizations that share the same policy space (but not necessarily the same policy orientation). Communities – unlike populations (in the PE sense) – consist of policy participants that organize or represent a broad range of interests that may compete for public policy outcomes. What they have in common is that they operate in, say, agricultural, health, or education policy (or some subdomain thereof). 'Populations', he suggests, ought to refer to a set of organizations that share the same basic resource environment: they compete with other population members for resources that are critical to sustaining them. In the group world, this is essentially financial support through members, supporters, and patrons. But it might also extend to competition over limited places as 'the' representative or spokesgroup for a given constituency or policy viewpoint.

In this context, and referring to Nownes' distinction, it seems that such models are most relevant to explaining organizational birth and death – that is, the formation and disbandment of organizations – within related populations. While studies show some explanatory value in using ecologically inspired models to understand changes in same-constituency competitor organizations, does the same ecological metaphor provide plausible mechanisms for the type of negative feedback systems that would regulate overall populations of competing groups in broad lobbying networks? PE illuminates problems and generates fresh expectations, but it should not be subject to an un-nuanced transfer from the biological to social sciences. Perhaps the commercial behavior of firms in markets is better suited as an analogy for group scholars.

In an interest group context, this means that populations are defined according to whether they contend for the same constituency. For instance, one would be justified in talking of a 'population' of gay and lesbian groups because they share a common desire to enhance the rights of gay and lesbian persons. Changing the language, they are brands in the same market. In contrast, a gay and lesbian 'community' would include all policy participants engaged in this area, which would presumably cover groups opposed to gay rights. This distinction raises some important issues with respect to applying theories to population data. As Lowery argues in his contribution, there is a need to think carefully about the data we plan to gather, and the research design for collection needs to reflect the use it is intended to serve.

Organized interests/pressure participants – including interest groups – seem more similar to organizations and firms than to birds and kangaroos. In other words, like firms, groups *respond* to their competition in different ways (see, e.g., Young 2010). Groups can seek out different income streams, can develop specialist skills and interests, can merge with competitors, and so on. In short, unlike animals adapting to ecological conditions, groups (and entrepreneurs of groups) have considerable agency in interpreting and attending to environmental change and challenges.

Getting to a sense of scale: prior concerns as shaping definitions

In trying to generate reliable numbers, one of the most basic, yet problematic, tasks in working with the whole enterprise of group, associational, or organized interest populations is how to draw the boundaries. Various contributors to this volume illustrate the unavoidable dilemmas. What is in and what is out?

The prior issue, though, is the underlying purpose of the count. Many political scientists probably accept the idea that public policies are in part shaped by collective action bodies that represent constituencies of members. It then seems natural in describing the political universe to want to get a feel for the number of groups, and to discover why some are more influential than others. But there is the question of what binds these organizations together such that it makes sense to take them as a unit of analysis.

Constituents/members might want benefits from the political system (e.g., pensioners seeking pension increases or a public sector trade union wanting terms and conditions of employment protected), or they might want a value advanced politically (e.g., abortion or anti-abortion). The constituents might want action to improve the lot of third parties such as endangered animals or abused children, or they might want simply to show solidarity with the interests of others they care about. The collective constituents might be firms wanting competitors restricted or regulations relaxed. In other words, there are a variety of kinds of groups embroiled in chaotic processes, but to count the relevant population one needs to refine the specific question being pursued (see Lowery, Chapter 3). The practical conclusion is that sensibly different underlying purposes suggest consequentially different boundaries in counting exercises. This, though, is a huge issue – *before* the researcher hits the next barrier of *how* to count for any understanding. Researchers interested in different problems are likely to have different casts in mind: there is no guarantee that different projects will have identical interests and choose to register identically defined participants. In other words, pressure participants recorded in any exercise are likely to be those that seem to be of interest in that particular project; there is no generally accepted list of participants that stands apart from the particular and which all 'normal' research would measure. This is not to say that with care and reservations, sensible comparisons cannot be made, but it is not a routine, unthinking kind of comparison.

Different research questions imply different phenomena to count: is the goal to count all cause groups, self-interest groups, or organized interests more broadly, and how is each to be defined empirically? And, of course, this decision may be effectively determined by access to an immediately available data source. But is the source really coincident with the definition that would best satisfy the research goal? Again, there are cases where interesting findings can be extracted by exploiting existing data, but care is obviously needed in interpretation.

The volume has suggested two very broad perspectives underpinning inclusion decisions. One is the recording of empirical action as a signal of relevance for political science analysis: actors are the subject of the counting. The other approach is more about organizational structure: is there a formally organized collective actor to be included? In this latter approach, structure rather than action is the essential requirement. These are very different exercises, but to date the evidence seems to suggest that the take-away conclusions are in similar ballparks (with predictable differences).

By way of illustration, Figure 12.1 reports data on changes in the population of policy-active interest groups in Scotland (see Halpin *et al.*, Chapter 6 for details). The data here are calculated as a three-year moving average, which requires one full year before and after the year being calculated, so we start with 1983 and end with 2005. This allows us to map any organizations active *at least once* in a rolling three-year period. The method substantially reduces (but does not eliminate) any potential distortions that lurk in the pooled data arising from organizational disbandment, name changes, and mergers.[4] Perhaps the most salient observation here is that over a 25-year period, the overall number of unions has been very constant, with levels of professional bodies and trade associations growing moderately. In contrast, the citizen group

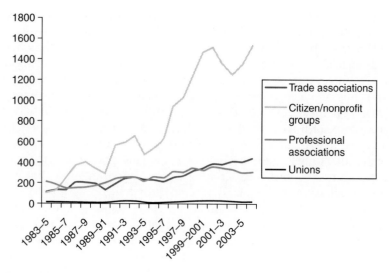

Figure 12.1   Frequency of interest group types in Scotland, 1983–2005

population has grown almost year on year. To reiterate, this type of data counts active groups in a rolling three-year period; the groups counted in 1983 may be different from those in 1985, and so on. This activity-based measure is a very different sort of lens from the directory-based studies reported in this volume (see Jordan and Greenan, Chapter 4; Jordan *et al.*, Chapter 7), but the results can be seen as reflecting the same underlying processes and tendencies. This style of triangulation only strengthens confidence in the broad message. And, in so doing, it underlines the value of allowing for a broad range of methods and data approaches.

Pressures on group numbers

One of the difficulties in getting a handle on the numbers that mapping produces is regulating our expectations. In this respect, perhaps the biggest hurdle is the discussion around the rise and fall of group and organized interest numbers.

Driving numbers up?

As set out by Jordan *et al.* in Chapter 7, there is a well-developed assumption that group numbers are growing inexorably – the explosion thesis. One important source establishing these expectations was David Truman's *The Governmental Process* (1951). This contribution was undermined by Olson (1965), leading to the marginalization of Truman; nonetheless, Truman was a powerful influence in framing notions about growth. He both reflected and prompted an idea of irresistible automatic growth. He drew attention to the 'rapid proliferation of associations in recent years' (1951, p. 66). He noted 'the tremendous growth in the number of formally organized groups in the United States within the last few decades' (p. 47) and commented upon the 'sort of mosaic of groups ... a bewildering array of groups' (p. 32). He presented a picture of groups emerging 'spontaneously' as a result of new circumstances, 'In compensation for disturbances in the equilibrium of existing institutionalized groups' (p. 32). Truman saw group emergence prompt other mobilizations to try to restore 'stability', so group emergence often occurred in waves. Truman's suggestion was that increased technological, economic, and other change increases the level of representable interests. He saw economic interests as often stemming from the rapid and extensive change in technical methods in industry (p. 61). Certainly, developments such as solar, wind, and other renewable energies have sponsored group proliferation, just as Truman anticipated. In the UK, for instance, the 'solar power solution' sustains the British Photovoltaic Association, the Renewable Energy Association, the Glass and Glazing Federation, the Network for Alternative Technology and Technology Assessment, the Scottish Solar Energy Group, the Solar Trade Association, and the Solar Energy Group.

Another specific pressure to increased numbers was noted by Heinz *et al.* (1993, pp. 375–76). They remarked on a tendency for niches and individual businesses to self-represent and not rely wholly on umbrella or peak organizations. They said, 'peak organizations cannot always satisfy the policy preferences of their diverse constituencies. Larger associations tend to take positions that minimize internal conflict, thus encouraging specialized interests to develop independent strategies' (p. 376). This suggests a potential complementarity to the work of general umbrella business groups and the sectoral specialists.

Downward pressures?

There are a various reasons to quickly reject any idea of tendencies toward infinite replication and proliferation within the associational and organized interest world. There is (as PE rightly suggests) likely to be some competition for market share for support which prevents groups proliferating ceaselessly. Larger groups can emerge to squeeze out the smaller groups. This might be enhanced by governments *de facto* granting representational quasi-monopoly to small numbers of groups, and this privileged access undercuts the membership appeal for some other groups – though, of course, avoiding too-close contact with government is positive for some potential members. The bias toward larger groups at the cost of smaller ones is reinforced as more successful groups gain a higher profile that in turn attracts enhanced support: common sense suggests it is easier to recruit a sympathetic potential supporter to a prominent group than a low-key example. And larger groups can make use of proactive recruitment techniques that are important in explaining modern 'supportership'. There are economies of scale in, say, research backup or top-level executives if groups in a similar field merge. This pressure is directly opposite to the fragmentation tendency noted by Heinz *et al.* (1993), but which factor wins out is at best explained by organizational fashion – and possibly only by randomness.

Although there may be pressures to simplify the representation system, there can be stubborn geographical factors of differentiation – where, if anything, the tendency is to pull apart in the face of devolved political arrangements. There may be subtle niche differences that are more powerful to insiders than is obvious to observers. So, while a major factor driving down group numbers is the organizational efficiency argument that reducing the population allows the units to be more efficiently organized (economies of scale) and perhaps affords better research or avoids governmental 'play' in selecting which group to consult, there are often countervailing arguments.

Olson's temptation?

Olson offered an ingenious and counterintuitive argument that not all groups were similarly easy to mobilize. The implication was that the group population did not reflect the balance of societal views because groups that could offer selective incentives (especially those with smaller potential memberships subject to peer pressure) would be easier to organize. Other groups would be undermined by the free-riding of collective incentives. Of course, business groups fitted these requirements, and business groups seemed to proliferate easily. Accordingly, Olson was seen as discrediting pluralist assumptions that the group contest was an acceptable substitute for wider political competition. Business numerically dominated the organizational scrimmage – and that was held to *cause* a business dominance of outcomes.

Olson certainly won the logical argument about the advantage for certain types of groups of the possibility of providing selective incentives to those who joined (and the impact of small numbers in a constituency with visible nonmembership), although there is much doubt about his strong implication that noneconomic interests could not be mobilized (a point perhaps underlined by Figure 12.1). But perhaps his pro-business-bias argument was so convenient for the political preferences of most political scientists that they accepted it uncritically. In fact, the argument that political outcomes are determined by counting the groups in favor is a deterministic mechanical image that misleads.[5] The idea that some interests with less easily organized groups are therefore politically handicapped through the group contest is widespread. For example, David Held claims that the 'Poor resource base of many groups prevents their full participation' (2006, p. 17). But what if this weakness is simply one dimension in a democratic mix? In the reverse way, elites presumably do badly at the ballot box and are weak on the electoral strength dimension, but they might be dominant in other democratic contests. Do the unemployed lack power because they do not possess the basic organizational requirements (i.e., a group), or are other types of weakness as important or more important? Are abused children left out of political consideration because they are not organized, or can political importance emerge with nongroup manifestations and ensure attention to their problems?

The problem, as we have seen across several chapters, with arguing that *more groups = more power* is that the trends toward reduced business group numbers then have to be read as *fewer groups = less power*. In fact, if the trends toward business group reduction are as strong as they initially appear, might this not be about enhancing business power and not undermining it? Arguably, Olson tempted political science to lazily assume that power derives from numbers – because the business numbers were large. But the basis of the power may lie elsewhere.

Quite another suspicion of the premise that more business groups reflects more business power was hinted at by Heinz *et al.* (1993, p. 379). They quote Salisbury (1990, pp. 25–26.), who had set out how 'The descent upon Washington of so many hundreds of associations, institutions, and their agents does not mean that these private interests have acquired greater sway or even a more articulate voice in the shaping of national policy. In many ways, the opposite is true.' Heinz *et al.* present the mobilization in Washington as a defensive response to government regulation and a search for reduced uncertainty by the organizations. The wave of business mobilization in this light is the business response to governmental impacts on their business environment. If anything, it is a signal of growing weakness.

Accounting for the proportions of interests before government is therefore a rather salient question. The standard approach has been to focus on formation issues (where business has an advantage), and this was the preoccupation of the collective action and maintenance literatures (see Olson 1965; Salisbury 1969). More recently, emphasis has been placed on the issue of entry to and exit from populations through temporary policy 'hibernation' (see especially Schlozman, Chapter 2). Here it is the lobby function itself that changes – and signals exit from and entry to our populations (as identified by action) – among a set of surviving organizations. These are two rather different phenomena to be explaining. The same theory might struggle to explain both well. But this is a topic worthy of exploration and explanation.

Changing patterns of diversity?

Population work has hitherto focused on counting broad numbers of groups. Less attention has been paid to how we label and type organizations. More attention to this will aid comparison. There is a basic distinction between (collective action) interest groups and pressure participants (i.e., policy-influencing organizations). But within the interest group category, we tend to focus on categories such as unions, citizen groups, and professional groups. These are helpful, but there is also the issue of the organizational form in which groups survive in populations – that is, their structural features and core identity (see Halpin and Nownes 2011). This issue is particularly salient when it comes to assessing things such as participatory contribution. Claims that old groups structured on branches are being replaced by new groups organized centrally with remote supporters have been gathering momentum (see Skocpol 1999). If this were an accurate representation (see McCarthy 2005) it would be of critical importance to our assessment of the democratic functions of group systems. We might also expect it – at least in principle – to be salient with respect to explaining the breadth of a group's policy engagement, the style of tactics it might use. In sum, noting that there are more or fewer groups over time might be vastly more interesting if we could say something about the changing mix of organizational forms within them. This might also add value to ecological work: entry to and exit from populations might be better explained with attention to any changes in the 'dominant' or 'legitimate' organizational model used by group entrepreneurs. After all, Skocpol (1999) claims that – today – no right-minded entrepreneur would bother to create groups from the grass roots up using branches based on face-to-face engagement (but see evidence from Walker *et al.* 2011).

Mapping data might usefully bolt on measurements related to dimensions – such as group form or other features (see Chapter 2) – in order to allow insight into the qualitative transformation that accompanies population changes. Such dimensions would be useful, in particular, where the headline total numbers are not very volatile. This might underestimate subterranean shifts in form that come with significant implications for, among other things, the quality of citizen participation in interest group life.

Prospects for comparative work?

This volume opened with the assertion that US work in this area was comparatively advanced, and that Europeans lag somewhat behind, but that there has been considerable recent rebalancing. However, does the availability of new data inside and outside the US simply exacerbate the temptation to compare apples and oranges?

Most of the comparative work has tended to be in an EU setting – comparing the access or influence of groups from specific member states at the EU level. In this context, studies cannot first agree on whether the EU system itself can be characterized as pluralist or corporatist in nature (see discussion in Berkhout and Lowery 2011). Yet even when study designs explicitly surmise that groups from corporatist countries will do better than those from pluralist settings, researchers using actual data struggle to find any clear effect and consequently conclude with a statement about the doubtful nature of a 'national systems' effect (see, e.g., Eising 2007, pp. 335, 357).

If there *is* a system effect, perhaps it is interpretive and maybe even beyond the reach of our counting data. A brief empirical example gets at the broader point. In the face of criticism from a new and vociferous Danish farm group (Bæredygtigt Landbrug [Sustainable Agriculture]) agitating on the fringe of the 'official' farm union's annual meeting (Landbrug og Fødevarer [Agriculture and Food]), the Danish environment minister advised, 'You do not get influence by standing in the corner and yelling.'[6] To researchers in pluralist systems (Australia, the US, and the UK), this kind of advice sounds consistent with what we 'know' about policy processing and insider politics. Generations of studies have reported that ministers, and civil servants, *prefer* to hear a single view. At the same time, they do not want to hear a single view if that means important views are filtered out (see the discussion for the UK in Jordan and Halpin 2006). Perhaps, then, the real difference is that the advice offered by the Danish environment minister is taken even *more* seriously in so-called corporatist systems than in pluralist ones. It is a matter of emphasis and not of outright difference. This might explain the clear absence of any fundamental difference in the pictures presented in this volume, and in the various attempts to conduct national comparisons within the EU member states. In pluralist systems, a finding of *few* (and weak) groups or organized interests advocating for a set of interests is viewed as normatively deficient. There is a willingness to see 'more' as evidence of increased power. A rule of thumb might simply be that in so-called corporatist systems, the emphasis is placed on 'speaking with one voice', whereas in the same scenario in pluralist systems, this urging is interpreted as a call to 'listen with one ear'.[7] Thus, differences in 'system' really work at the level of establishing what the numbers 'mean', and this interpretive exercise is best done close to the coalface.

In addition to leaning on some soft notion of 'emphasis', we might point to other nuggets of evidence from the contributions to this volume. In several chapters, there appears to be more variation *within* national settings than between. That is to say that the search for a comparative theory of policy participant or interest group populations might best be replaced with a search for a more general theory of policy processes and institutional venues. For instance, there is the finding that populations of pressure participants vary within national settings across arenas (see Halpin *et al.*, Chapter 6; Salisbury 1984). A national comparative theory might make sense, but only if it is attuned to within-case variations based on choice of arena.

There is a vibrant literature that focuses on collective coordination which rests on a range of institutional formulations. But, as Baumgartner *et al.* (2011) make clear, there is a 'second-level collective action problem', and that is with respect to the mobilization of already formed organizations. This is a frequent focus of contributors to this volume. Schlozman (Chapter 2), Lowery (Chapter 3), Hanegraff *et al.* (Chapter 9), and Halpin *et al.* (Chapter 6) all stress that much of the volatility in populations over time is a consequence of participation hibernation by collective bodies and the *ad hoc* involvement of policy amateurs.

Developing data sets and making them available to fellow scholars is a welcome development. In Chapter 1, we reflected on the comparative sophistication of the party literature, which benefits from well-crafted and accumulating data sets. The more that successive generations of group scholars can be provided with data, the better chance there will be to identify – with some confidence – firm trends. However, as these chapters show, there has to be an emphasis on maintaining comparability during data-accumulation phases. 'More' is not the same as 'more comparable'.

Directories are a convenient shortcut that may allow scholars a sense of the scope and diversity of a group system. However, for more sophisticated purposes, directories are rarely suitable as directly exploitable political science instruments without some adaptation. For example, the original coding may not serve political science purposes, and may require effort to tie into broader systems of classification. Directories alone do not suffice as summaries of interest populations. This is clearly evident at the EU level, where beyond dedicated EU associations, it is simply impossible to list out all potentially relevant interest groups. In the face of this challenge, several recent efforts have sought to *combine* sources – to find overlaps between what are at face value incomplete sources – to arrive at an overview of the population (see Wonka *et al.* 2010; Berkhout and Lowery 2011).[8] In fact, this is an approach that has been utilized by students of local voluntary associations for some time (see Grønbjerg 2002). But working from such 'foundation' sources means grafting meaningful labels onto them, which requires work and resources.

For those interested in mapping policy participants, the target is policy activity by organizations. One of the lessons from this style of policy activity data collection (see Halpin *et al.*, Chapter 6) is that for many organized interests, the choice of arena to participate in is just that, a choice. And, consequently, mapping one arena cannot substitute for a multi-arena approach. While it may be tempting to take data on participation in US congressional hearings as addressing *the* Washington system, it is more accurately a depiction of the congressional system.

Exploring the world of associations/pressure participants/organized interests/interest groups typically seems to suck researchers into unwieldy research projects with large numbers and rather finicky problems about inclusion. It is a mix of industrial-scale research and constant craft-scale decisions. Some projects have been counting organizations because they are organizations; others have focused on those active in a political way. These difficulties mean that the seductively simple questions in this area are chimera-like and are difficult to engage directly. How many organized interests are there in different societies? How quickly are they growing? Do different types grow at different rates? These are very difficult questions to answer directly, and this volume has tried to sketch some of the research impediments.

But some broad differences do emerge. Without empirical research, would UK/US differences be on the agenda? Without research, would the pattern of the transformation of business representation be so stark? Would the increases in cause representation be fixed as opposed to remaining a speculation? Above all, the various contributions have underlined the importance of a focus that sees democratic policy making as involving a cast of thousands of organizations to partner the cast of thousands of mid-level civil servants captured by Page and Jenkins (2005). Having struggled to avoid being swamped by the volume of associations, researchers are unlikely to neglect their policy impact.

Notes

1. This probably arises from the influence of Lijphart (1999) and then of the corporatist literature (see Schmitter 1982).
2. One of the key authors in the organizational ecology literature makes plain that the word 'ecology' does not imply that the theory deploys ecological thinking (Hannan 2005).
3. It is important to keep in mind that the work by Gray and Lowery concentrates on explaining density among state lobby populations, while that of Nownes focuses on explaining the mortality of individual groups. That is, in their foundational work on US states Gray and Lowery treat density as their dependent variable, while Nownes uses density as an independent variable in explaining formation (and mortality).
4. The only possible source is double-counting arising from an organization changing its name or merging. But this arises only in the year that its name was changed, and only if it was active under the old and new names in a single rolling period.
5. This 'weighing the publics' assumption is of course rarely articulated, but arguably it is smuggled into considerations.
6. The original Danish quote was 'Man ikke får indflydelse ved at stå I hjørnet og hyle op.'
7. See Campbell (1971), who uses these terms in discussing the issue of amalgamation among Australian farm groups in the late 1960s.
8. This approach is also being used in various national comparative projects underway at the time of writing; see, e.g., Dür and Mateo (2011) and a Swiss project comparing populations in Germany, the UK, and Switzerland (www.nccr-democracy.uzh.ch/research/module-3/ip-8-mediatization-of-political-interest-groups-changes-of-organizational-structure-and-communication-repertoire).

References

Baumgartner, F., H. Larsen-Price, B. Leech, and P. Rutledge (2011) 'Congressional and Presidential Effects on the Demand for Lobbying', *Political Research Quarterly*, 64(1), 3–16.

Berkhout, J. and D. Lowery (2011) 'Short-Term Volatility in the EU Interest Community', *Journal of European Public Policy*, 18(1), 1–16.

Berry, J. (1999) *The New Liberalism: The Rising Power of Citizen Groups* (Washington, DC: Brookings Institution Press).

Campbell, K. (1971) 'Australian Farm Organisations: The Unity Issue', *Politics*, 6(2), 148–60.

Carroll, G. R. and M. T. Hannan (2000) *The Demography of Corporations and Industries* (Princeton, NJ: Princeton University Press).

Dür, A. and G. Mateo (2011) 'National Associations and Lobbying on EU Legislation: Is Access Biased?', paper prepared for a workshop on 'Interest Groups, European Integration and the State', Oxford University, May 21, 2011.

Eising, R. (2007) 'Institutional Context, Organizational Resources and Strategic Choices: Explaining Interest Group Access in the European Union', *European Union Politics*, 8(3), 329–62.

Grønbjerg, K. A. (2002) 'Evaluating Nonprofit Databases', *American Behavioral Scientist*, 45(11), 1741–77.

Halpin, D. and G. Jordan (2009) 'Interpreting Environments: Interest Group Response to Population Ecology Pressures', *British Journal of Political Science*, 39(2), 243–65.

Halpin, D. and A. Nownes (2011) 'Reappraising the Survival Question: Why We Should Focus on Interest Group "Organizational Form" and "Careers"', in A. Cigler and B. Loomis (eds.) *Interest Group Politics* 8th edn. (Washington, DC: Congressional Quarterly Press).

Hannan, M. T. (2005) 'Ecologies of Organizations: Diversity and Identity', *Journal of Economic Perspectives*, 19, 51–70.

Heinz, J., E. Laumann, R. Nelson, and R. Salisbury (1993) *The Hollow Core* (Cambridge, MA: Harvard University Press).

Held, D. (2006) *Models of Democracy* (Cambridge: Polity).

Jordan, G. and D. Halpin (2006) 'The Political Costs of Policy Coherence? Constructing a "Rural" Policy for Scotland', *Journal of Public Policy*, 26, 21–41.

Lijphart, A. (1999) *Patterns of Democracy: Government Forms and Performance in Thirty-Six Countries* (New Haven, CT: Yale University Press).

McCarthy, J. (2005) 'Persistence and Change among Nationally Federated Social Movements', in G. Davis, D. McAdam, W. Scott, and M. Zald (eds.) *Social Movements and Organization Theory* (New York: Cambridge University Press).

Olson, M. (1965) *The Logic of Collective Action: Public Goods and the Theory of Groups* (Cambridge, MA: Harvard University Press).

Page, E. and B. Jenkins (2005) *Policy Bureaucracy: Government with a Cast of Thousands* (Oxford: Oxford University Press).

Salisbury, R. H. (1969) 'An Exchange Theory of Interest Groups', *Midwest Journal of Political Science*, 13, 1–32.

Salisbury, R. H. (1984) 'Interest Representation: The Dominance of Interest Groups', *American Political Science Review*, 78(1), 64–78.

Salisbury, R. H. (1990) 'The Paradox of Interest Groups in Washington, DC', in A. King (ed.) *The New American Political System*, 2nd edn (Washington, DC: American Enterprise Institute).

Schmitter, P. C. (1982) 'Reflections on Where the Theory of Neo-Corporatism Has Gone and Where the Praxis of Neo-Corporatism May Be Going', in

G. Lembruch and P. Schmitter (eds.) *Patterns of Corporatist Policy-Making* (London: Sage).

Skocpol, T. (1999) 'Advocates without Members: The Recent Transformation of American Civic Life', in T. Skocpol and M. P. Fiorina (eds.) *Civic Engagement in American Democracy* (Washington, DC: Brookings Institution Press).

Truman, D. B. (1951) *The Governmental Process* (New York: Alfred A. Knopf).

Walker, E. T., J. D. McCarthy, and F. Baumgartner (2011) 'Replacing Members with Managers? Mutualism among Membership and Nonmembership Advocacy Organizations in the United States', *American Journal of Sociology*, 116(4), 1284–1337.

Wonka, A., F. Baumgartner, C. Mahoney, and J. Berkhout (2010) 'Measuring the Size and Scope of the EU Interest Group Population', *European Union Politics*, 11(3), 463–76.

Young, M. (2010) 'The Price of Advocacy: Mobilization and Maintenance in Advocacy Organizations', in A. Prakash and M. K. Gugerty (eds.) *Advocacy Organizations and Collective Action* (Cambridge: Cambridge University Press).

Index